BREAK THROUGH

MASTER YOUR DEFAULT MODE AND THRIVE

HOSEIN KOUROS-MEHR, MD, PhD

Break Through: Master Your Default Mode and Thrive

Print ISBN: 979-8-9894665-0-4
Published by Hosein Kouros-Mehr, MD, PhD

Published in the United States of America

Contact information: yourdefaultmode@gmail.com

Cover design by Victoria Wolf, wolfdesignandmarketing.com.

For Lumi, Bowin, and Kylin

CONTENTS

A NOTE FROM THE AUTHOR

AS SOMEONE TRAINED IN WESTERN MEDICINE, I have witnessed remarkable advancements in the management of diseases like diabetes and hepatitis. We are developing effective therapies for cancer using engineered antibodies and cell therapies.

While advancements in medicine during the last century have increased our life span, many of us are more anxious and depressed than ever before. Rates of suicide and drug addiction are increasing in the developed world, just as mental and spiritual health are in decline.

Our physicians and nurses are equipped to treat the manifestations of disease but not to prevent illnesses from sprouting at the root level, beginning with the basic elements of thought and emotion. Many healthcare providers suffer from the same anxiety and burnout that afflict their patients.

As a physician-scientist, I have dedicated more than two decades to the challenging task of translating cutting-edge scientific discoveries into innovative medicines for patients. With this background, I recognized (and personally experienced) the profound implications of a recent scientific breakthrough—the discovery of the default mode network, the part of the brain that gives rise to your ego.

This advancement provides an objective framework to understand your thoughts, emotions, and behaviors. The default mode is the "wandering mind" that takes you away from the present moment to the past and future. When it is overactive, it can lead to painful mental conditions like stress, anxiety, emotional pain, and addictive craving.

By combining this cutting-edge research with classical remedies at the heart of clinical medicine, psychology, and religion (including Judeo-Christian and Buddhist teachings), *Break Through* bridges the gap between the medical and spiritual realms and presents a healing process that resolves these imbalances of the body and mind.

By learning to master your default mode, you will powerfully unlock the natural freedom and bliss within. The journey also awakens your higher self, bringing to light the true immensity of your worth.

You are a miracle of nature.

Regardless of your gender, religion, or income level, you can embark on the path to health, happiness, and inner peace. May you thrive on your journey.

JOURNEY OF INNER HEALING

THE ENERGY OF THE UNIVERSE FLOWS through your capillaries every second, fueling 100 trillion cells that work together to give rise to you. Deep in your core, you have a self-healing vitality that radiates outward to nourish you, your family, and your community. This tranquil power forms the fabric of your soul, capable of healing your deepest afflictions.

While it is always available to access, the inner spirit may lie dormant inside of you, trapped by negative emotions and behaviors that form painful mental entanglements, or "knots," that restrict your access to a reservoir of well-being. You may spend your life searching externally for happiness and fulfillment, unaware that the source of physical and spiritual suffering lies within.

Fortunately, you can *break through* these barriers and reconnect with your core to awaken profound bliss, wisdom, and connection with others.

The key to success is self-understanding. In life, we all experience a series of psychological states that create substantial tension, trapping us in pain. We are conditioned to believe that happiness depends on our individual success, so we approach the world with a self-focused mentality, unknowingly heading down a road of distress and unhappiness.

Recently, in a remarkable scientific breakthrough, scientists have discovered the location of the human ego, the source of our self-obsession. It is known as the *default mode network* (DMN), a part of the brain that turns on when the mind wanders. The DMN (the ego) is responsible for eleven mental knots that give rise to significant tension:

- Stress
- Emotional pain
- Addictive craving
- Loneliness
- Negativity
- Anxiety and anger
- Dishonesty and denial
- Inaction
- Dissatisfaction
- Poor lifestyle
- Resistance to change

The good news is that you can break through your mental knots to find freedom and contentment. By resolving these conditions, you can rejuvenate your soul, restore inner peace, and awaken your higher self. The key is to understand the root causes of the mental knots and then apply specific measures that allow your mind to heal them.

A knot is an unpleasant tension in the mind or body that signals an unmet need. You may have experienced a muscle knot in your neck or shoulder. During times of stress or overexertion, muscle fibers tighten and bundle together, leading to throbbing pain, fatigue, and tension. The remedy is simple—apply intense pressure to loosen the constriction, improve blood flow, and promote healing of the damaged area. A neck or shoulder massage may feel painful, but by releasing the knot you allow the body to restore its original state.

When you untie the knots in a rope, it automatically returns to its original shape. When you release the eleven mental knots, you allow the mind to naturally restore itself—a process called *homeostasis*. Your body has remarkable self-healing properties, just as a sprained ankle will repair itself if given proper time and nourishment.

As you loosen each mental knot, you feel the healing process take hold. The progress gradually accelerates and guides you to an awakened state of freedom. You will identify the root causes of your distress, leading to permanent rejuvenation and a new understanding that prevents knots from forming in the future.

By understanding these negative mental states and resolving them, you open the door to inner peace and happiness. In the process, you discover the higher self and your soul—the spiritual essence of your being—to reach the peace and bliss of the enlightened state.

Chipping the Knots Away

"The sculpture is already complete within the marble block before I start my work," the Renaissance artist Michaelangelo said. "I just have to chisel away the superfluous material." When you chip away at your internal knots and allow inner healing to take hold, you gain access to a deep peace that lies at the heart of your consciousness.

In our turbulent times, few people experience the rare and enigmatic quality of serenity. We grasp for instant happiness and gratification, hoping it will last, but the euphoria is often followed by unfulfillment or dissatisfaction. Life drags us along from highs to lows as if we are not in control. Thoughts toss us from one place to the next, triggering waves of emotions and exhausting us.

When we lose contact with inner peace, troubles arise. Restlessness and anxiety erupt as we grasp for an elusive fulfillment that slips away from our hands like sand. At times, it may seem that life is unfair or pointless.

You may wonder, "Am I on this Earth to suffer with some occasional moments of satisfaction? Is life a hamster wheel with no purpose?"

The answer is no. Life is a journey with profound meaning. When you look inside and identify the obstacles within, you see the road to an awakened state of being. "Peace comes from within," Buddha said. "Do not seek it without."

When you lose inner peace, you are like a boat drifting in a turbulent ocean of thoughts and emotions. Waves of anger, judgment, and craving pull you in different directions, and soon you are lost at sea. While the turbulence may make you feel helpless, in your most desperate moments you can arouse your spirit and anchor yourself into the bedrock of the ocean. Finding stability, you watch as waves of negativity pass without your involvement. Soon the storm clouds disappear, and you sail home with a new appreciation for the immaculate majesty of the ocean and sky.

Inner Peace Is Freedom

As you break through the mental knots, you awaken inner peace and free yourself from the prison of suffering. You discover the tranquility of being present as life unfolds and gratitude for the world's infinite beauty. You find blissful calm smiling in the face of adversity, wishing well-being for friends and foes alike.

This energy is the grace of the Holy Spirit, limitless in its power to sanctify and available to everyone regardless of background or circumstance. It's the awakening of your soul and the Christ-like, inner Buddha that is present inside you. A life in peace is a state where mind and body are in harmony. The ancient Greeks referred to this as *eudaemonia*, a state of serenity deeper than the fleeting joy of the senses.

The path within changes your worldview and frames daily tasks in a much larger perspective. You become aware of the Infinite Unknown, a force that provides grace and guidance as described in the Book of Psalms: "Your word is a lamp to guide my feet and a light for my path." In times of need, the energy guides you to a higher purpose.

The healing process allows you to gaze beyond your limited shadow, beholding the vastness of life's wonder. Freed from cravings and negative thought patterns, you live more effortlessly like a bird soaring through the sky. In daily activities, you experience an unconditional bliss and gratitude that is not dependent on external circumstances, in contrast with fleeting happiness that is triggered by money, food, or possessions and does not last.

Inner tranquility provides positive thoughts and a longer, healthier life. A study of 97,000 women examined the impact of thought patterns on health outcomes. All participants were free of cancer and heart disease at the start of the study and were then followed for eight years. Remarkably, optimistic women were much less likely to develop heart disease or die from cancer. Women with cynical and hostile attitudes had the highest rates of heart disease and early death.

Although this study cannot definitively prove that positive thinking leads to better health, it raises important questions. You may be wondering, "Are negative thoughts damaging my health? Could a positive mindset reduce my chances of disease and death?" Based on the totality of medical evidence, the answer to both questions is a resounding yes!

Inner peace enhances health and well-being in many ways, from stress management to improved sleep. It also unlocks other qualities, such as patience, compassion, and wisdom, which awaken your higher self. You connect more easily with your subconscious mind and receive insights to solve life's challenges. You recognize negative states, like anxiety and anger, as they appear and stop them in their tracks. Free from the fog of unwholesome thought patterns, you achieve ambitions naturally and with less effort, unlocking your creative and intellectual potential to fulfill your namesake as a *Homo sapiens*—a wise human being.

Inner peace grants freedom in the form of self-acceptance and love, mental clarity, and positive energy. When you access this vitality, past stressors no longer trigger harmful behaviors. You resolve emotional pain and forgive yourself and others for past wrongs. Tense or angry moments are short lived, and you return more naturally to a state of calm. You experience a greater connection with friends, family, and community. Your baseline mood goes from an egocentric, cynical, or judgmental state to one that is more selfless, accepting, and at peace.

As the knots further unravel, you find bliss and gratitude even in the quiet moments of the day, and the tranquility of Sunday morning lasts throughout the week. Life has more freshness and color. You no longer need external substances like alcohol or social media to distract from misery. Instead, you view negative thoughts and unwholesome impulses as opportunities to advance your spiritual practice.

With inner peace, the accomplishments and promotions that previously eluded you appear unexpectedly. Insights into your problems arrive as if on demand. Aggressive people do not impact you as much, and compassion for others dominates as a force for happiness and satisfaction.

You were born with the serenity of inner peace. To find your way home and reconnect with your core, you must break through the mental knots blocking the way. The recent discovery of the default mode network (the ego) provides a reliable way to understand how the eleven mental knots take hold and lead to suffering. This breakthrough provides a new objective framework for the age-old journey of self-discovery. Because the default mode is at the center of the healing process, let's take a closer look at it.

Master Your Default Mode

Tranquil presence is a hallmark of infancy and the end of life, but during most of our lives we are in a state of self-obsession driven by our ego.

By age two, toddlers have started to develop a sense of self. The word *mine* becomes a favorite, and a new concept arises—me versus others. This separate self strengthens during adolescence, when an egocentric perspective of the world takes hold with thoughts like, "I'm right, they're wrong. The world is against me. I'm so alone."

We form an identity based on our friends, desires, or aspirations, and our energy focuses on self-growth and self-reflection. These changes help shape us into successful adults. However, later in life this self-centered thought pattern can restrict our view of the world, trapping us in dissatisfaction and suffering.

Over the years, philosophers and psychologists have given various names to the separate self—ego, id, mind, or self. As mentioned earlier, scientists have discovered that the human ego is generated in the brain via the default mode network (DMN), a set of neural connections between the prefrontal cortex, posterior cingulate cortex, and inferior parietal lobe. This is a groundbreaking, revolutionary breakthrough that helps explain the complexity of human behavior!

The DMN (the ego) selectively focuses on information relating to our own lives and drives our self-centered perception of reality. It also creates the sense that we are distinct and different from others. The DMN connects with other parts of the brain containing emotion and memory, controlling how we respond to information. Our default mode is to make judgments and decisions that are in our own perceived best interest. The brain conserves energy by ignoring information that does not directly pertain to the self.

We can recognize our DMN every time our minds wander into thought, like when we're waiting for a taxi, brushing our teeth, or engaging in other mundane activities. Memories of recent events or thoughts of future plans can surface, along with cravings, judgments, and powerful emotions such as anger or anxiety.

Negative or anxious thoughts can bubble up, seemingly from nowhere. "Why did he say that to me? My life is so hard. Will I finally get promoted next year?"

Our brain's default mode network is often characterized by self-obsession, leading to narrow or erroneous views of the world. It can trap us in addictive craving, stress, loneliness, emotional pain, anger, anxiety, and a host of unwholesome thoughts and behaviors. While a healthy ego may be beneficial in certain situations, more often than not our default mode leads to conflict and painful emotions.

Thankfully, our brain has another pathway that can become active when the default mode network turns off. It is called the *central executive network* (CEN), a set of neural connections between the prefrontal cortex and parietal cortex. The CEN starts to develop during adolescence and encodes a more expansive consciousness that goes beyond the limited egotistical self.

While the default mode network has restricted awareness and judgmental tendencies, the CEN has far-reaching perception and control over complex decision-making. It is activated when we are fully engaged in activities, such as sports, music performances, prayer, or mindfulness exercises. This state of mind is often referred to as "flow" or being "in the zone," a state of energized focus, complete involvement, and presence in the now—free from mental chatter, doubt, judgment, and negativity. Athletes, musicians, and other highly accomplished people tune into the CEN for peak performance.

While you may spend most of your time operating in the default mode network, with intention and practice you can access the central executive network and learn to live "in the zone," not only for productivity and success but also for happiness, freedom, physical health, spiritual well-being, and closeness with divine inner love. You can cultivate qualities such as virtue, restraint, and equanimity that lead to an enlightened state. This book will show you how.

What Is Enlightenment?

Enlightenment has had different meanings over the years. It originates from the Sanskrit word *bodhi* meaning *awakening*—as in waking from a bad dream to realize suffering has ended.

Twenty-five hundred years ago, Buddha described enlightenment as a spiritual state marked by the absence of dukkha (dissatisfaction caused by craving, aversion, or ignorance). He did not vividly describe the qualities of an awakened soul but instead focused on the unwholesome forces to be overcome for it to occur. In the West, this has led to confusion—"spiritual enlightenment" has taken on a self-centered, romantic concept far from its original definition.

In seventeenth- and eighteenth-century Europe, the Enlightenment movement was something quite different. It referred to the clash of science and philosophy against religious dogma. Logic and rational thought became the light of human progress.

In 1637, the French philosopher Rene Descartes captured this movement in a simple yet profound statement: "I think, therefore I am."

In the following decades, English scientist Isaac Newton unlocked the physical laws of the universe, the French chemist Antoine Lavoisier opened the door to modern chemistry, and the Scottish mechanical engineer James Watt invented the steam engine. New concepts of religious tolerance and individual liberty gave birth to the United States of America. To be enlightened was to have reason and uphold science, regardless of religious or spiritual backgrounds.

Now, in the twenty-first century, enlightenment has a much deeper meaning. It is the awakening of our spiritual consciousness, giving rise to inner peace and compassion. To be enlightened is to realize the limited self and arouse our soul to heal ourselves and our community. It is to walk away from darkness and turn on the light of love and gratitude.

Enlightened people have some shared virtues. They are fully present in the moment to experience the glory of reality without judgment, negativity, or worries about the past and future. This allows them to be patient, positive-thinking, and forgiving. Like children, they have a deep joy and curiosity for life.

Having transcended the obsession about "me" and "mine," they also have a deep awareness of the interconnectedness of all living beings, which grants a profound sense of altruism and awe. They are insightful yet modest, led by a durable inner strength that confers resilience to life's challenges. Whether or not someone is watching, they lead their lives with integrity, stability, and calm regardless of the day's circumstances.

You can take the road to the enlightened state. The Industrial Age connected the planet with roads and highways, while today's Information Age links human beings with smartphones and computers. As society grows increasingly restless, it is time for a period of self-healing and a return to center. You can commit to enlightenment for health, happiness, and inner peace.

Path to the Higher Self

The journey to your higher self begins when you decide to end suffering in search of deeper contentment. The first step is to learn your true condition and how the eleven knots listed earlier in this chapter manifest themselves. This understanding is a critical part of the process; without awareness your problems will remain unresolved. When you look inside with honesty and intention, you will see the path to the higher self. This is the ultimate journey in life. "It's your road and yours alone," Rumi, the thirteenth-century Persian poet, said. "Others may walk it with you, but no one can walk it for you."

Progress may be slow at the beginning. As you release each of the mental knots, you may not notice any recognizable changes for the first few weeks. But one day, you will experience moments of serenity free from anxiety, stress, or anger. These fleeting glimmers are previews of a greater bliss that is to come. As you commit to a daily intention, more light shines, and an inner peace becomes palpable. With time, the process gains momentum and strengthens on its own.

Honesty with yourself is important. You may blame your problems on a boss, parent, or partner and feel a need to escape them—to a retreat, a vacation, or a new town or country.

"Once I find the right job, I'll have peace. I can't wait for that vacation. When I make it, I'll be free." Does this sound like something you might say?

Recognize this tendency as the ego deflecting internal problems on others, blaming the world when your pain originates within. Believing that peace will be found only through the right relationship or occupation is an invitation to suffering. Becoming jaded with the material world and running away to a retreat or tropical island is not the way. The path to freedom lies within.

The beginning of your journey may be difficult or tense. You may have lived with negative thoughts for a long time, even developing a bond with them. Freeing yourself may feel frightening or unnatural at first. As with an unhealthy relationship, acknowledging these unwholesome tendencies and truthfully seeing how they affect your life will allow you to peacefully part ways with them and embrace positive change.

The journey is an adventure—a liberating and, at times, challenging one with blissful moments and a glorious destination. You cannot reach the finish line overnight, and you will experience bumps along the way.

Initially, it may feel like being lost in a desert as negative thoughts sap your strength and will. But in your most difficult time, a spectacular desert rose lifts your spirits and energizes you to press on. As you continue forward, more flowers and plants appear, bringing more hope. Eventually, the desert gives way to a green oasis, and the final destination—the lake of your soul, full and wholesome—replenishes you back to health. "Dig deep," the Roman emperor Marcus Aurelius said. "The water—goodness—is down there, and as long as you keep digging it will keep bubbling."

The light may be dim at the start of the journey, but with time it shines brighter and eventually erases all darkness. Be prepared for adversity and embrace an attitude of openness and curiosity. The Zen Buddhist concept of shoshin—or the "beginner's mind"—teaches us to set aside preconceptions and judgments.

As we gain knowledge in life, our minds can become rigid and locked in their ways, with thoughts like, "I already know this. This doesn't apply to me. Get to the point." Recognize this resistance as the ego, and set it aside for shoshin—this will save you time and effort on your journey.

If you are stalled and not making progress, give yourself time and trust the process of healing. If you are drawn back to darkness, turn on the light of positive intent. "The secret of change is to focus all of your energy, not on fighting the old, but on building the new," the Greek philosopher Socrates said.

The ego often puts up stiff resistance, thwarting change and ridiculing the process of moving forward. When this happens, take notice, and acknowledge that you want to be in a better place. Repeat your intentions.

May I be happy. May I be healthy. May I have peace.

Grant yourself patience and space. With a relaxed and persistent attitude, progress will resume. In challenging times, remember that throughout history millions of people have taken the path to the higher self by taking refuge in the Infinite Unknown.

The journey is like planting an orange tree. You will provide the right soil and water it daily, watching it grow for several months until fruits appear. In the same way, you will cultivate the right conditions for your mind to blossom and awaken.

The process of inner healing ultimately leads to a higher self that transcends your default mode and reveals a greater purpose. Take your time and savor the journey. A world of happiness awaits.

KNOT 1

STRESS—FREE YOURSELF FROM ITS CHAINS

STRESS IS A COMMON FEATURE OF MODERN LIFE. The fast-paced nature of society and rapid access to information exacerbates daily pressures. To cope with mental tension, we often turn to digital stimulation—news streams, social media, video games, texting—that further worsens the problem. Over time, stress destroys our health and robs us of creativity and spontaneity, trapping us in a prison of suffering. Fortunately, with some simple adjustments you can free yourself from its chains.

In this chapter, you will learn about the science of stress and the toll it can take on you physically, mentally, and spiritually. You will understand the triggers of stress along with an effective remedy—mindful relaxation. With practice, you will find that breathing exercises, concentration meditation, and other mindfulness exercises will tame your "wandering mind" and the stress it propagates. These preventive measures help foster your inner peace, granting you greater bliss in the present moment.

The Purpose of Stress

Stress is a natural response to physical, emotional, or psychological tension. It allows you to stay focused and energized in the face of life's challenges. If you respond positively to the pressure, you will adapt and become stronger and smarter.

However, when experienced repeatedly, stress will damage your mind and body, promoting the aging process and contributing to deadly diseases like cancer and stroke. Understanding your triggers will help you develop healthy coping habits, enabling you to find inner peace and improve your mental and physical well-being.

Stress is subjective, and the same conditions may not be taxing for everyone. In the past, our ancestors faced external pressures from predators, invasions, famine, and natural disasters.

Imagine a family living in a cave 20,000 years ago. Sleeping by a fire, they are abruptly awakened by the noise of growling four-legged animals. As the fight response kicks in and adrenaline surges, the adults grab weapons and pump their fists. With hearts racing and pupils dilated, they chase the creatures away.

In the rush of the moment, someone accidentally sets fire to the fur bedding, triggering a panic-filled flight response. The elders grab the infants as the family rushes from the cave to safe ground. Reality sets in when they discover the sudden disappearance of their food supply, which triggers the stress hormone cortisol.

Cortisol shifts the body's energy usage away from less critical areas (such as the immune and reproductive systems) toward more vital ones (like the brain). Ultimately, the family survives with limited food and soon gets back on its feet.

Fast-forward to modern times, and our pressure points have changed considerably. Food and water are bountiful for most people in our society, and we can overcome a wide variety of challenging circumstances that occur in any given month. Instead, we now experience internal stressors like thoughts, perceptions, and feelings that may not threaten our survival. A politically charged social media post, the boss's frown, or road rage can trigger the same stress pathways that saved us from life-threatening conditions in the past.

Your stress response evolved to help you rapidly tackle or escape immediate dangers and survive long-term challenges with lower energy needs. When a threat is detected, the brain activates the fight-or-flight response (also known as the *sympathetic pathway*) by releasing hormones (like adrenaline and cortisol) into the bloodstream. This increases heart rate and blood pressure, dilates the pupils, sharpens senses, and emotionally prepares you to fight or flee.

If the threat persists, the brain triggers a second wave by raising cortisol levels. As mentioned, this hormone redirects energy away from the immune and reproductive systems to other vital areas, such as the brain. In the short term, adrenaline and cortisol help you adapt to life's pressures. You could not survive without them.

For example, you may be in good spirits during an afternoon drive when you suddenly notice a large pothole in the road ahead. Without hesitation, the stress response kicks in—you become alert and focused as your heart races, tightening your grip on the steering wheel to navigate around the pothole while avoiding a collision with oncoming traffic. Having saved your life, the stress hormones start to fade as the danger recedes.

But as you continue driving, your mind begins to wander, and painful thoughts arrive. The memories of recent conflicts arise, along with future worries.

Thoughts like these surface: "Why did she talk to me like that? My father did this to me. Am I going to get fired because of that mistake?"

Unfortunately, this internal chatter can trigger the same level of stress as the pothole, even though you are no longer in harm's way. As before, hormones like adrenaline and cortisol flood your bloodstream and make your heart pound. Excessive amounts of these chemicals can cause serious harm to your body, leading to overeating and weight gain, diabetes, sleep disturbances, mental health disorders, and much more.

Clinical studies have shown the detrimental health consequences of chronic stress, which can lead to heart attacks and life-threatening cancers. Within the brain, chronic stress impairs the hippocampus and prefrontal cortex, resulting in poor memory and cognitive function. It also causes profound changes in the immune system, leading to infections, ulcers, and delayed wound healing.

The Signs of Stress

Short-term stress is easy to recognize. For example, when you are at ease and then suddenly an email makes your temper boil and face flush—this is the stress response. Triggers can come from memories, digital or verbal communication, news, and much more. Many of us are in a constant state of stress.

Chronic (long-term) stress may be more challenging to recognize. It is important to understand its signs before long-term health consequences occur. Symptoms may include:

- Fatigue
- Feeling helpless or hopeless
- Loss of appetite
- Bursts of anger or depression
- Eating or sleeping too much or too little
- Headaches and stomach aches
- Smoking, drinking, or using drugs
- Frequently checking your smartphone or other electronics
- Lack of interest in normal activities
- Suicidal thoughts

Chronic stress can manifest in many ways. Feelings of guilt or shame may arise and lead to a withdrawal from family and friends. You may forgo activities that used to bring joy and satisfaction in favor of those that merely distract from bad feelings. This makes it difficult to stay present in the moment.

In children, the signs of stress may be subtle and overlooked by loved ones. Kids may not want to leave home, even for fun activities, or they may withdraw from their social group. As an outlet, they may express themselves aggressively, ramping up conflict with peers and parents.

The first step in the healing process is self-discovery. When the signs of chronic stress appear, it is important to reflect on how you are feeling and why. Sometimes the objects of your consternation may not be entirely clear. Take a moment to reflect on these questions:

"What triggers my tension?"

"Does it come from a single source or multiple sources?"

"Can I live without these triggers? If not, can I react differently the next time they arise?"

Self-understanding will bring some relief. When you identify your coping methods and how they impact your emotions and behaviors, you will start to regain some control. With this knowledge, you can then apply an effective remedy to significantly reduce the stress in your life.

How Thoughts Trigger Stress

Stress originates from thoughts in the mind. The brain is home to 86 billion neurons that communicate with each other through neurotransmitter signals like glutamate. When you watch a TV show or scan a social media feed, glutamate activates neural networks that interpret the incoming information.

To prevent overstimulation, your brain has counterbalancing signals that return you to center. GABA (gamma-aminobutyric acid) is one such opposing neurotransmitter that blocks neurons from firing. You need GABA to sleep at night. People addicted to their smartphones have too much glutamate and not enough GABA, leading to difficulties falling asleep and staying asleep.

Thoughts are a normal part of our human experience. On average, you have a thought every 2 to 6 seconds (about 10,000 to 40,000 per day). Most of them usually pass without reaction or recognition, but occasionally some thoughts will activate the brain's limbic system and trigger emotions such as anger, anxiety, fear, sadness, or irritability.

The limbic system guides your emotional and behavioral responses to thoughts. When it perceives a threat, it sends signals to other parts of the brain to activate the stress response. For example, if you receive a threatening email, the amygdala (a part of the limbic system) triggers the fight-or-flight response by communicating with the hypothalamus, which then releases stress hormones like adrenaline into your bloodstream.

While you cannot control your thoughts, you can better understand and modify how you *respond* to them. Instead of reacting to the email, you can acknowledge it from a place of neutrality with a nonjudgmental attitude. The Greek philosopher Epictetus said, "We cannot choose our external circumstances, but we can always choose how we respond to them."

Many of the thoughts that trigger emotional responses originate in the brain's default mode network (DMN), the part of the brain responsible for self-focused thinking. You can recognize the DMN anytime your mind wanders. For example, you may be fully engaged in a movie when suddenly you are reminded of a recent emotional event and grow tense. This takes you away from the present moment, turning a serene moment sour.

In a scientific study, researchers found that people were in a less happy state when their minds began to drift off, which happened frequently throughout the day. Being in this "wandering state" was more stressful and unpleasant than performing the task at hand, even if the thoughts were positive. Surprisingly, the type of activity (work or play) did not predict how often people became lost in thought, except for one particular activity where there was a high degree of focus (sex).

We spend most of our day in rumination, and it often leads to stress and unease. That raises some questions—what is the purpose of the default mode network, and why did it evolve?

In the early 2000s, neuroscientists discovered that our brains are just as active when we perform a task as when we sit idle. Our brains are never truly at rest. We spend a large portion of our day wondering about the past and future. This is when the brain's default mode network switches on.

The function of the DMN is to analyze and process the information that is relevant to our lives, particularly recent events and upcoming activities, and to ignore the rest. The DMN attempts to make sense of our current circumstances in relation to our past and future, allowing us to react accordingly. We tend to align with conditions that support our well-being while rejecting those that challenge it.

A healthy default mode is important in many ways:

- ***Self-reflection***—We analyze the results of our actions and learn good versus bad behaviors.
- ***Social evaluation***—We exercise emotional intelligence and either strengthen relationships or avoid troublesome people.
- ***Memories***—We recollect past circumstances and form new memories of current events.
- ***Looking ahead***—We process present conditions and develop a plan to deal with future situations.

When your mind drifts off, it helps you process the events and emotions of the day. You may come to terms with a heated conversation, devise a solution to a problem, or better understand the recent behavior of a friend. A healthy DMN helps you recollect memories and maintain emotional well-balance. When it malfunctions, it can lead to deficits in memory processing, a challenge that is experienced by millions of people with Alzheimer's and Parkinson's diseases.

Your brain's default mode network allows you to predictably respond to life's situations. However, one downside is that it filters reality through a self-centered lens, leading to a biased and erroneous view of the world that becomes more deeply ingrained over time. The DMN ignores information that does not concern the self, and sadly the beauty of the universe can pass by without recognition. Many of us never realize that a way of living and thinking exists that transcends "me" and "mine," a path that leads to an enlightened state of health, happiness, and inner peace. More on that later.

While a balanced DMN is important for peace and happiness, an overactive one can be a source of harm and distress. It can lead to hypercriticality, rigid thought patterns, and negative thought loops. When you overthink, it can build your stress.

For instance, let's say a tense argument unleashes your inner anger, but you manage to stay composed in the moment. Later in the day, the DMN forces you to recollect the disagreement, making you fume and act out in irrational ways. Over time, the ruminations can lead to wild emotional swings, leading to distress and unhappiness.

The situation can escalate if you lose control of your thoughts, unleashing stress hormones in your bloodstream. The mental distress intensifies. Buddha referred to this as the "second arrow" that strikes you in the wake of the first.

A Constant State of Stress

A feature of modern society is continuous stress caused by information overload. This is further intensified by the DMN. Our thoughts, emotions, and behaviors are in overdrive, making us more tense and anxious than ever before. Regrettably, some companies exploit this craving for information to keep us disengaged from reality as we respond to every notification, sound, and alert coming from our digital devices.

The average American spends nearly four hours a day glued to their smartphone and has it within arm's reach almost twenty-four hours a day. Studies have linked excessive smartphone usage to anxiety, depression, poor sleep, lower academic and work performance, reduced social interaction, eye strain, repetitive stress injuries, low self-esteem, and addiction.

Staring at a screen for many hours contributes to an overstimulated mental state, leading to irregular sleep patterns, lack of creativity, and bad decision-making. The surge in glutamate activity creates the ideal environment for stress to take hold and ravage our lives. In some ways, the addiction to information can be as detrimental as nicotine or alcohol dependency.

We might cope with stress by trying to mask it with social media, gaming, and online videos. Unfortunately, these electronic coping mechanisms only further compound the problem by triggering an unhealthy release of glutamate and cortisol. Every beep and chime is like Pavlov's bell, triggering an anticipation of reward that may or may not be fulfilled. By continuously dipping into the digital world to escape reality, we further escalate the stress response.

Society's rapid pace has had detrimental effects on our mental tension, contributing to conditions like anxiety and depression, which are the third-highest causes of US healthcare costs after heart disease and cancer (both of which are also aggravated by stress). Chronic stress has been linked to obesity, diabetes, depression, hypertension, stroke, heart attack, and dementia.

Researchers have confirmed that stress accelerates aging and turns hair gray. It restricts the brain's capacity to adjust to change, a process known as *neuroplasticity*. This causes deficits in various brain regions, including the hippocampus, which leads to learning, memory, and attention impairments. As a result, we become less able to effectively manage real dangers when they arise.

Stress-fueled hormones can worsen negative thought patterns and mental illnesses like anxiety, depression, addiction, and attention-deficit/

hyperactivity disorder (ADHD). Our default mode network (the ego) revisits painful memories and future anxieties, which contributes to a state of overthinking known as the "monkey mind." Through its role in mind-wandering, the DMN further intensifies our tension and contributes to an overactive brain with too much glutamate.

Stress and its manifestations shorten our lifespan and rob us of our peace and joy. It can lead to deep misery and hopelessness. Rather than preventing stress from occurring, we often resort to short-term "solutions"—medication, alcohol, and other forms of pleasure—that only exacerbate our stress and drag us in life from highs to lows.

Our body was not designed for nonstop agitation. A functioning brain requires a balance of excitatory (glutamate) and inhibitory (GABA) signals. The stress response and sympathetic pathway were meant to be activated occasionally, not all the time.

The good news is that suffering is an opportunity for positive change. When we experience physical or emotional pain, our hearts and minds grow receptive to a greater purpose, allowing us to embark on the road to a higher self. "Not until we are lost do we begin to understand ourselves," American poet Henry David Thoreau said.

If you are one of the millions of people who experience chronic stress, there is a path to peace. Once you identify stress as the cause of your condition, you have taken the first step. You can then proactively apply a remedy known as the *relaxation response*, the body's natural process to eliminate stress. By turning off the fight-or-flight mode, you can activate the rest-and-digest process and allow your mind and body to heal.

The Power of Mindful Relaxation

Some triggers of stress are unavoidable. An impending final exam or work deadline can spark worry and apprehension, which you can alleviate by creating a plan and following through with it. But when stress arises from internal thoughts and mental overactivity, the best coping mechanism is to relax the mind and turn on the GABA neurotransmitter.

Human beings love quick solutions, and what is the fastest way to turn off glutamate and turn on GABA in the brain? If you guessed alcohol, you are right. While a glass of wine during dinner may have some health benefits, relying on it to manage stress is not recommended. Alcohol consumption is known to cause numerous diseases, including cancer and heart failure, and in the long term it can create more stress than it resolves.

A healthier way to relieve stress is to practice exercises that prevent it from arising. Described by Harvard Medical School professor Herbert Benson, the relaxation response (also known as the *parasympathetic pathway*) is a technique that activates GABA and turns off the fight-or-flight response. This can help restore your heart rate and blood pressure to a normal state, promote deeper sleep, and generate positive emotions like gratitude and contentment.

The relaxation response is a palpable sensation of tension release. You can feel the waves of calm as your mind and body unwind. For example, recognizing that your shoulders are hunched can make them immediately relax. You can also feel it after exercising when feel-good endorphins counteract the effects of stress hormones.

When you learn to cultivate a state of relaxation, your mental and physical health can significantly improve. A study of 13,000 patients at Massachusetts General Hospital found that relaxation exercises reduced the need for healthcare services because of faster recovery and better health.

You can activate the relaxation response in many different ways, such as breathing exercises, meditation, yoga, or prayer. A bath, a walk in nature, or a warm breeze will stimulate GABA and bring immediate peace. Music is an effective way to reduce cortisol, particularly nature sounds (like ocean waves) and calm songs with a tempo matching your heartbeat (sixty beats per minute or less). Exercise also releases endorphins, which counter the effects of cortisol to improve pain and mood.

Understanding which activities work best for you is a key step toward alleviating stress in your life. However, it is essential to practice the relaxation technique *mindfully.*

Mindful relaxation means being fully present, savoring the moment, and letting go of the past and the future. In this ten- to fifteen-minute period, you stay focused in the now and avoid reacting to your thoughts, but rather watch them come and go. Anytime a stressful impulse arises, you make a conscious decision to disengage from it and return to the present state.

For example, during a pleasant bath your mind may ruminate on the future, prompting you to check your smartphone. If you reach for the phone, you are not mindfully relaxed. But if you shake off the thought and return to the bath, then you can deepen the relaxation and allow GABA to protect you from potential stress.

At first, it may be difficult to savor the moment for more than a few seconds. However, with effort you can train yourself to stay focused for longer periods and prevent intrusive thoughts from disrupting your tranquility. When you learn to recognize interruptions and let go, you will spend more time in a relaxed state.

Many of us falsely believe we don't have time to unwind. In reality, it only takes a few minutes to activate the relaxation response, which in turn reduces stress for several hours. Investing a few minutes for mindful relaxation can set you up for a more efficient, productive day.

We must make use of our free time to relax mindfully. "Guard well your spare moments," American poet Ralph Waldo Emerson said. "They are like uncut diamonds. Discard them and their value will never be known. Improve them and they will become the brightest gems in a useful life."

To trigger the relaxation response, you can start by carving out ten to fifteen minutes in the morning and evening to mute your smartphone, turn off any other distractions, find a quiet place, close your eyes, and breathe. Initially, it may be difficult to stay mindful as your thoughts race.

Depending on your age, health, and other factors, the relaxation response may last for just a few seconds. Do not look at this as a sign of failure. You may have conditioned yourself to avoid being present, and unlearning this tendency may take time. When you try to unplug, your brain might react like a fish out of water, panicking and looking for a way to flop back into the water of constant stimulation. The good news is that you can resolve old habits and promote new behaviors.

Three Deep-Breathing Exercises

During stress, anxiety, or panic, the breath becomes shallow and irregular, depriving the body of oxygen and causing shortness of breath and lightheadedness. Deep-breathing techniques can reverse this process and induce the relaxation response.

Just as a yawn slows down heart rate and mental activity, these exercises can calm the mind and body. They cultivate mindfulness and tranquility by reducing stress hormones and quieting your default mode network. With regular practice, you will learn to deepen and prolong the relaxation response, generating peace within.

The following paragraphs describe three different deep-breathing techniques. Before beginning an exercise, take a moment to observe the state of your mind. Notice any tension in your neck, forehead, eyes, jaw, and muscles. Allow any emotions that arise to be present without reacting to them. Recognize and let go. After the practice, observe the mind and body once again to track if any changes took place. This will help you learn which techniques are most beneficial for your health and well-being.

4-7-8 Breathing Exercise

With eyes closed, inhale for 4 seconds, hold your breath for 7 seconds, and then exhale for 8 seconds. Feel the waves of relaxation in your head, chest, and legs when you breathe out, focusing on areas of tension in your body. When you locate an area of tightness or strain, allow it to relax. Calm your mind and notice the transition from in-breath to out-breath. Practice for 5 to 10 minutes, but if you experience shortness of breath, return to normal breathing.

Mouth Exhalation Exercise

Inhale through the nose for 4 seconds, paying attention to the air as it goes through the nostrils and throat. Exhale through the mouth for 4 seconds, feeling the relaxation take hold. With each in-breath, tell yourself, "Breathing in, my mind clears." As you exhale, tell yourself, "Breathing out, my body relaxes." Place your hand on your chest or abdomen and focus on the sensation of breathing. If a thought or distraction interrupts, acknowledge it kindly and return to the exercise. Stop the exercise if you feel lightheaded or dizzy.

After a few minutes, the relaxation response will take place. To deepen it, slow yourself down and try breathing in for 4 seconds and breathing out for 6 seconds. Feel your mind and body unwind as GABA takes hold, and spend a few minutes afterward to savor the calm. To further enhance the feeling, practice gratitude with positive self-affirmations.

I am grateful for this moment. I am rising to my best self. In this moment, I feel peace.

Box Breathing Exercise

Breathe in deeply for 4 seconds, pause for 4 seconds, breathe out for 4 seconds, and then pause for 4 seconds. Visualize each step as the sides of a box and mentally draw the shape. As the relaxation response takes hold, focus on slowing and deepening your breathing.

After 5 to 10 minutes of practice, spend a few minutes maintaining awareness of your breath, feeling the waves of calm traveling through your body. To further enhance the relaxation, gently tense and then release each part of your body for a few seconds without causing any strain. This is particularly effective when stress manifests as body tension. Start with the forehead and continue to the jaws, shoulders, arms, hands, thighs, calves, and feet.

Breathing exercises are powerful techniques that trigger the relaxation response, reduce the heart rate, and calm the body. When practiced regularly, they can alleviate pain and improve sleep quality. The ancient text *Hatha Yoga Pradipika*, written in the fifteenth century, says, "When the breath is unsteady, the mind is unsteady. When the breath is steady, the mind is steady, and the yogi becomes steady. Therefore, one should restrain the breath."

It is important to identify the deep-breathing methods that work best and track your findings. In addition, take time to understand and document the specific sources of stress you may experience during your week. Is it related to a difficult boss, rush-hour traffic, excessive caffeine, or something else? This knowledge will help you anticipate and manage stress before it escalates.

Deepen the Relaxation Response

Breathing exercises will cultivate a state of deep relaxation, but sometimes thoughts can disrupt your calm. As the default mode network turns on, memories of a recent argument, for example, can unexpectedly bring anger, frustration, or anxiety. Reflect on this question for a moment: How do thoughts interrupt your peace?

The brain is a thinking machine and thoughts are a natural part of its activity, coming and going like clouds in the sky. You cannot control when a thought arrives, but you can learn to restrain the emotional reaction to it.

To extend the calming benefits of a breathing exercise, maintain a relaxed, nonjudgmental attitude toward your thoughts, observing them from a distance. When you learn to acknowledge them without reacting, you can avoid the fight-or-flight response and prevent stress altogether.

You can awaken inner peace by developing a deeper awareness of your thoughts and, in particular, the gap between them. At the end of a breathing exercise, observe the mind when it is not wandering. Watch the canvas of your mind when it is in between thoughts and emotions. How does it feel? What is the quality of your "observing mind"?

By tuning into the gap between thoughts, you will get a glimpse of the peaceful nature of the brain's resting state. It is the home of inner peace, a place of clarity and serenity. This is the foundation of your mind on which thoughts and emotions arise.

Gaze into the eyes of toddlers as they explore the world around them, and you will experience a playful presence that is hard to resist. Their baseline emotional state is one of curiosity and joy; they feel and exist rather than think and interpret. This is the same bedrock of inner peace on which your ego, thought patterns, and impulsive behaviors develop over time.

Your mind's peaceful nature is like an ocean of stability. Nothing can destroy its core. But when you lose awareness of your serene depths and float to the surface—where your thoughts, cravings, and emotions reside—you may find yourself in a state of turbulence and unease.

Fighting the ocean tides results in pain and difficulty. The currents of your thoughts can violently toss you around without mercy, until you are lost at sea. Fortunately, the surface waves do not touch the permanent peace down below. To find freedom from the turbulence, you must reconnect with your core. "Your heart is the size of an ocean," Rumi said. "Go find yourself in its hidden depths."

Developing an awareness of your vast inner peace allows you to tune into your higher self and the Infinite Unknown. People of faith accomplish this by listening to God, being mindful of His presence, and following His will. This allows Christians to open their hearts and accept the grace of the Holy Trinity. It guides Muslims to take a break from worldly activities five times a day to pray.

At first, this peace may seem difficult to grasp and maintain. The gap between your thoughts and emotions may last for a few seconds and be drowned out by mental chatter. Fortunately, you can train your mind to prolong this period of freeing silence, allowing you to deeply experience the blissful peace at your core.

Through mindfulness exercises, you can learn to live longer in the present moment and extend the bliss of the relaxation response, allowing your brain's natural state to play a greater role in your life. Mindfulness also helps you neutralize the reactions to thoughts and emotions, helping you reduce and ultimately eliminate daily stress to leave you feeling more content and fulfilled.

The Essence of Mindfulness

Mindfulness means focusing your attention on the present moment and becoming aware of what you are sensing and feeling from a place of truth and acceptance, without judgment. Prayer is an example of a mindful activity where you can form an intimate, truthful connection with the divine.

Popularized by Buddha as meditation, mindfulness has been practiced by many cultures, traditions, and religions since antiquity. Ancient wall art in India dating back as far as 5000 BC depicts people sitting in a meditative posture with their eyes half closed. Meditation has been practiced in Hindu traditions and Taoist China for thousands of years, and it is also documented in Christian traditions. In Matthew 6:5, Jesus taught his disciples to "pray alone and to use few words."

Hundreds of clinical studies have demonstrated the healing effects of mindfulness exercises. By lowering stress hormones like adrenaline and cortisol, these techniques improve concentration and attention, enhance memory, and improve emotional regulation.

In one clinical study, an 8-week meditation course involving breathing and body exercises was as effective as the antidepressant medication Lexapro in reducing anxiety. In other studies, mindfulness practice improved physical and mental health through changes in blood pressure, immune function, pain, and inflammation.

Concentration Meditation

Concentration meditation is a type of mindfulness practice that reduces stress and cultivates inner peace. The technique involves maintaining present-moment awareness by anchoring to your breath, sounds, or body sensations. This keeps you connected to your core and trains you to disconnect from impulsive thoughts and feelings. By becoming aware of inner tension and letting go, you can prevent the stress response from taking hold.

To start, spend a few minutes becoming mindful of the present moment by anchoring to your breath, noticing the flow of air entering and leaving your nostrils and mouth. Notice the quality of your breath as you inhale and exhale, your chest and abdomen rising and falling, and the air hitting the back of your throat. Then count your breaths from 1 to 5 at the end of each exhalation. Anytime you lose focus, start again with 1. After 5 to 10 minutes, notice the state of your mind as it relaxes back to baseline.

During concentration meditation, the act of returning to the present moment is the key to developing mindfulness. You want to become aware when your mind has wandered; the more interruptions you recognize, the stronger the practice becomes. This empowers your "observing mind," a powerful force that will help you break through mental knots.

For example, during a 4-7-8 breathing exercise, your shoulders may tense as recent memories race through your mind. However, when you recognize this strain and return to the present, your body will relax. Simply noticing the unconscious strain is enough to stop it. In that moment when you develop awareness, the stress response subsides.

Other Types of Mindfulness Practice

You can try various forms of mindfulness practice that will empower your deeper mind. These practices help you stay rooted in the present moment, so the "observing mind" can strengthen. Depending on your individual personality and preferences, you may be drawn to particular practices, such as:

- ***Prayer***—Acknowledging the Infinite Unknown
- ***Breath meditation***—Watching or counting your breaths in the present moment, feeling the flow of the air and the rise and fall of your chest and abdomen
- ***Body scan***—Scanning your body for physical sensations, starting from the top of your head to your feet
- ***Sound***—Listening to each and every sound in your environment
- ***Walking meditation or yoga***—Being aware of your body as you walk or exercise

With any mindfulness practice, you will want to follow three essential steps to cultivate a state of mindfulness:

1. Maintain presence in the now, focusing on the prayer, breathing, or body sensations. You can begin by acknowledging your current state of mind with honesty, evaluating if it is positive or negative. You should not judge or react to your condition, and you should be comfortable with either ease or unease. Once you make this acknowledgment, return to present-moment awareness.
2. Recognize that any unfavorable thought you encounter is transient. Do not focus excessively on it or attempt to change it, medicate to avoid it, or

escape from it. Thoughts are passing phenomena (like clouds), so allow them to fade away on their own. Take note of the signals your emotions may be giving you but then release them and return to the present.

3. Realize that good states are also temporary, and savor them while they last. Accept that these moments will eventually pass, and fully experience them with gratitude. Avoid getting angry or irritated when these pleasant conditions inevitably end.

For people of faith, prayer is a form of mindfulness practice where you can break away from internal mental chatter and tune into the present moment to communicate with the Infinite Unknown. Speak in full honesty and end the prayer with Amen, which means *the truth*. You can pray to a higher power to help improve your life, reduce stress, and awaken inner peace.

Lord God, the Infinite Unknown, the energy of the universe, as I fill my lungs with air, I fill my heart with Your grace. I breathe in Your benevolence, and I breathe out my restlessness and my pride. Lord God, help me see the light of this moment so that I have the strength to end the darkness of stress.

The Science of Mindfulness

Scientists are beginning to understand the effects of mindfulness on the brain and how it unlocks peace and well-being. When your mind wanders, the default mode network turns on and takes you on a rollercoaster ride of thoughts, memories, and emotions. It causes you to lose awareness of the present moment.

However, during a prayer or meditation, your awareness shuts off the DMN and liberates you from a major source of stress and anxiety. When you are mindful, negative thoughts subside, which in turn reduces stress hormones like cortisol and grants you greater calm in the face of adversity.

During a breath exercise when you recognize a distraction and return to the now, the DMN disengages, and the brain's central executive network (CEN) takes control. In this state, you are more aware of the present moment, living "in the zone" with greater focus and concentration. The increased activity in your brain's prefrontal cortex and parietal cortex leads to improved attention and presence.

With daily mindfulness practice, the power of the CEN will grow and activate the brain's deeper consciousness, eventually guiding you to the higher self and the peace and harmony of the enlightened state. As inner peace replaces stress, you will discover greater bliss in the present moment. Rumi said, "Your task is not to seek for love, but merely to seek and find all the barriers within yourself that you have built against it."

Meditation also allows you to be aware of your thoughts without becoming attached to them, learning to let go. You can avoid your DMN, the state of being lost in thought, by stepping back and recognizing that DMN-driven thoughts have appeared. In that moment, you have used your CEN, or "observing mind," to become aware that ruminating is occurring.

MRI imaging studies of meditators have shown a reconfiguration in their neural networks, with reduced activity of the DMN ("wandering mind") and greater connectivity in the CEN ("observing mind"). When you observe your thoughts and emotions from a distance, you activate the CEN and stop mind-wandering in its tracks. This "observing mind" is inherently peaceful, rational, and curious. Through mindfulness practice, you can turn off the DMN and strengthen the CEN to become the dominant mode in your life.

Two aspects of mindfulness are critical to foster the CEN and your "observing mind"—attention and acceptance.

Attention is the ability to tune out your thoughts and distractions and focus on the now. Buddha said, "Do not dwell in the past, do not dream of the future, concentrate the mind on the present moment."

You can anchor to the present moment by focusing on your breathing, your state of mind, physical sensations in your body, or prayer. Initially, undivided attention may last for only a few seconds at a time. With practice, you can deepen your "in the zone" attention span to several minutes and even hours. Concentrating your mind on the present moment will give rise to profound inner peace.

The acceptance aspect of mindfulness involves acknowledging your thoughts and feelings without judgment and then examining and letting them go, rather than allowing them to control you. In this way, you will learn more about the triggers of stress, so you can recognize them as they arise. Remember, a trigger could be thinking about a past argument, worrying about a future event, or ruminating on any other thought or memory that stirs anger, anxiety, or emotional pain. Over time, you can train your brain to identify early stress and prevent it from escalating.

During mindfulness practice, attention and acceptance enable you to explore the root causes of your problems. When in a state of focus and concentration, your brain is a remarkable self-learning organ that can identify triggers of stress and stop them from exploding into distress. "The power of concentration is the only key to the treasure house of knowledge," said the Indian monk Swami Vivekananda.

Everyone has the capacity to be mindful; it's not a secret club exclusive to certain people. With time and commitment, you can cultivate this essential mental quality that brings health, happiness, and inner peace. Just as weight-lifting strengthens muscles, mindfulness practice empowers your "observing mind" to play a more vital role in your life.

Sometimes when you practice prayer or meditation, you will come into contact with negative emotions, frustrations, or problems that have been lingering beneath the surface. When this occurs, remind yourself to be present and accepting, never judging or criticizing. Self-condemnation is unhelpful and counterproductive.

When this happens, the turbulence can be overwhelming. To counter it, start each practice with positive affirmations.

May I be happy, healthy, and at peace.

Smile and foster gratitude for the mindful moments, no matter how short they might be, while allowing the negative tendencies to subside.

Do not reject the emotions that arise in quiet moments. Rather than reacting to them instinctively, take a step back and observe them objectively, learning more about yourself. The truth will set you free. By seeing your true condition, you allow the mind an opportunity to understand and heal itself.

How to Practice Mindfulness Exercises

There is no proper way to practice mindfulness exercises, but there are ways to maximize their benefits. Some people prefer guided meditation (by an instructor or apps like Balance or Headspace), while others like to practice alone. Some may find it easier to develop awareness of sounds, while others prefer following the breath or body sensations. To get the most out of mindfulness practice, choose the method and style that best grounds you to the present and provides the greatest stress relief.

It is essential to set a daily intention for your practice. While a goal is a specific accomplishment you want to achieve in the future, an intention describes how you want to feel as you work toward that goal. It is the guiding principle for how you want to live, based on your values. For example, on New Year's Day, a goal of losing ten pounds can be coupled with an intention to do so with patience and happiness, in a relaxed and healthy manner.

Whenever you communicate your goals and intentions, you send powerful signals to your subconscious mind—a force that can bring them to fruition without your conscious awareness. The more fervently you wish to achieve something, the more likely it will come to fruition. "You become what you think about all day long," said Ralph Waldo Emerson.

Follow these additional guidelines to maximize the benefits of mindfulness practice:

- Daily practice will deliver better results; a fifteen- to twenty-minute exercise is most effective, particularly in the morning and/or late afternoon.
- Apply a relaxed attitude with presence and alertness; avoid being rigid, strained, or overly focused.
- Find a comfortable posture where you can be alert and present; sitting in a chair with an upright posture or sitting cross-legged on a cushion are good options (avoid lying down or slouching).
- Being outdoors activates the relaxation response more naturally than an indoor setting, particularly when tuning into nature.
- When distracting memories, thoughts, or emotions interrupt you, acknowledge them gently by labeling what they are and then return to the present.
- Practice kindness, self-acceptance, and compassion and avoid judgment, criticism, and self-bullying; praise yourself for taking the road to the higher self, and enjoy the journey.

- Begin to meditate or pray with your eyes closed but learn to practice with your eyes open, so you can perform a mindfulness exercise in real-world circumstances.
- Pay attention to cravings, aversions, or delusions. This topic will be discussed later; for now, simply pay attention when they bubble up, gently acknowledge them, and return to the present.

The Importance of Silence

Silence can be uncomfortable, but it is an essential component for peace and enlightenment. We are often conditioned to embellish the present moment with music, podcasts, TV shows and movies, social media, electronic games, or gadgets. Why? Distractions may help us bury negative states of mind, troubling memories, and nagging worries or help us avoid feeling socially awkward or lonely.

However, this tendency to "fill the silence" can prevent us from understanding the truth of reality and connecting with our higher self. To master our default mode, we must learn to embrace silence and be comfortable with it. "Silence is the language of God," Rumi said. "All else is poor translation."

Silence is a powerful tool for promoting health and learning, as several research studies have demonstrated. A Duke University study found that two hours of silence per day stimulated neuronal growth in the hippocampus, a part of the brain that encodes memories. Silence can also reduce stress, lower blood pressure, improve focus, and promote creativity.

A strong mind is one that is at peace. During quiet times, you will receive critical insights from your subconscious mind to help solve your problems and foster inner growth. For people of faith, these messages come from God, the Infinite Unknown. By tuning into your deeper consciousness in silence, you will cultivate inner peace and spiritual development.

Final Thoughts on Stress

Stress is a common feature of today's world and can be a major driver of your negative thought patterns, addictive cravings, and even diseases. If not managed effectively, it can explode and wreak havoc on your life. Reacting to stress with substances such as alcohol or distractions like social media can worsen the problem.

Instead, preventive measures like breathing techniques and mindfulness exercises can stop the stress response from occurring. "An ounce of prevention is worth a pound of cure," wrote Benjamin Franklin, a founding father of the United States. Investing fifteen minutes each morning to breathe deeply in silence and become aware of sounds and sensations will significantly reduce your stress during the day.

Mindfulness also helps you identify your life stressors and modify your reactions to them. You become better equipped to recover quickly from tense moments instead of letting them overpower you, avoiding the sting of the second arrow. Life's difficulties become more bearable and are short lived. "A man endures his pain and does not add to it," Marcus Aurelius said.

With regular practice, you will learn to prevent stress from occurring. The brain's self-learning capabilities will guide you away from the fight-or-flight reaction toward inner peace. Studies have revealed that mindfulness rewires the brain's neural circuits, shutting off the "wandering mind" and the stress it compounds.

In today's digital era, you may be expected to respond to a continuous stream of information, which can make it difficult to practice mindfulness during the day. You do not have to react to this nonstop stream of data—you have the freedom to ignore nonessential information. You can exercise restraint and learn to decline requests that are not worth your time, deliberately choosing a path of relaxation.

During stressful moments, instead of reaching for your smartphone as a distraction, use that energy to practice a breathing exercise. Mindfulness will help you more peacefully react to your ever-changing external and internal world.

When you identify a trigger of stress, you can respond in one of two ways—you can remove the bad actor from your life, or you can modify how you react to it.

Ideally, you should end bad habits that cause you harm. If preventable triggers like social media or certain acquaintances cause stress, limit them to find peace. Saying no to your impulse to yell at someone or to drink another glass of alcohol may be inconvenient in the short term, but it is worth a future state of peace and happiness. You can improve your mental state by removing harmful catalysts and creating healthier habits that will prevent overstimulation and excess.

However, some stressful situations may be out of your control. You cannot ignore the boss's demands or your kid's outbursts, but you can change your reactions to them. Recognizing early signs of stress and practicing a breathing or mindfulness exercise will have an immediate effect and prevent negative emotions from escalating.

Investing in mindfulness exercises will help you cultivate the "observing mind," which is controlled by the central executive network. Thoughts and emotions are transitory states, and by observing them you will recognize their impermanent and illusory nature. When you learn to use your "observing mind," you can access the deeper consciousness of your central executive network.

During prayer or meditation, it is essential to notice when your default mode network switches on and self-obsessive thought patterns arise with thoughts like, "Why did she talk to me like that? How will I make the deadline? I don't know if I can do this." The DMN's "wandering mind" might show up at other times, when not in prayer or meditation. You may tune out during simple tasks like cooking, cleaning, exercising, or showering and find yourself ruminating about negative memories or future worries. These moments when the ego rears its head are great opportunities to practice mindfulness. By becoming aware of the default mode network, you can switch it off, be present, and enter a relaxed state.

The key to lasting change is to extend mindfulness beyond the exercises and into your daily life. You can maintain awareness during heated conversations, feeling early sensations that might turn to anger, fear, or anxiety. You can maximize bliss by being mindful during joyful moments like listening to music or taking a bath. You can show respect to family members, partners, friends, and coworkers by being present and listening to them. You can also practice mindfulness while eating, taking the time to savor and taste every bite instead of rushing to the next activity.

Studies have shown lasting positive health benefits of mindfulness exercises, beginning just six to eight weeks after regular practice. Incorporating mindful relaxation into your daily life will help you reduce stress and promote inner peace and contentment. Setting a daily intention and dedicating yourself to positive change will help you reach your goals.

KNOT
2

EMOTIONAL PAIN—HEAL YOUR INNER WOUNDS

LIFE CAN BE PAINFUL, not only from our physical aches and breaks but also from the emotional trauma we encounter along the way. Pain can arise from many sources, including our ancestral history, parents, friends, and partners, and it impacts our daily lives. Even in the happiest moments, unresolved pain can lurk in the background, dragging us back to a place of dread or despair. If you suffer from emotional pain, you can permanently resolve it through a healing remedy that is at the heart of religion, a power that grants you freedom, inner peace, and bliss.

In this chapter, you will learn how your brain sustains emotional pain and its impact on health and relationships. One major driver is your default mode network (DMN), which can repeatedly revisit painful memories and prevent you from moving on. By understanding your mind's inner workings, you will learn to create space from and ultimately heal the roots of emotional pain through the practices of forgiveness and concentration meditation.

The Effects of Emotional Pain

Many of us carry unsettled grief and heartache that can affect the quality of our lives. This suffering can originate from a traumatic event such as a divorce, illness, passing of a family member, vehicle accident, or altercation. For some, the origin of the pain may be familial, passed down across generations from our parents and ancestors. These experiences can create deep-rooted pain that influences our daily thoughts, decisions, and behaviors.

Regardless of the source, emotional pain shapes our relationships, guiding us toward or away from certain people. It exerts a constant pull on us, spawning a range of emotions such as fear, guilt, anger, grief, despair, sadness, shame, and envy. It is one of the most complex and difficult mental knots to unravel, because it can fester for years and even decades, coexisting with us like a close companion. Sadly, our long-lasting ties with difficult memories can lead to addiction, depression, and many other mental health issues.

Emotional trauma can become so severe that it can lead to suicide. According to the Centers for Disease Control and Prevention, suicide rates in the US have risen by 30 percent over the past two decades, with nearly 46,000 in 2020 (or one every 11 minutes). It has become the second-leading cause of death for the 10 to 14 age group and the 25 to 34 age group. These figures do not include the countless other people who contemplate, plan, or attempt it.

If left unresolved for an extended period, emotional trauma can alter brain chemistry and lead to unhealthy coping behaviors like drinking, taking drugs, or smoking. We may hope for permanent peace from the pain, but these unhealthy measures only provide temporary relief. If we do not address the issue at its source, emotional pain can exacerbate over time as we ruminate and blame ourselves or others for it.

If you suffer from this mental knot, there is hope. By developing an understanding of your pain and how it influences your actions, you can break through to a new chapter in your life.

The Roots of Pain

Emotional pain can manifest at any age, occurring suddenly or developing gradually over time. Our upbringing is often a direct source, coming from parents who were critical, abusive, or neglectful. Children who view their parents as perfect may internalize blame and derision made by careless parents during times of conflict. These beliefs may follow teenagers into adulthood, reinforced by painful memories that can frequently recur.

Have you noticed that recollections of your past experiences can evoke powerful emotions? When you recall a painful memory, it can bring up fear, stress, sadness, and other unbearable feelings. Of course, not all memories are bad; wedding days, Christmas mornings, and first days of school are also deeply ingrained and linked to powerful, positive emotions.

Remembering a distressing event may force you not only to relive the past but also to revisit painful emotions. Bitter memories can directly activate your brain's limbic system, which is responsible for generating emotions like fear, anxiety, anger, and remorse. On any given morning, you may be feeling relaxed or focused on a task when suddenly a recollection of a past event sends you spiraling into emotional pain. You may even relive old trauma constantly throughout the day, which takes you away from the present moment and back into a hurtful past experience.

The key to transcending the turmoil of the limbic system lies in recognizing that it does not dictate your identity. Remarkably, even the ancient Egyptians were aware of this, as evidenced by the Eye of Horus. They used this symbol, which originally derived from the myth of Isis and Osiris, in funerary and spiritual contexts. Other cultures refer to it as the *all-seeing eye.*

It served as a reminder that a life of prosperity and protection is only possible by freeing ourselves from the constraints of our emotions.

Composed of six distinct parts, the Eye of Horus accurately represents the neuroanatomy of our brain's limbic system, depicting key centers involved in memory, stress, and fear. Despite lacking X-ray technology, ancient Egyptians recognized the important role of the brain's emotional center in our lives. According to their beliefs, it was only when our soul reached a spiritual level that the "third eye" would open, allowing us to develop deeper self-awareness and heal our spirit.

Found in fish, amphibians, reptiles, and mammals, the limbic system is evolutionarily one of the oldest brain structures in nature. It consists of the amygdala, hippocampus, thalamus, hypothalamus, basal ganglia, and cingulate gyrus, which work in concert to control our emotions and memories. Whenever we relate an emotion to a life event, the limbic system is activated.

The hippocampus, part of the brain's limbic system, is a cashew-shaped structure that stores our memories. An old melody, a familiar smell, or the memory of our grandparents are kept as distinct engrams, or networks of neuronal connections. A recent study found that the hippocampus stores "good" and "bad" engrams in distinct areas—pleasant recollections in the top half and hurtful ones in the bottom half. These regions have different gene expression and seem to connect to different parts of the brain, indicating that the brain processes positive and negative memories differently.

When you recollect a painful experience (like a breakup or car accident), the hippocampus sends a signal from the engram to the emotional centers of the limbic system, such as the amygdala or the "fear center." Recurrent memories of past traumas can lead to an overwhelming emotional and physical stress response that can be debilitating. If left unresolved, emotional pain will take you on an emotional rollercoaster ride and cause significant damage to your body. In a split second, you may be overcome by physical tension, with a rapidly increasing heart rate and blood pressure. A feeling of terror can arise as your fight-or-flight response takes hold.

Engrams not only encode the sensory information from an event but also the emotional impressions associated with it. For example, you may be able to manage an occasional bout of heartache from a breakup, but if you suffer from an overactive default mode network, you may repeatedly revisit the unpleasant memories of your old relationship. This forces you to repeatedly experience the painful sting of anger, betrayal, and loss.

The DMN becomes active anytime you lose touch with the present moment and ruminate on the past. As we discussed, because of the brain's inherent negativity bias, you are more likely to dwell on distressing memories than happy ones.

While a healthy DMN is important to process your daily events and help you navigate through life, it can become agitated after emotionally traumatic experiences. In this state, the DMN continually takes you to painful recollections and disrupts your present-moment awareness.

The more harshly you react to these memories, the more the DMN believes they are important, so it steps up its mind-wandering campaign and unwittingly adds to your emotional trauma by forcing you to relive your old wounds. Because the DMN amplifies your hurtful memories, it can give rise to intense emotional pain that can haunt you for a long time.

Sometimes the memories stored in the hippocampus may not reflect reality but rather your interpretation of it. Emotional pain can also arise because of a self-centered or erroneous view that you may apply toward the past. As the Greek philosopher Epictetus said, "It's not the events that upset us but our judgments about them." For instance, you may have unrealistic expectations of others that can taint memories of your loved ones. By recognizing this false view, you can right the past and rediscover the charm of old times.

However, in other cases emotional pain is unequivocally caused by traumatic events. If you suffer from unresolved heartache, there is hope. To find peace, you must first recognize the DMN and understand how your brain interprets and relives past events. With practice, you can learn to resolve even the most intensely hurtful memories, untangling the mental knot of emotional pain and finding a path to inner peace.

Finding Space from Emotional Pain

Two drivers sustain emotional pain. The first is mind-wandering, a process where the DMN revisits old memories. The second is the activation of painful emotions associated with these memories. By understanding how this process unfolds, you can learn to create space from your emotional distress and work to resolve it.

Mind-Wandering

To reduce the recurrence of old memories, you must first stop mind-wandering by silencing the DMN. Mindfulness practices such as meditation, prayer, and affirmations can shut down this "monkey mind" and keep you present in the moment, thereby pulling you out of the DMN's tendency to ruminate on the past.

When practiced for at least fifteen to twenty minutes daily, concentration meditation cultivates mindfulness and quiets the DMN. This provides a respite from painful memories and anxious thoughts, enabling you to spend more time being aware of the present. American psychologist William James said, "The faculty of voluntarily bringing back a wandering attention, over and over again, is the very root of judgment, character, and will."

Mindfulness will reduce the occurrence of painful memories, though it may not completely prevent them from resurfacing. Even with dedicated practice, a single thought can trigger a traumatic memory and plunge you back into emotional pain.

The Memory/Emotion Connection

To permanently resolve emotional pain, you must sever the connection between a memory and its associated feelings. This can be challenging, especially when deep-rooted negative emotions grow over time and become entrenched in your daily routines.

You have the power to break through the mental knot of emotional pain and find lasting inner peace. It will take courage and tenacity to get there, which will mean having faith that freedom is possible. As President Franklin Delano Roosevelt once said, "The only thing we have to fear is fear itself."

This key insight reveals an effective strategy to counter the power of emotional pain—to accept and experience your emotions, no matter how negative they are, rather than attempting to avoid or medicate them. Learn to be objective about your feelings, and do not allow them to rule your life.

When a painful memory arises during a prayer or mindfulness exercise, turn on your "observing mind" and tune into these emotions without succumbing to them. By stepping back and seeing the traumatic event from a detached point of view, you will better understand the root causes of your suffering. You will activate your brain's central executive network, the gateway to wisdom, which gleans insights into your habitual tendencies. The light of self-awareness will ultimately dispel the darkness of existential pain.

Emotional pain persists because you have learned to live with it, rather than resolving it and moving on. It is like enduring the physical discomfort from a chronic condition like acid reflux. You may take medication for a temporary relief from the pressure in your throat, knowing that the symptoms will return once again. In the same way, you may have unconsciously accepted that emotional pain is an unavoidable part of life, thus never able to find permanent freedom from it.

Rather than acknowledging your negative emotions and allowing them to pass, you may have tried to avoid them with alcohol, work, video games, drugs, nicotine, shopping, or gambling. Unfortunately, this only serves to postpone the discomfort, and as the pain recurs, you may have resorted to increasingly heavier doses of distractions to avoid it. This can end up wasting considerable energy and time, even placing you at risk of addiction. Instead of running away from your memories and their related emotional pain, consider using your effort to accept and understand your memories and thoughts.

When you run away from negative emotions like fear, grief, regret, resentment, shame, envy, anger, or sadness, you become the polar opposite of the hero in children's books. You opt to flee instead of confronting the monster.

Instead, think of it this way: if you can simply experience the rain and wait out the storm, you will be rewarded with sunshine and clear skies. Finding peace means accepting and observing your negative feelings and then allowing them to drift toward the horizon.

It is like a pilot who steers around clouds, frightened of the turbulence they may bring. This fear leads the pilot to act irrationally and waste fuel. It would be more prudent to gain composure and simply fly through the clouds—on the other side lies a blue sky and an understanding that turbulence is a normal part of flying. Do not be afraid to fly through the clouds of emotional pain; you will emerge stronger on the other side.

If you prefer to work with a therapist to resolve your emotional pain, dialectical behavior therapy and cognitive behavioral therapy can offer effective help. With the aim of improving your overall quality of life, professionals may use a technique called *radical acceptance* to help you process emotional pain by learning to recognize its many facets. This approach fosters self-understanding and teaches new skills that will replace unhealthy behaviors.

Even with the guidance of a trained therapist, it may be difficult to resolve emotional pain associated with trauma or deep-rooted issues. It might feel daunting to turn off your distractions and truly experience the raw emotions underlying your emotional pain. You may have become accustomed to negative memories and feelings dominating your life, leaving you worn down and uncertain of your ability to overcome them. You may have even taken out the pain on others, damaging relationships and reputations in the process.

To effectively break the link between a memory and its emotion, you can turn to an age-old remedy found in the world's major religions. This power will help you reclaim your life and break through one of the most challenging mental knots.

The Power of Forgiveness

"The weak can never forgive," the Indian leader Mahatma Gandhi said. "Forgiveness is the attribute of the strong." A renowned peace broker, Gandhi fought against British oppression in India for over three decades, enduring arrests, imprisonment, and sanctions without resorting to violence. Through his commitment to peaceful protest, Gandhi ultimately achieved his goal of a free India and served as an inspiration to millions by forgiving the British for the centuries of injustices they had inflicted on India.

For Christians, the power of forgiveness is the most Christ-like quality we can foster. Pope John Paul II famously forgave his would-be assassin, recognizing that anger, fear, and anxiety ultimately cause the most suffering for the one experiencing them. He commented that forgiveness is a personal decision of the heart to go against the instinct to pay back evil with evil.

Resentment and ill will toward others prevent you from living in peace and achieving true happiness. The power of forgiveness is not for the benefit of others but for your own benefit.

Forgiving those who have hurt you may not be easy. The ego puts up stiff resistance as the default mode network locks you into emotional pain. But carrying this anger forward only brings more hurt. Will a lifetime of resentment toward a parent, relative, previous spouse, or other person who wronged you make them repent or change the past? No. Your ill will toward someone for their wrongdoings will only adversely affect you, not them.

Jesus Christ said, "You have heard that it was said, 'Love your neighbor and hate your enemy.' But I tell you, love your enemies and pray for those who persecute you, that you may be children of your Father in heaven. He causes His sun to rise on the evil and the good and sends rain on the righteous and the unrighteous." Christ reminded us that God provides grace and benevolence for all beings, regardless of their sins or defilements. When you forgive others, you enter the realm of the divine. "Be perfect," Jesus said, "as your heavenly Father is perfect."

Buddha taught that the power of forgiveness aids you in the journey toward enlightenment. The Noble Eightfold Path, an essential tenet of Buddhism, forbids anger and instead encourages metta (loving-kindness), sympathetic joy, and compassion. By forgoing the oppressive energy of anger and blame, you will embrace positive karma that frees you from suffering, bringing you closer to nirvana, a spiritual awakening where you are freed from the flames of desire, anger, hatred, and jealousy.

In Judaism, a person who causes harm should apologize sincerely and honestly, and the victim is encouraged to grant forgiveness. The *Torah* reads, "When asked for forgiveness, one should forgive with a sincere mind and a willing spirit." Similarly, the *Koran* and hadiths contain numerous texts that promote Muslims to be forgiving. Hinduism considers forgiveness to be one of its six cardinal virtues.

Forgiveness lies at the heart of the world's major religions for good reason. When the memory of a painful experience causes you to feel anger or resentment toward another person, the solution is to release those feelings instead of holding onto them and letting them rule your thoughts, behaviors, and emotions. You must forgive. "It is in pardoning that we are pardoned," St. Francis of Assisi said.

If you choose not to forgive, emotional pain will continue to fester beneath the surface, digging deeper and deeper into your thoughts, emotions, and views until it causes irreparable damage. It is like pouring red dye into the pond of your mind; the red particles will spread throughout the body of water. Unchecked anger, anxiety, and fear will eventually consume you.

What good is there in getting angry at someone's wrongful deeds? It will not change their actions and only guides you to negative emotions that cause suffering. Instead, view the actions of others with calm and restraint. "Patience is the companion of wisdom," St. Augustine said. When you choose not to react to your negative emotions but rather smile in the face of them, you develop a superpower. The hero is the one who faces hardship not with anger and prejudice but with compassion and wisdom.

At times, you may need a refuge or safe space when negative emotions appear. It will help to have a trusted friend or partner to help you process your feelings, but not everyone is always available. Thankfully, your higher power is always there. Whether it is Almighty God, the Infinite Unknown, the all-encompassing energy of the universe, or the infinite power of your subconscious mind, this higher force will listen and guide you through your most challenging times.

Communicating with the divine is a highly effective way to release emotional pain. Through prayer and meditation, you can open yourself to salvation by granting forgiveness to those who have wronged you and forgive yourself for old transgressions. By taking the time to directly communicate with the divine, you will find the peace and freedom you seek.

Lord God, the Infinite Unknown, the energy of the universe, I fill my lungs with Your grace. I breathe in Your benevolence, and I breathe out my pain. As I let go of the past, I forgive those who have wronged me, and I forgive myself for past mistakes.

When you are willing to forgive and let go of the burdens of the past, you will be set free to enjoy the present moment and the inherent beauty of life. Breaking through the mental knot of emotional pain will allow inner peace to flourish and nurture you. Forgiving others and reconnecting with them will help rekindle the light at your core. "To err is human," Alexander Pope said, "To forgive, divine."

In your journey of healing, the DMN (your ego) will put up a fight to prevent you from genuinely granting forgiveness. An exercise practiced by Buddhists may aid in lifting this weight from your shoulders. Imagine receiving a phone call from your physician with sudden and unexpected bad news—you have a terminal illness and will pass away in the next week. Your physician urges you to make amends and prepare for your final days.

In this moment of grief, who will you reach out to and what will you say? Is there an estranged person toward whom you would like to show genuine forgiveness? Consider any deep-rooted burdens that are no longer worth hiding. Will you let them go? Who would you like to see in your last few days on Earth? What will you share on social media, and who will you thank?

This exercise causes the DMN to relinquish its control and allows you to access the divine inner love radiating from your soul. When you are no longer burdened by the past, you will be present in the moment and free to experience life and its unbridled glory. St. John of the Cross said, "In the inner stillness where meditation leads, the Spirit secretly anoints the soul and heals our deepest wounds."

Tackling trauma on your own might feel daunting, but by invoking the strength of your spirit, you can take the difficult steps on your healing journey. With determination and a daily intention to resolve past emotional pain, you will find lasting peace and happiness. By forgiving and breaking the root of emotional pain at its source, you will permanently resolve the past and find peace in the present.

The Importance of Self-Forgiveness

If you have experienced self-inflicted trauma, you may find yourself in a cycle of overwhelming blame and guilt. Perhaps you made choices based on emotions you did not understand or acted on conditions that were beyond your control. Whatever the cause, self-forgiveness will set you free from the negative memories and emotions that consume you.

Granting acceptance and forgiveness for yourself is an essential step on the path to enlightenment. You may blame misfortunes on your appearance, background, upbringing, or misdeeds, which sow the seeds of shame, self-hatred, regret, and remorse. This can lead to poor decisions and judgments during daily life. To ensure your health and well-being, it is critical to let go of the hurtful past and accept who are you in this moment.

The four essential elements for self-forgiveness are accountability, remorse, restoration, and renewal.

The first essential element in the process of self-forgiveness, accountability, may seem odd to you. Avoiding responsibility for emotional pain is a major reason why it continues unresolved. The DMN (your ego) may want to blame the pain on your upbringing, ancestry, or other external factors. However, it is important to realize that *you* may be responsible for the hurt you feel. Acknowledging this can be difficult, but it is necessary to break free from suffering.

When you take responsibility for your emotional pain, you must do so wholeheartedly and sincerely, without trying to pass the blame. By ending the pattern of avoidance and greeting your innermost emotions with bravery, patience, and kindness, you will lay the groundwork for the healing process to take place. "Your own soul is nourished when you are kind," King Solomon, a monarch of ancient Israel, said. "It is destroyed when you are cruel." Accepting responsibility for the errors of the past brings tremendous relief, lightening the load that you have been bearing.

Remorse is the second essential element in the process of self-forgiveness.

During prayers and meditations, stay present and genuinely experience this feeling from a place of honesty and acceptance. This may be challenging, particularly if you have blamed others, portrayed yourself as the victim, disregarded the emotions of others, or ignored the harm done. St. Augustine said, "Repentant tears wash out the stain of guilt."

The truth is that guilt and remorse are beneficial emotions that signal a need for change. They will help you heal and grow, granting you wisdom from your most difficult life experiences. Rather than denying or ignoring these feelings, accept them and understand their significance. Once you do, the emotions will pass and allow the next phase of healing to begin.

The third essential element is restoration, which begins as soon as you take action to restore the damage of past actions and undo the effects of emotional pain. This can involve letting go of internal ill will and judgment, restoring relationships or partnerships that have gone sour, or restoring a healthy connection with your workplace or community.

Restoration is an act of faith for a brighter tomorrow. A simple apology may sometimes suffice, although a greater effort might be needed to make amends. Face-to-face dialogue is the most effective way to communicate and restore old bonds, although setting it up might require some effort. Restoring your relationships can bring tremendous relief, far greater than the pride and inconvenience you may need to overcome in the process.

When restoration is complete, the fourth element of renewal kicks off as the fruits of self-forgiveness begin to emerge. This can be an overwhelmingly positive, euphoric experience. As you heal from the wounds of guilt and remorse, the light of inner peace starts to shine. You will experience greater compassion toward yourself and others, an energy that relieves stress and improves health.

In fact, clinical studies have demonstrated the positive impact of forgiveness. In a randomized trial of 4,600 participants, a workbook intervention designed to promote forgiveness led to reduced depression and anxiety symptoms. Other studies have found a similar link between forgiveness and improved well-being.

The power of forgiveness enables you to break through the mental knot of emotional pain. By accepting and letting go of the past, you can open a new chapter and take back control of your life. Old habits of blame and regret will be replaced with peace and acceptance. Free from the grip of negative thought patterns, you will become rooted in life's natural serenity. Regardless of past mistakes, it is never too late to look within and heal yourself.

For some people, emotional pain can be so intense that it requires the care of a healthcare professional. PTSD is among the most debilitating emotional disorders. In some cases, past trauma can be so overwhelming that it can trigger a cascade of neurobiological events that result in long-lasting changes in the brain. This can lead to unconscious behaviors and impairments in memory, attention, and executive function.

People suffering from PTSD often battle to stay present in the moment, making it challenging to practice mindfulness and forgiveness. They may yearn for a few moments of tranquility, aching for the mental and emotional balance that many of us take for granted. We must be especially mindful to show empathy and compassion for those who suffer from PTSD, including victims of war, rape, violence, and other traumatic circumstances.

Symptoms of PTSD may include intrusive flashbacks and nightmares that disrupt daily life, leading to avoidance of places, activities, or people associated with the traumatic event. Other symptoms may include suicidal ideation, self-destructive behavior, and overwhelming feelings of hopelessness, isolation, depression, fear, or anger. In some cases, people may experience extreme disorientation and psychosis due to involuntary distress that recurs throughout the day and night.

Due to the potential for self-harm and suicide, PTSD requires the care of a medical professional. Several approved drug therapies and psychotherapy-based approaches can improve the severity of symptoms, with new treatment options on the horizon. Recently, clinical studies have shown that MDMA-assisted therapy leads to significant, lasting benefit in the majority of treated PTSD patients, with major improvements in empathy and a decrease in suicidal ideation and emotional pain. FDA approval of MDMA-assisted therapy for PTSD is expected in the future.

Final Thoughts on Emotional Pain

Painful emotions are signals of an unmet need. When unaddressed and left to fester, your emotional pain can become intense and overwhelming, manifesting as depression, jealousy, guilt, or worthlessness. You may brush them off and blame them on your family or upbringing, but their roots may actually arise elsewhere.

Past trauma can revisit you daily, disrupting your life with gripping memories. Triggered by the amygdala (the "fear center" of your brain), fear can paralyze you, keeping you from making good decisions. Anxiety and anger obstruct the light of love that naturally radiates from your soul, trapping you in a state of unrest. Making matters worse, your default mode network may ensnare you with gripping memories and negative emotions as you bounce from one painful state to the next, making you your own biggest victim and depriving you from experiencing life's natural bliss and serenity.

You can break through the mental knot of emotional pain and find a path out of the darkness. Rather than running away from or numbing the distress, strive to understand the cause of your troubles and forgive those who have wronged you. Accept and embrace your suffering with compassion, so you can heal and find freedom. "Blessed are the merciful," Jesus said, "for they will be shown mercy."

Prayer and mindfulness exercises grant peace by decreasing rumination and severing the link between negative memories and their associated feelings, thereby disrupting the cycle of emotional pain. When you switch off the "wandering mind" (your DMN) and turn on the "observing mind" (your CEN), past trauma no longer exerts power over you. Instead of acting at its mercy, you will regain control and observe emotions like fear or anger as transient clouds that appear and pass in the sky of your mind.

Mindfulness and faith are powerful tools that help you heal and resolve emotional trauma once and for all. They are aided by the power of forgiveness, a cornerstone of religion and an essential step for enlightenment. Jesus Christ said, as recounted in the Bible, "Forgive, and you will be forgiven."

While it may be challenging to forgive those who have harmed you, remember that you cannot control other people's will, and how you feel inside will not impact them. You may not comprehend their motivations and cannot influence their choices, but you can manage your reactions to them. When you realize that your emotions affect your own health and wellness, you can more easily accept others without needing to control or change them. The eighteenth-century English poet Alexander Pope said, "Forgiving those who have wronged us is the key to personal happiness."

You cannot effectively grant forgiveness to others until you accept and forgive yourself. Self-forgiveness starts with looking in the mirror, acknowledging the truth, and saying, "I'm sorry." This can be challenging if you have blamed others for your emotions. To overcome this, take responsibility, experience remorse, and commit to restoration and renewal. With an intention to find inner peace and joy, you can use empathy and compassion to forgive, apologize, and make amends.

Emotional pain is a formidable mental knot that can disconnect you from your true self. But as you start to unravel and resolve it, you will once again access the inner peace in your core, the divine energy you were born with. This is your highest and most natural state, one that is inherently understanding, patient, and blissful. When the flame of emotional pain is finally extinguished, the light of love rises from its ashes.

Love is an unconditional state of affection not only for our family and friends but for all living beings. It is naturally a permanent, all-encompassing force that does not require anything to maintain its strength. "Love is the bridge between you and everything," Rumi said.

Some may believe love is conditional, meaning it only happens at certain times, such as on a Friday night dinner date. But true love is an inherent, unshakable force that radiates from your soul. It is a state of total presence and awareness of the present moment, composed of calmness, peace, and forgiveness. To find and share love with others, you must first discover it within yourself.

KNOT 3

ADDICTIVE CRAVING— OVERCOME ITS PRESSURE

ADDICTIVE CRAVING IS A SOURCE of significant mental and physical distress. It is a state of mind where the present moment is not good enough and needs to be enhanced. We obsessively pursue experiences or substances to seek a fulfillment that rarely lasts. While habits such as smoking, drinking alcohol, or taking drugs may come to mind, addictive cravings also include overeating to soothe emotions, escaping into your digital device for endless hours, or indulging in shopping sprees to relieve stress. For the illusion of gratification, you may place yourself in harm's way and suffer disappointment or depression when the experience or substance no longer satisfies. You may even unknowingly place yourself at risk for disease, imprisonment, and death.

In this chapter, you will learn about the science of addictive craving and the central role of the default mode network. Through the power of insightful awareness, you can overcome this mental knot and rediscover natural joy and fulfillment. In the process, you will improve your confidence and awaken your higher self.

Addiction Starts with Good Intentions

During times of stress, trauma, or grief, it is natural to seek relief from pain. When you feel overwhelmed, it is common and understandable to seek pleasure as an outlet. Ice cream, video games, or social media can counter the tension of a stressful experience. The euphoric release of reward hormones—serotonin and dopamine—helps to balance the effects of stress hormones like adrenaline and cortisol.

While craving is not inherently wrong, it can lead to a cycle of abuse and trap you in a state of suffering. Addictive craving arises when you habitually desire euphoric activities or substances, even as you no longer face the stressors you sought to alleviate. You may build a narrative that these habits are important for well-being and happiness, even though they can cause significant emotional and physical distress.

When you learn to properly manage and prevent stress, you can avoid the trap of addictive craving. Unfortunately, our fast-paced lives and consumer culture increase our chances of falling into addiction. That is because we learn to cope with our stress by pursuing pleasure, which releases high levels of habit-forming serotonin and dopamine. It is the perfect recipe for a dependency to arise.

When cravings become uncontrollable, they can lead to a debilitating and painful way of life. Those of us who are afflicted will go to extreme lengths to indulge in habitual behavior, often to the detriment of our relationships, health, and career. We may even break the law to access the addiction. We may conceal it from others and often from ourselves, constructing false narratives that the activities or substances are beneficial.

Although we may appear composed in public, a part of our brain is constantly preoccupied with the fixation of our indulgence. Our mind may continually wonder, "Where can I smoke? What's on my social media feed? What should I buy next?"

For those who have never suffered from an addictive craving, it can be difficult to understand why it is so challenging to break free. Family, friends, and partners may express frustration, urging their loved ones to "stop doing it." However, an addictive craving is a reflexive behavior due to the rewiring of the brain, resulting in a lack of control.

To overcome an addictive craving, it is helpful to first understand its causes and manifestations. The power of knowledge will help you untangle one of the most challenging mental knots. You will find by recognizing and eliminating your addictive craving, you will experience profound freedom, joy, and inner peace.

The Many Faces of Addictive Craving

Addictive craving is a condition where you repeatedly engage in a behavior that causes harm to yourself and others. Its defining characteristic is the inability to control the habitual tendency despite the associated risks, which can lead to a range of detrimental physical, psychological, and social consequences.

The most innocuous pursuit can become an addictive craving, from seemingly healthy interests like dieting and exercising to everyday activities like shopping, eating, and drinking coffee. Drugs, alcohol, cigarettes, vapes, stocks, and casinos are known to be habit forming. Recently, social media, gaming, and smartphones have joined the list of cravings that, for some, can be as crippling as drugs and alcohol.

Addictive cravings can take the form of food cravings for caffeine, sugar, or salt. In this case, your brain becomes conditioned to believe these substances are essential and living without them will cause distress. When deprived of these foods, you may experience withdrawal symptoms like anxiety and depression.

Social media is a new and dangerous source of addiction. Online platforms are designed to activate the brain's reward areas and release dopamine, similar to drugs like cocaine. Teens are particularly vulnerable; a recent study found that more than three hours of social media use per day increases the risk of depression, anxiety, eating disorders, and sleep problems.

Ironically, although social media is intended to build social connections, for some users it can cause feelings of isolation. Because loneliness reflects a need for human interaction, this may be a signal that social media has become an addiction and should be replaced by genuine connection.

According to the American Psychological Association, 40 million Americans suffer from addiction to drugs, alcohol, or nicotine—substances that are known to cause lethal diseases like cancer. Cravings often compel people to chase many forms of pleasure, resulting in a dependency on more than one substance or activity.

The addictive nature of sex and easy accessibility of online pornography have made it a prevalent dependency for millions. According to the Mayo Clinic, up to 24 million Americans are addicted to sex, a number that is rising with the abundance of online sexual content as well as apps that promote and facilitate casual encounters. It is estimated that 4.7 million Americans spend more than 11 hours a week viewing pornography online.

For many of us, money is an addiction that is encouraged by family and friends. We may begin with good intentions, pursuing money to buy our first home, start a family, and help others. But when it becomes an addictive craving, money fails to bring fulfillment and leaves us wanting more. We desire bigger houses, newer cars, and extravagant vacations, but they are never enough. We work overtime, sacrificing our time and health and even engaging in unethical practices, all in the pursuit of "more." We may gamble or trade the stock market to increase our net worth, but it leaves us feeling increasingly anxious, stressed, and restless, plunging us further into the addictive cycle as we seek the illusion of gratification.

The craving for status, title, and promotion can also become addictive. We strive to climb the corporate or academic ladder as if our lives depend on it. We may embellish our backgrounds and exaggerate in interviews to secure positions with grander titles, taking credit for the ideas of others. We do everything in our power to improve the appearance of our resumes and pad our bank accounts. But does it ultimately bring us fulfillment and happiness?

A timeless fable illustrates the nature of addictive craving. A corporate executive who leads a large company takes a walk on the beach one evening. He sees a fisherman lying on the sand with his hat pulled down over his face and his pole buried in the sand.

Being a master of business success, the executive decides to give the fisherman valuable advice. He stops and declares, "Hey, you're not going to catch many fish that way! You should be standing up, checking the line, and trying out different bait."

The fisherman looks up and asks, "If I do that, what will my reward be?"

The bigwig smiles and says, "For starters, you could invest in a better fishing pole with more range. You could buy more bait and catch more fish!"

"Okay," the fisherman nods. "But if I do that, what will my reward be?"

The executive laughs, wondering how anyone could be so dense. "Are you kidding? You can sell the extra fish for more money and start a business. You can buy a stall in the market and cash in. Then you can save up and buy a large boat and really start catching fish!"

"Sure, but if I do that, what will my reward be?"

"Don't you see? You can make so much money you can buy more than one boat, hire a crew, and eventually have a whole fleet and earn more money than you can possibly imagine!"

The fisherman appears more confused. "If I do that, what will my reward be?"

"You'll be rich, you idiot! You'll never have to worry about money again.

In fact, you'll never have to work a single day. You can just sit on the beach and enjoy the sunset."

The fisherman finally smiles and says, "Oh, isn't that what I'm doing right now?"

The executive returns to his corporate life, frustrated and angry.

This story addresses an age-old question: Does money buy happiness? Certainly, a minimum salary is necessary for well-being, and even the fisherman needs money for shelter, clothing, food, and water. How much is enough?

Research from Purdue University suggests that emotional well-being can be achieved with a salary of $60,000 to $75,000 per year, with peak satisfaction at $95,000 per year. Beyond these amounts, more money does not necessarily lead to increased happiness.

Given the immense toll involved in making excessive amounts of money, why do we persist in striving for riches? Are we truly trying to "achieve happiness," or are we instead caught in the cycle of addictive craving?

"Wealth is the ability to fully experience life," Henry David Thoreau said. If our lives are emotionally and spiritually poor, could it be that we are not as affluent as our bank accounts would suggest?

Addictive Craving Can Impact Your Health

Addictive craving can create a vicious cycle of use and abuse, resulting in a wide range of mental and physical health complications. Stress, anxiety, suicidal ideation, insomnia, and depression are just a few of the mental health conditions that can arise. Addictive craving can also cause serious repercussions to your physical well-being, resulting in diseases like stroke, heart failure, diabetes, and cancer.

An insidious aspect of addictive craving is that more and more of the pleasurable activity or substance becomes necessary to provide the desired reward, leading to a worsening dependency. For example, smartphone addiction can lead to poor sleep, creating a new reliance on coffee, soft drinks, or nicotine to stay awake.

Over time, cravings can become more prominent and ever-more damaging to your welfare, often without your awareness. For example, a medication addiction may start off with using prescription drugs once a week, gradually increasing to three times a week, then daily, and eventually multiple times a day. A gambling addiction could begin with a $5 lottery purchase each week, escalate to daily scratch-off purchases, and further escalate to virtual slot machines and poker.

One of the first manifestations of addictive craving is poor sleep. You may struggle to fall asleep or stay asleep or even avoid snoozing altogether in order to engage in your habit. This can deprive your body of needed rest, resulting in unhealed aches and pains from the previous day. Lack of sleep can lead to fatigue, anxiety, depression, gastrointestinal problems, and headaches and increase your risk of a car accident or work mishap.

You may also find that addictive craving makes you irritable and contentious, leading to a withdrawal from loved ones. Your brain becomes rewired for pleasure-seeking activities and substances, so you may deprioritize personal responsibilities such as family, work, and health.

Perhaps you have made excuses for your issues, refusing to believe that habitual craving may be involved and instead convincing yourself that the activity or substance is your *raison d'être*—the most important purpose for your existence. If you were simply to acknowledge the problem, you would have a chance of regaining freedom.

The cycle of addiction is characterized by a never-ending search for satisfaction. In Buddhism, this quest is the hamster wheel of samsara, a repetitive cycle of highs and lows. It is critical to understand that addiction does not offer lasting gratification, only momentary relief that is part of an ongoing cycle of dependence.

The intensification of the craving and its harmful effects will persist until those destructive consequences are no longer tolerable. In fact, many people are oblivious to the damage they are causing to themselves and to those closest to them until they experience a traumatic event that finally brings them to awareness. Hitting rock bottom may finally motivate these people to seek help and overcome their addictive craving, but this is not always the case.

Rock bottom is the point where you feel broken and emotionally overwhelmed, and it can take many different forms—fatigue, sickness, suicidal ideation, bankruptcy, divorce, criminal charges, or imprisonment. Despite the immense pain and damage it brings, hitting this depth offers a chance to seek help and start restoring what addiction has taken away. It is an opportunity for change and growth.

Fortunately, you can break the cycle of addictive craving before reaching the lows, thereby preserving your family and work relationships and improving your health before irreversible consequences take place. Examining yourself honestly and understanding your triggers is the first step to breaking through the mental knot of addictive craving.

Triggers of Addictive Craving

A single precipitating event can lead to addictive craving, even if you were in a comfortable mental state just minutes before. These triggers can be thoughts, feelings, images, sounds, or smells that cause cravings to stir. A random spark from a TV commercial, a song, or a stray thought can start the cycle. This makes it difficult to fight the urge, especially when the brain has been rewired from repeatedly experiencing the addictive activity or substance.

The rates of many types of addiction are steadily rising, driven in part by the increasing number of distractions in modern society. For example, employees are expected to process an avalanche of electronic information in the form of email, news feeds, websites, social media, and text messages. Employers often actively encourage the consumption of this mass information. Unfortunately, the combination of high stress and bountiful stimuli creates an ideal environment for addictive cravings to take hold.

In many cases, the triggers of impulsive behaviors originate in your own thoughts. As with stress, the culprit is often the brain's default mode network (DMN), which, as you know, can lead to the "wandering mind" or the "monkey mind." When you are focused and present in your activities, the DMN is off. But if you are caught in the cycle of addictive craving, the DMN becomes overly active, to the point that it overrides your awareness of the present moment.

In addiction, the DMN works in concert with the nucleus accumbens and limbic system to form a circuit where impulsive thoughts trigger pleasure-seeking emotions and behaviors. This loop comes to dominate the brain, leading to a continuous cycle of craving, seeking, and reward. Any one of your 40,000 daily thoughts can feed the dependency. As conscious control diminishes, you may become a prisoner of a rewired brain. And even if the pleasurable addictive activity or substance were to disappear, cravings for it can persist for months and even years.

The Science of Addiction

Let's take a closer look at how addictive urges manifest in the brain. When you open the refrigerator and see a slice of chocolate cake, a signal is sent to your nucleus accumbens, a part of the brain that generates feelings of desire. This "pleasure center" is the interface between your motivation and action, guiding your cravings and reward-seeking behaviors. It plays a key role in connecting the idea of wanting with the impulse of acting.

When you spot the cake, the nucleus accumbens releases neurotransmitters like dopamine and glutamate. Often referred to as the "happy hormone," dopamine motivates you to take action to satisfy a craving. It also produces feelings of euphoria when you consume an object of desire. For example, dopamine creates the yearning for your favorite food or TV show and then motivates you to act on it.

Scientists have confirmed that people who are addicted to drugs or alcohol have neural changes in their nucleus accumbens and their default mode network, allowing these parts of the brain to act independently of the brain's rational centers. This leads to a loss of conscious oversight over cravings and denial of any possible consequences. In short, addiction gains control of the brain and takes over its normal function. Like cancer, it's a disease that grows outside of our control.

To compare the difference between a healthy brain and an addicted brain, let's consider an example of a pleasant dessert that most people enjoy. Ice cream is a nice delight on a hot, sunny day, a treat to enjoy with family and friends. It's also a great stress reliever during tough times.

During a challenging week, you may drive by an ice cream parlor on your way to work. A healthy brain may think, "It's been a long week, and I deserve a break. A hot-fudge sundae after work today sounds wonderful!" The idea resolves some tension, and on your way home you swing by the ice cream parlor for your dessert, a great reward for a tough week.

An addicted brain may spot the same ice cream parlor on the way to work and think, "I need ice cream right now!" In this case, your intense craving triggers a spate of erratic behaviors, like turning the car around to check if the ice cream parlor is open, even if it means being late for work. If it is closed, your stress may escalate. As the pain intensifies, you might rush to a convenience store in search of a substitute, only to be met with disappointment.

At work, you feel annoyed and distracted, searching online for other ice cream parlors or convenience stores nearby. You neglect your tasks and keep an eye on the clock, wondering how you will get through the day. You venture into the break room with anxiety, hoping to find ice cream in the freezer but come up empty, which aggravates your disappointment.

The day passes in agony until you leave work early and head straight to the ice cream parlor. Instead of ordering two scoops in a cone, you indulge in a massive sundae with five toppings and a brownie on top, devouring it to the point of feeling sick. You go home somewhat content but foggy, forgoing dinner and crashing on the couch as a sugar rush sets in. The next morning, you wake up feeling hungry and sick. Grabbing your smartphone, you spot an ad for a new ice cream parlor in the area, and the cycle of craving starts anew.

You may chuckle at the idea of an ice cream addiction. It may be hard to imagine devouring something to the point of passing out. But what if you replace ice cream with social media, overeating, online shopping, workaholism, electronic gaming, sex, alcohol, drugs, or nicotine? The resulting scenario would describe daily life for millions of people struggling with one of the many types of addictive cravings.

Addictive craving is a barren road of pain and misery. The addiction can sneak up on you, consuming your body and soul until you hit rock bottom. It is common to become increasingly dependent on activities and substances to feel satisfied from a desired high. All forms of addiction are destructive cycles that override your rational thoughts and needs, ultimately damaging you inside and out.

Fortunately, there is a way out of the darkness. Even in your most challenging time, you can break the cycle and reclaim your life by harnessing a powerful force that lies at the heart of religion.

The Power of Surrender

Addiction rewires the neural circuits in your brain, making you unaware of your cravings and their damaging effects. Acknowledging the severity of the problem can be daunting, so you may choose to ignore it. The cycle of pain can reduce your self-worth and self-esteem, leaving you increasingly powerless to act.

At the core of this condition lies a false narrative crafted by your brain's default mode network (the ego), convincing you that your survival depends upon desires being met. It forces you to believe that forsaking the cravings will lead to catastrophic losses. The default mode network perpetuates this falsehood, compelling you to overlook your inner moral compass. It continually revisits the addictive thought patterns and ensnares you in an unrelenting prison of suffering, like a pathological beggar you feed who incessantly demands more, because he is never satisfied.

A better life awaits if you choose to want it. There is a path to freedom from addictive craving, and the first step is to recognize the falseness of your ego's narrative. You can surrender the ego to find freedom and salvation. Accepting that you have lost your way amid the overwhelming nature of craving, you can open your heart to a higher power to be forgiven and release the heavy burdens.

For people of faith, this means surrendering to God—the Infinite Unknown—to guide you back to health and peace. You can take refuge in His compassionate grace, seeking salvation from your worldly cravings and relying on the divine to lead you to freedom. With a daily prayer, you can free yourself from the burden of addiction and seek refuge toward the healing light.

Lord God, the Infinite Unknown, the energy of the universe, I fill my lungs with Your grace. I breathe in Your benevolence, and I breathe out my sins and my desires.

As I surrender the throne of my life to You, help me to see the light, so I can find a way out of this darkness.

During times of intense pain and suffering, the default mode network's harmful grip on us becomes apparent, and we start to yearn for freedom. By confessing our sins to our higher power, we can release the ego's grasp and start to recognize divine love and a path to recovery. Because God's mercy and compassion are infinite like the sun's rays, He will help us regardless of our weaknesses. Surrendering brings freedom.

Buddhists surrender to the dharma, or the nature of reality, which means letting go and fully embracing the present moment. Buddha said, "It is a man's own mind, not his enemy or foe, that lures him to evil ways." He described the Four Noble Truths as a way to end our suffering. By developing present-moment awareness of our impulses and cravings, we can surrender to the now and find freedom from our ego. This unlocks nirvana, a state of freedom where harmful desire is finally absolved.

If you do not have a religious background, surrendering the ego means acknowledging that the pleasure-seeking centers of your brain have taken control of your life. You can surrender to the infinite power of your subconscious mind, which will provide the insights to solve your challenges. Doing so can be difficult, as it requires abandoning the ego's illusion of control. However, by doing so you will open your mind and heart to the ocean of inner peace, allowing you to calm the turbulent waves of addictive craving and break through to health, happiness, and your higher self.

Surrendering does not mean blaming yourself or others but rather accepting and turning a page. When you can honestly see the ravages caused by your addictive craving, you will realize that your pain is caused by your own cravings and aversions. A lightbulb moment occurs—there is a path to freedom. When you become aware of the infinite grace of your higher power, a sudden mental shift occurs—your suffering can come to an end.

You start to see the path to freedom from your addictive craving, one that points toward peace—a deep spiritual peace you may have forgotten or perhaps never before experienced. The Roman philosopher Seneca said, "Every new beginning comes from some other beginning's end."

Breakthrough in Understanding Addiction

For thousands of years, Native Americans have recognized the healing powers of plant medicines like the peyote cactus. Mescaline, the active ingredient in peyote, belongs to the family of substances known as *psychedelics*, which can alter the brain's perception, mood, and cognitive processes.

Recent breakthroughs have shed light on the medicinal effects of psychedelics like psilocybin, ayahuasca, and peyote. Clinical studies have found them to be highly effective in managing and curing severe addictions to alcohol and opiates. In one trial, two doses of psilocybin combined with psychotherapy led to an 83 percent reduction in heavy drinking in a group of alcoholics.

This therapeutic effect is linked to the ability of these compounds to shut down the default mode network and ease the ego's stranglehold on our lives. A temporary reprieve from cravings brings moments of insightful awareness. During the psychedelic experience, we discover awe for life's radiant beauty as a cosmic consciousness takes hold.

By shutting off our brain's default mode network, psychedelics induce a phenomenon known as *ego dissolution*, where our superficial identity temporarily fades away, akin to surrendering our ego to a higher power. This reduces the power of our cravings and reconnects regions of the brain that have become silenced, such as the central executive network.

The experience forces us to confront our addiction and the harm it has caused to ourselves and others, a journey that can prove both liberating and excruciating. It can also be a powerful spur to action that opens our minds and hearts to the world and the people in it. "Be not afraid of life," the American writer William James once wrote. "Believe that life is worth living, and your belief will help create the fact."

Brain imaging studies have shown that psychedelics significantly decrease activity in the brain's default mode network, quite similar to mindfulness practice. Like meditation, these compounds can reduce negative rumination, provide temporary relief from anxiety and depression, and break through repetitive, self-obsessive thoughts. For people struggling with addiction, they can provide healing transformation.

However, while mindfulness practice activates the central executive network and guides our awareness of the present moment, psychedelics activate many parts of the brain in an arbitrary manner, even connecting regions that would not normally communicate. This explains some of their bizarre effects, like seeing geometric shapes, the feeling of colors as emotions, and the perception of sounds as vibrations.

Psychedelics may provide assistance in the healing process of surrender, but they are not a reliable way to battle addiction in the long term. These drugs give rise to an altered reality that can precipitate mental illnesses like drug-induced schizophrenia. They also impair judgment and control, potentially leading to physical or emotional harm. Psychedelics provide a temporary, morphine-like relief from addictive craving, but they may not permanently heal the underlying issues.

While their therapeutic role is still under investigation, psychedelics have taught us about the nature of addiction. In the craving cycle, the pleasure-seeking parts of the brain—in particular, the nucleus accumbens and the default mode network—come to dominate our lives and trap us in inescapable suffering. To regain control, the first step is to surrender our ego by silencing our default mode network, whether through God and prayer, mindfulness practice, or (in severe cases) assisted psychedelic therapy.

With a recognition of the underlying problem, the next step in the process of healing is to develop insightful awareness. Insights, whether from God or from deep within our subconscious mind, provide the tools to end the cycle of addiction.

The Power of Insight

Surrendering to a higher power enables you to see the truth of your present condition, granting you moments of mental clarity. Unfortunately, this freedom may be transient as resurfaced cravings test your will. It is common to relapse back into darkness.

To permanently resolve addictive craving, you must strengthen your will by communicating your deepest intentions to your higher power. Whether it is God, the Infinite Unknown, or your vast subconscious mind, tapping into a force mightier than yourself will guide you toward the light. You can trust that this higher power will provide the critical insights for you to achieve your aspirations.

An insight is an intuitive solution to a problem. It is a capacity to perceive the reality of your life situation and take effective action. Insights can provide a new perspective to help you tackle your challenges. They may inspire you to reevaluate old views and motivate you to take action, often appearing like a bolt of lightning when you least expect it. "A moment's insight is sometimes worth a life's experience," the American physician and poet Oliver Wendell Holmes wrote.

Your subconscious mind will deliver the insights that will solve your deepest problems. If the brain is like an ocean, its conscious portion—the sights and sounds of the present moment—is like a small spotlight shining on the surface. In contrast, the subconscious mind is the vast depths of the ocean, constantly working to solve your problems without your awareness.

At any given time, you use a tiny fraction of your brain. But if you learn to listen to the ocean within, you will access a power that will solve your most complex issues. Sigmund Freud, the founder of psychoanalysis, said, "The mind is like an iceberg; it floats with one-seventh of its bulk above water."

You can actively cultivate a mind that is more receptive to powerful insights. When you relax or meditate, you create the ideal conditions for these revelations to arise. I explored this concept in my novel, *Project Bodi:*

Awaken the Power of Insight, where meditation techniques help the main character develop his insightful awareness.

Another popular, real-life story illustrates this concept. As a PhD student at the University of Cambridge, Rishi Rajpopat attempted to crack the enigmatic Sanskrit code. Thousands of years ago, a scholar named Panini devised a complex language machine to encode the ancient language of Sanskrit. For centuries, scholars had been unable to decode its message, and Rajpopat was no different. After months of attempting to crack it, he was close to giving up.

Frustrated, he decided to take a month-long break to focus on exercising and meditating. On his return to work and with a fresh look at Panini's code, the answer to the riddle suddenly became clear. His subconscious mind had solved the 2,500-year-old enigma during his time away and delivered the insight to him.

In many ways, battling an addictive craving can be as difficult as cracking the Sanskrit code, making it nearly impossible to differentiate between the truth and the lies you may have told yourself for years. By developing the power of insight, you can arrive at an honest self-understanding and liberate yourself from suffering, allowing you to reconnect with inner peace and joy. Like Rajpopat, you can unlock the enigma of yourself by heeding insights when they arrive.

Developing Insightful Awareness

Insightful awareness means truly understanding what you are doing when you are doing it. This in-the-moment awareness allows you to overcome a rewired brain and regain conscious control of your life. With this self-understanding comes wisdom, a force that guides you to the higher self. In the *Tao Te Ching* (a foundational work of Taoism), the Chinese philosopher Lao Tzu said, "He who knows others is wise; he who knows himself is enlightened."

Earlier, you used concentration meditation to deepen relaxation and cultivate inner peace, which can prove helpful for the discomforts and withdrawal symptoms that appear on the road to recovery. Here you will explore how you can use mindfulness exercises to foster the insightful awareness that will help you overcome your addictive craving and advance you socially, spiritually, and professionally.

Insight meditation, or vipassana, is a powerful technique where you observe your mind from a place of curious interest and neutrality. You start by developing present-moment awareness through a mindfulness exercise and then ask yourself, "Am I at ease? What am I feeling right now?" Just as you scan a painting to glean the artist's message, you study the canvas of your mind objectively to understand its inner workings.

As with concentration meditation, it is important to anchor to the present moment and turn on your "observing mind." However, while previously the goal was to notice interruptions and return to the now, during insight meditation you identify three types of thoughts—cravings, aversions, and delusions. After you recognize and label each thought that comes to you, you then watch each of them fade away as you return to the present moment.

During the exercise, anytime you are interrupted by a thought or impulse, take note of its quality—whether positive or negative—and then label it with your "observing mind." Is it a craving (desire), aversion (dislike), or delusion (thought rooted in ignorance)? When practiced every day, insight meditation allows your brain to understand its true condition and generate the insights that will improve your life.

For example, during a prayer or breathing exercise, you may experience a distinct sensation in your throat. When this happens, tune into the feeling and observe it. You may recognize it as a strong craving to vape, drink alcohol, or check your smartphone. Instead of reacting to this impulse or avoiding it, practice the RAIN technique:

R—Recognize when a strong emotion is present.

A—Accept the emotion without judgment.

I—Investigate the emotion and sensations it gives rise to from a place of honesty and detachment.

N—Non-identify with your emotions and watch them as an observer.

With this approach, you will find space from your cravings and aversions, giving you freedom from their power. With repeated practice, you will recognize unhealthy impulses when they interrupt you and learn to watch them with restraint, overcoming their pressure. You also gain insight into how early sensations evolve into harmful behaviors. This is how wisdom develops over time.

The process of observing your thoughts with curiosity and impartiality gives you a deeper understanding of the addictive cycle. When you apply insight meditation to your daily life, you begin to recognize the triggers of addictive craving when they arise. For instance, that extra cup of coffee in the morning might be the catalyst that leads you to feel overwhelmed later in the day. With this insight, you can avoid the extra cup and reduce afternoon stress.

Let's put these ideas into practice.

Insight Meditation Exercise

Begin by setting the intention for the exercise, such as, "I want to be happy more often." After repeating this several times, spend five minutes developing present-moment awareness. This can involve feeling body sensations, observing your breath, listening to sounds, or saying a prayer. When thoughts arrive, notice them, and return to the present.

Once you are fully in the now, tune into the state of your mind. Ask yourself, "How am I feeling?" Are you tired, stressed, irritable, calm, happy, or something else? Next, pause and ask yourself, "Am I at ease right now?" Repeat these questions at the end of the practice to see the changes that have taken place. The most critical driver of success is seeing the truth of reality, so self-honesty is key.

Spend fifteen to twenty minutes scanning your body from the top of your head to the bottom of your feet, noticing sensations along the way. Focus on one body region at a time, tuning in to feel any subtle pain points, vibrations, or pulsations. Simply notice their presence, intensity, and how they change over time. Take note of any reactions you have to your body sensations, separating your reaction from the sensation itself.

Identify thoughts as they arise and pay close attention to cravings (desires), aversions (dislikes), or delusions (thoughts rooted in ignorance), watching them closely and taking note of their quality without fixating on them for too long. Notice when your "wandering mind" gets taken over by these cravings, aversions, or delusions, and return back to the present with your "observing mind."

When difficult emotions arise, observe them calmly without too much strain or focus. Are they signaling an unmet need or conveying a hidden message? Remain relaxed and label feelings as they arise and fade. Be kind to yourself and stay curious about your thoughts, no matter what they are.

With daily practice, insight meditation reveals the roots of addictive behavior, uncovering the cravings, aversions, and delusions that fuel it. Each of these thoughts is like a piece of a larger puzzle. Initially, the pieces may be difficult to interpret, but as you become more adept at recognizing and assembling them into the full picture, you gain a deeper and more accurate understanding of yourself. This is the essence of insightful awareness, a powerful tool that can transform your life.

For example, a traumatic experience may have been the initial trigger for an alcohol or social media addiction. With time, the default mode network (the ego) may have created a false narrative that booze is a helpful relaxant or that social media connects you with friends, when in fact, these addictions might be the cause of recurrent sleep problems. Armed with this insight, you can cut the roots and break the cycle of addiction. The truth will set you free.

A few tips will help ensure you get the most from insight meditation:

- It is important not to judge or react to your present condition. Sometimes your view inside may be cloudy or scattered, which is normal. Rather than being annoyed, express gratitude that you were able to recognize a state of distraction, an act that strengthens your "observing mind." With a regular meditation practice that is accepting and unbiased, the right view—one of crystal-clear clarity—will soon arrive.
- Thoughts are a natural product of the mind. Remember, your mind may generate 40,000 thoughts a day. Do not be annoyed or dismayed by them. By observing them from a distance with your "observing mind," you will begin to understand their intrinsic character. You will start to recognize that they are temporary phenomena that do not require any action. You also will develop an understanding of how they change over time, which helps to find space and manage them.
- Consistent practice helps you develop deeper awareness of subtle sensations and thoughts, which will further strengthen your insightful awareness. The more deeply you can focus, the greater the benefit. For example, you may recognize lower back pain along with an aversion to it as two separate sensations.

Insights are valuable tools for seeing the truth of reality and discovering the path to inner peace and happiness. Your DMN may prefer to ignore the truth out of inconvenience or shame, but this only prolongs suffering. Take action when insights arrive, heeding their messages with discipline and conscious effort. St. Augustine said, "God provides the wind, but man must raise the sails."

When you set a consistent intention every day, the power of insight meditation will gain momentum and become a source of grace that transforms your life. Awareness and wisdom start to counterbalance craving, aversion, and delusion, leading to a new beginning. Through the knowledge you gain from insightful awareness, you can break the cycle of addictive craving and find health, happiness, and peace within.

The Science of the "Observing Mind"

Thanks to recent scientific breakthroughs, researchers are beginning to understand how insightful awareness arises in the brain. During mindfulness exercises, your brain's default mode network is less active. Because the DMN drives your self-obsessive, emotionally charged thought patterns, its silence brings peace. You become less preoccupied with the past and future when you fully engage in the present moment. This raises a question: What turns on in the brain during mindfulness?

When you switch on your "observing mind," you activate task-positive networks in the brain. As discussed, chief among these task-positive networks is the central executive network (CEN), a relatively recent evolutionary development in humans. Compared to the DMN, the CEN is more rational and expansive, enabling you to solve complex problems, set goals, and maintain focus. It is a power that will deliver the insights to solve your most pressing issues. The key is to learn how to use it.

When practiced daily with intention, insight meditation allows you to spend less time in the DMN (your "wandering mind") and more time in the CEN (your "observing mind"). When you learn to stay present and recognize cravings, aversions, and delusions, you develop insightful awareness. Worries and fears are replaced with solutions and decisions, enabling you to overcome life's challenges with greater ease.

Just like exercising helps to build a muscle, you can strengthen the CEN over time. Whenever your default mode network traps you in thoughts and cravings, turn it off and activate your CEN by simply asking yourself, "Am I at ease right now?" Observing your mind will bring peace. When you learn to become aware of your "wandering mind" and return to the present moment, you learn to harness your CEN—your "observing mind"—and build its power.

Scientists have also discovered how we transition back and forth between the DMN and the CEN. The salience network is a third brain network that acts like a switch on a railway track, directing you between different mental states based on your current experience. For instance, the salience network can recognize that you have started a mundane activity, like brushing your teeth, and switch you over to the DMN so that you tune out.

By acting as a "train conductor," the salience network guides how the brain responds to incoming information, controlling its attention while conserving energy. By directing information to the appropriate brain pathway, the salience network controls mental traits like social behavior and self-awareness. It helps coordinate the balance between sensory information, emotions, and consciousness.

Insight meditation trains the salience network to spend more time in the CEN, thereby strengthening your power of insight. For example, when you start a mindfulness exercise and watch your thoughts from a place of curiosity and interest, you flip on your CEN. Moments later, the salience network switches you to the DMN as your mind begins to wander. But by becoming aware of this transition and reorienting your attention back to the present, you will train your salience network to stay in the CEN.

With time and practice, sustaining the CEN's "observing mind" will bring peace, happiness, and well-being. Through the wisdom of your "observing mind," you will become more resilient, adaptable, and self-aware, able to navigate life's challenges with ease and confidence. By harnessing your CEN, you will strengthen your intelligence, productivity, efficiency, and decision-making capabilities. You will acquire qualities typically associated with personal and business success, such as leadership, presence, focus, and communication. All this is possible as you learn to engage the deepest, most powerful part of your brain.

Insight meditation teaches you how to control and ultimately eliminate your counter-productive impulses and cravings. You gain the upper hand to break through the cycle of addictive craving. With fewer distractions, you will find a new energy and purpose in life, no longer needing to seek the illusion of gratification as happiness starts to find you. The light of your higher self will start to shine as you walk away from darkness.

You will learn to live "in the zone," a state of flow free from doubt, mental chatter, fear, or anxiety, which allows you to achieve more with less effort, leading to improved emotional and physical health as well as professional recognition and promotion. These developments attract the attention of your family, friends, and employers, and as you strengthen your bonds with them you will become a magnet for positive change.

Other Solutions for Addictive Craving

Insight meditation is just one solution to tackle your addictive craving; you can find many other types of support. Medications, therapists, counselors, and support groups are all viable options, now more accessible and affordable than ever before. Online therapy has broken down the barriers to accessing psychotherapy, making it easier for people to get the help they need. Finding the right solution will accelerate your journey to recovery.

Cognitive behavioral therapy is an effective method to overcome an addictive craving. As with insight meditation, this involves identifying the thoughts and behaviors that trigger the addictive cycle, but this time with the help of a therapist. For some people, the support of an experienced coach or mentor can be invaluable.

Support groups are also highly effective. Alcoholics Anonymous (AA) is the most well-known group of its kind. Founded in 1935 through the work of psychotherapist Carl Jung, AA has grown to over 2 million members in 180 nations. During weekly meetings, participants identify themselves by their first names and share life stories in an environment that fosters safety, honesty, and progress without pressure.

AA is guided by the "Big Book," a twelve-step program that requires surrendering oneself, being honest, gaining insights from a higher power, and growing spiritually. The first step involves writing down the history of your addiction and sharing it with the group. This cathartic experience relieves the burden of carrying secrets alone. Later in the process, you make amends by apologizing to those you may have harmed, cultivating the important quality of compassion.

During AA therapy, you find connection with peers who recognize your courage with applause—something that may have seemed impossible during your darkest days. The strength of the group guides and supports you, offering relief from your struggles. This shared experience often leads to transformative moments where you realize your self-worth and the potential to live a life beyond addiction.

In addition to therapy and support groups, medications can also be useful in reducing addictive craving and managing the symptoms of substance withdrawal. These include methadone and naloxone for opioid addiction, bupropion and varenicline for nicotine dependence, and acamprosate for alcoholism. Contact your healthcare provider for more information about these medicines.

Final Thoughts on Addictive Craving

Not all cravings are bad. Social media can be a great way to stay connected with your family, while a glass of wine with friends can cultivate healthy bonds. Intimacy with your partner is a natural expression of love, and shopping for your children can be immensely rewarding. However, these joyful cravings can lead to harm if you abuse them.

Distinguishing between beneficial and harmful cravings is the key to a long and happy life. Before pursuing pleasure, you must acknowledge any potential risks. Actions that bring happiness and growth to your family and friends are invaluable, but if you sense even a slight chance of harm, be sure to exercise restraint and prioritize moral conduct. Avoid gambling with your inner peace by succumbing to your cravings.

If you have strayed from the path and become ensnared in addiction, then it is best to surrender to reality before it is too late. Overcoming your cravings may cause short-term pain (and in some cases physical withdrawal), but it is worth the inconvenience. Your default mode network will urge you to ignore the truth, but a far greater joy awaits when you triumph over harmful desires.

To break through the mental knot of addictive craving, it is not enough to simply silence the default mode network. For lasting change, you must garner wisdom into your true condition through the power of insightful awareness. By exercising your "observing mind," you will open the door to insights into your true condition. These powerful eureka moments will advance you spiritually, physically, and professionally. You will become better equipped to tackle life's challenges, navigating through them with greater ease and comfort.

For the best results, it is important to perform insight meditation daily and set an intention for your practice. By observing your thoughts and emotions from a place of curiosity, you will identify cravings, aversions, and delusions, which will help you develop a deeper understanding of yourself. The root causes of your suffering will become apparent, allowing your subconscious mind to grant you the insights that will bring about positive change. Be attentive and take action when these messages arrive.

It is common to experience relapse on the road to recovery. To avoid falling back into darkness, turn on the light of positive intent and exercise your morality. This means restraining yourself from harmful temptations and rewarding positive behaviors (this is known as *right effort* in Buddhism). Try to observe your cravings and aversions rather than getting swept away by them.

Morality is the ethical compass for determining right from wrong, and it is an essential part of enlightenment. Society may value profits or productivity as the barometer for success, but this does not always translate to inner happiness. If you want to awaken lasting peace, it is best to advocate virtue and integrity.

Research has shown that morality is encoded in our genes and wired in certain regions of our brain, such as the medial prefrontal cortex. Children can distinguish between positive and negative behaviors and provide comfort to others in times of distress. It is often later in life that we learn the behaviors of deception and misconduct.

In life, you will encounter pressures that test these ingrained moral principles. Stress, loneliness, and emotional pain may tempt you to indulge in the illusion of gratification or even reckless behavior as a way of relief. To awaken your higher self, learn to break through the mental knot of addictive craving—and maintain your moral principles above all else—so nothing can touch your inner peace.

KNOT 4

LONELINESS—BREAK FREE FROM ITS GRIP

LONELINESS IS NOT SIMPLY A FEELING of sadness when you are apart from others, but it is also a debilitating mental knot that can severely impact your health and happiness. It can lead to depression and anxiety, increasing your risk of an early death. While external circumstances can contribute to it, loneliness is an internal phenomenon that you can reverse. Through simple techniques, you can break free from it and strengthen your bonds with others, allowing you to live life to its fullest.

In this chapter, you'll discover how loneliness develops in the mind and impacts your mental and physical health. You will learn how to reverse and break free from its grip through the powerful remedy of compassion. As you strengthen empathy and tolerance, you will build your bonds with others and dissolve feelings of isolation.

A Growing Epidemic

Loneliness is a common and serious public health issue that affects millions of people worldwide. The US Census Bureau estimates that in 2010 about 31 million people lived alone, and it is fair to say that many of these people regularly experience loneliness. By 2050, this number could rise to 60 million. In industrialized nations, loneliness affects nearly one in three individuals at some point in their lives.

No one is safe from its effects. Loneliness is a universal experience that crosses all ages, genders, races, ethnicities, incomes, and educational backgrounds. Like a virus, it can be highly contagious. If you suffer from loneliness, you may face stigma and have your condition minimized, making it feel like it is your fault for not being sociable or popular. Your "wandering mind"—your brain's default mode network (DMN)—can further escalate this guilt and shame, leaving you trapped in an endless cycle of pain.

Humans are social creatures who thrive when united in support of one another. We build communities and work in teams, encouraging others to be at their best. Our institutions, from bustling airports to crowded shopping malls, rely on collective interactions. Yet amid the hustle and bustle of these busy environments, loneliness can take hold. Even if you have the love and support of family, friends, and colleagues, you may still find yourself in the grip of solitude.

The COVID-19 pandemic highlighted the detrimental effects of social isolation on our emotional health and development. When the virus struck in early 2020, governments and other organizations implemented drastic measures to contain its spread. These included government lockdowns and mask mandates that had an unforeseen impact on mental and physical well-being. Psychiatrists and psychologists saw a large influx of people suffering from anxiety, depression, addiction, and other illnesses related to social isolation.

For older people, the separation from family brought particular hardship, as they were isolated from their loved ones and other seniors when the virus spread through retirement homes. The pandemic also had a damaging effect on the workplace, a key social circle. This was especially hard for younger workers who were transitioning from college to their careers. Junior employees learn from their more seasoned colleagues, and replacing face-to-face interaction with Zoom calls and instant messaging was an abrupt change that limited the professional growth of new hires.

How Loneliness Affects Health

A renowned Harvard study conducted over eighty years followed the lives of thousands of people to discover the secrets of health and well-being. The data showed that having strong relationships, rather than wealth or possessions, was the single most reliable indicator of happiness and longevity. For people over age fifty, close bonds were better than low cholesterol levels at predicting the quality of life, and those without social support had the worst outcomes.

Like other species, human beings are social animals who require companionship to thrive and overcome life's challenges. Rich social environments enhance the development of neurons in the brain. Conversely, social isolation hinders mental growth and damages health outcomes.

Loneliness serves as an alarm bell that the need for social support is not being met. Instead of responding to this warning by building relationships, we often withdraw further, resulting in a downward spiral of worsening loneliness. Even those of us with plenty of family and friends can feel lonely if our needs are not being fulfilled or if we feel misunderstood.

Loneliness is distinct from introversion, which also involves a lower level of social involvement. Introverts may not feel lonely as long as their limited social needs are being met. Regardless of whether you are an introvert or extrovert, whenever your desired level of social interaction is not satisfied you will experience feelings of loneliness.

We may blame our environment for our emotions, but it is often our own outlook that causes us to isolate. For example, a business professional may approach life with a self-centered attitude where success depends on outperforming peers, like a game of musical chairs where the person fears being left behind. In this and many other types of situations, we mistakenly believe the world is against us, even though we are a part of it. This illusory mindset of a "separate self" leads to feelings of loneliness, fear, suspicion, and anger.

Research has shown that loneliness is associated with increased risk of depression, anxiety, and cardiovascular disease. It is also a significant contributor to sleep fragmentation, cognitive decline, and premature mortality. The chronic stress triggered by loneliness can lead to a weakened immune system and a higher susceptibility to illnesses.

Surprisingly, studies have shown that social isolation is as strong a risk factor for disease and early death as smoking, obesity, inactivity, and high blood pressure. Experiencing intense loneliness can predict the onset of dementia and other cognitive disorders, even after adjusting for education, gender, age, and overall health. Researchers estimate that loneliness can shorten a person's life by fifteen years. This is because we human beings (like many other species) need companionship to survive and thrive.

To counter the negative feelings of social isolation, some of us may pick up bad habits like smoking, drinking, excessive eating, online shopping, gaming, or inactivity, often leading to addictive cravings. All this contributes to cognitive decline and a heightened risk of dementia, something that animals exposed to prolonged social isolation also experience.

In addition, loneliness predicts how we will fare after the diagnosis of a serious illness. People with low social connection are almost twice as likely to be hospitalized than those with high levels of support. Conversely, those with strong social ties—family, friends, and peers—are less likely to report complications and more likely to have better outcomes after a diagnosis.

Studies have shown that when we go to bed feeling lonely, our sleep quality suffers, and we are more likely to wake up with anxiety and tension. The resulting spike in stress hormones, such as cortisol, can contribute to diseases like heart attack and stroke. Therefore, it is important to address loneliness before it irreversibly affects our health.

Unfortunately, when we are in the throes of loneliness, we often adopt a negative outlook and make decisions based on emotion rather than reason. This creates a vicious cycle of deepening isolation that can feel like a debilitating illness. We experience sleeplessness and fatigue, and our ambition may start to wane. We neglect our own well-being, straying from our usual diet and exercise, or even from basic habits like brushing our teeth and changing our clothes—all while feeling powerless to make changes due to feelings of fear, depression, or worthlessness.

The Illusion of Self

We are all connected—the air we breathe and the land we inhabit bind us together in the interconnected web of life. However, our egos deceive us into believing we are different from others. To judge our self-worth, we often compare ourselves to friends and foes, an act that opens the door to social isolation. What is responsible for upholding this belief that we are separate from others? You guessed it—the default mode network (DMN).

Remember, you can recognize the DMN anytime your mind drifts off. The "wandering mind" takes you away from the present moment and transports you to the past or future, forcing you to relive painful memories or nervously anticipate future events. The DMN can activate the brain's emotional center (the limbic system), which triggers a range of feelings from fear to hatred. When you disconnect from the now, you can end up in a place that is far removed from reality.

The DMN begins to develop at the age of two and strengthens during puberty. Its role is to keep the brain exclusively focused on our growth and survival. By prioritizing the self in this way, it secures the necessary resources for survival. Just as our ancestors believed the sun and planets revolved around Earth, as children we believe the world revolves around us. Those who disagree with our notion of self are ignored or deemed to be enemies.

It is helpful to remember that the DMN (the ego) selectively focuses on information relating to our own lives and drives our self-centered perception of reality. To conserve energy and ensure our success, the default mode network prioritizes judgments and decisions that are in our own perceived best interest, ignoring information that does not directly pertain to the self.

As we age, the DMN continues its obsessive focus on survival, dragging us on a journey of self-obsession. A self-centered mindset—"you versus me" and "us versus them"—drives a belief that we are better than others. Conflicts and violence arise as we portray ourselves as victims or scapegoats and others as the wrongdoer or enemy, a narrative that leads to racism, sexism, and xenophobia. Even the slightest perceived threat can rapidly escalate. In *Hamlet*, William Shakespeare wrote, "There is nothing either good or bad, but thinking makes it so."

When we allow our DMN to foment its selfish ideology, we can follow a desolate path of isolation. We neglect the outside world, and our social skills suffer. As we selfishly strive to satisfy our own needs and desires, our loneliness increases, because our innate need for companionship remains unfulfilled. Others tend to distance themselves from us, finding no value in being our companions.

Feelings of loneliness should, in theory, drive us to become more receptive and welcoming to connect with others. Instead, we tend to adopt a more hostile and competitive outlook toward others. Rather than engaging with others, we blame them for the issues we may have brought upon ourselves. A vicious cycle of negativity can hinder our relationships and exacerbate our sense of isolation.

It can be hard to break away from the ever-intensifying vortex of loneliness. While we may crave human contact and meaningful relationships, the DMN's ingrained prejudices lead us to view others with contempt and loathing, preventing us from accepting responsibility for our hurtful interactions. This worsens the spiral of loneliness as we find ourselves stuck in a cycle as crippling as a drug or alcohol addiction.

While the DMN may be useful during childhood, it can become a hazard to our health and happiness later in life if we do not manage it properly. Research has shown that the DMN is more active in the brains of lonely individuals, resulting in chronic activation that can lead to excessive rumination and stress, contributing to mental illnesses like dementia and depression and physical ailments like hypertension and diabetes.

Researchers have classified loneliness as a mental illness in which prolonged social isolation rewires the brain, shifting its focus to negative threats. An MRI study compared the brains of volunteers who were exposed to images depicting pleasant and unpleasant social scenarios. Results showed that the brains of lonely participants were more likely to be activated by unpleasant images compared to those of nonlonely people, suggesting that loneliness propels people toward more negative tendencies.

As we age, our DMN becomes increasingly rigid, resulting in a more constrained view of the world. We grow old and inflexible, convinced that our viewpoint is always correct and unwilling to consider other perspectives. It is as if we are peering through a telescope with an ever-shrinking lens.

Left unchecked, the DMN's self-obsession becomes a major roadblock to personal growth and the health, happiness, and peace of mind that comes with the enlightened state. Sadly, we are the biggest victims of our own loneliness. When we do not recognize this, we will be forced down a road of misery.

Breaking the Cycle of Loneliness

If you suffer from the mental knot of loneliness, it is possible to break free from its chains. To do so requires a daily intention and a commitment to change. You must be willing to take action and allow new habits to replace old ones. It may not be easy, but the rewards of empathy and social connection are immense and worth any short-term pain and difficulty.

You can free yourself from the chains of loneliness by actively challenging your negative biases and observing them for what they are. By stepping out of your traditional comfort zone, you can reframe your thinking and develop new behaviors that will help you engage with others more deeply. You can also practice exercises to reinforce positive change and maximize the chances of meaningful connection.

Your brain's default mode network is a key force that keeps you locked in a state of loneliness. Its activation can lead to painful memories and future worries, overwhelming you with negativity in the form of fear, anger, shame, failure, and regret. This makes it difficult to stay focused on the present moment, further deepening any feelings of loneliness, sadness, and depression.

An effective way to silence the DMN (the "wandering mind") is to practice mindfulness exercises like prayer or concentration meditation. This involves focusing on the present moment; observing your breath, bodily sensations, and sounds; or praying to God. A fifteen- to twenty-minute mindfulness practice is most effective in turning off the DMN.

During a prayer or meditation, the DMN will interrupt you with emotions, memories, and thoughts that disturb the peace of the moment. This is completely normal. Reacting with frustration or anger will only empower the DMN. Instead, practice observing these thoughts without reacting to them. As they fade, revert back to the present moment with a relaxed and nonjudgmental attitude.

By recognizing the DMN (your "wandering mind") and choosing to go back to the now, you will lessen its power over time. In doing so you will empower the brain's central executive network (CEN), which guides your "observing mind" and cultivates your wisdom and understanding.

Practiced over time, mindfulness exercises will weaken the DMN and strengthen the CEN. You will learn to create a distance between yourself and your thoughts, allowing them to drift away without impacting your emotions or actions. By fostering present-moment awareness, you can let go of internal pain and open up to new experiences and possibilities. Regular practice will significantly reduce feelings of loneliness and isolation while increasing happiness and inner peace.

For those of faith, prayer is an effective mindfulness exercise. It enables you to arrive in the present moment and communicate openly and honestly with the Infinite Unknown. You can share your struggles and listen for insights. Through His grace, God guides you to health and peace. His love is infinite like the sun's rays, and through prayer you will emerge from the darkness of loneliness and into the light.

Lord God, the Infinite Unknown, the energy of the universe, I fill my lungs with Your grace. I breathe in Your benevolence, and I breathe out my pride and anger. As I surrender the throne of my life to You, I open my heart and fill it with Your love.

As you practice your daily prayers and mindfulness, it is also important to foster one particular mental quality that will transform your life and permanently end your isolation. This powerful force will break the chains of loneliness, allowing you to experience life in a way that may have been out of reach.

The Power of Compassion

Compassion is the capacity to empathize with the suffering of others. We often blame our loneliness on other people, believing they should take better care of us or treat us differently, when our distress is actually caused by a lack of gratitude toward them. Rather than expecting others to meet our needs, we must cultivate a more welcoming heart and be more appreciative of what we have. This is key to overcoming our feelings of loneliness and despair.

You were born with the light of compassion. However, during life the mental knot of loneliness may have extinguished this light. Fortunately, you have the power to heal your wounds and rekindle the flame in your core. By doing so, you will rediscover happiness and freedom.

When you learn to let go of negative ruminations and open yourself up to compassion, you will break free from loneliness. If the idea of compassion sounds repulsive, it is a sign that your brain's default mode network (your ego) is in full control. To loosen its grip, you can change your thought processes and learn to feel positively toward others. "For it is in giving that we receive," St. Francis of Assisi said.

It may be easy to feel empathy for those who are kind to you, but what about those you may dislike—family members who have wronged you, coworkers who challenge you, or strangers who vote for a different political party? Should you feel empathy for them? Jesus Christ offers the answer: "Love your enemies and pray for those who persecute you."

You can alleviate your loneliness by cultivating compassion for all living things, humans and animals alike. But before you can extend this love to others, you must first grant it to yourself. This can be difficult, especially if you are in a state of blame, regret, or self-loathing. You may purposely neglect your own needs, either out of self-pity or a belief that you are undeserving. These negative attitudes may stem from feelings of guilt or shame related to your past.

One way to foster self-compassion is to practice it during a prayer or mindfulness exercise, such as a breath meditation. Breathing is essential for life, yet we often take it for granted until we experience an illness. You can experience every inhalation as an opportunity to heal, embrace the present moment, and experience self-gratitude and compassion. Let's try it now.

Self-Gratitude Exercise

Start by taking a few slow, deep breaths and relaxing into the now, expressing gratitude for this moment of life. As you inhale, say to yourself, "Breathing in, I clear my mind." As you exhale, say to yourself, "Breathing out, I relax my body." Feel the waves of peace and relaxation with each out-breath, extending them mindfully in the present moment.

Next, remind yourself of the intention of your practice, repeating this phrase several times:

May I be happy, healthy, and at peace.

If you encounter any resistance, observe the tension and return to the present moment. After a few minutes, repeat the phrase again until peace arrives.

When it does, raise your eyebrows and smile broadly as though you are taking a photo, sharing your feelings with the world. The act of smiling releases oxytocin, which will enhance your compassion and cultivate inner peace. American poet Walt Whitman said, "Keep your face always toward the sunshine—and shadows will fall behind you."

Compassion Exercise

You can perform the compassion exercise alone or with a loved one. Begin by mindfully arriving at the present moment through a prayer, breathing exercise, or other mindfulness practice. Calm the mind and body and develop awareness of the sights, sounds, and sensations of now.

Gently extend compassion to each of your family members by imagining them and sending them a wish: "May you be happy, healthy, and at peace." Take your time to truly feel the intention of granting well wishes. In a couples setting, directly express gratitude openly to one another.

Continue to share this grace with those whom you may not favor, such as a boss, an ex-partner, or someone who has upset you in life. It is important to recognize and let go of any negative feelings or biases toward others and see them as deserving of respect. Take your time to grant kindness to others and then return to present-moment awareness to allow change to take place. As before, smile at the end of the practice.

During these exercises, you may be interrupted by negative thoughts and emotions. The default mode network (the ego) shows up, mocking your good intentions and trying to drag you back into the darkness. It is a strong force that can feed off negativity, judgment, and remorse. However, it is not invincible; its downfall is your ability to be patient, persistent, and mindful.

When the ego rears its ugly head, stay objective and refrain from reacting. Instead of judging yourself, which will only strengthen the DMN, acknowledge the interruption and let it pass. Try to relax, smile, and gently come back to the present moment, countering the negativity with a deeper focus on your aspirations and filling your mind with the light of positive intent.

Remember that thoughts are temporary phenomena, like clouds, that will come and go on their own. You may not be able to control when they arrive, but you can choose how to respond to these thoughts and any associated emotions. It is important to recognize the tranquil space between thoughts and rest in the peaceful serenity, allowing it to expand.

We are all human beings who make mistakes, and we all deserve to be happy, peaceful, and loving. Developing compassion for yourself allows you to share it with others, and when you do, you will realize that all human beings are connected. As your empathy grows, so will your social bonds. The Scottish novelist and poet Robert Louis Stevenson wrote, "We are all travelers in the wilderness of this world, and the best we can find in our travels is an honest friend."

For example, when passing by strangers on the street, instead of avoiding eye contact you can wish them well. While waiting in a long line at the airport or standing next to someone with a screaming toddler, instead of reacting with impatience or frustration you can remind yourself of our shared experience, which is precious and priceless. Life is too short to spend it alone; it is critical to value human connection and strive to share your peace and joy with others.

Just as a sprained ankle will heal with the right nourishment, your capacity for compassion will grow if you provide the necessary conditions for it to thrive. As it does, you will keenly become aware of the interconnectedness of all living beings. It is remarkable that we exist on this planet with the ability to interact, share, and love. Every human, animal, and plant shares the same four-letter DNA code. We all rely on each other; the air we exhale is absorbed by plants, which release the oxygen that our friends and family breathe.

Studies have even shown that going to bed feeling alone or angry increases the likelihood of waking up with a cortisol-fueled stress response that can last all day. Generating compassion during your prayers and mindfulness exercises can significantly reduce cortisol levels (in one study by more than 50 percent), leading to reduced stress, better health, and greater inner peace, along with a deeper connection to those around you.

This is one of many reasons why compassion lies at the core of Christianity, as written in Ephesians 4:32: "Be kind and compassionate to one another, forgiving each other, just as Christ God forgave you."

Compassion is also central to Buddhism, where it is one of the four divine abodes that are necessary for enlightenment. "Thousands of candles can be lighted from a single candle, and the life of the candle will not be shortened," Buddha said. "Happiness never decreases by being shared."

Kindness is often viewed as a weak trait in a society that values individual success and domination. We are taught that success requires ruthlessness and disregard. In reality, compassion is far more potent and powerful than selfishness. As Marcus Aurelius said, "Kindness is invincible, provided it is sincere, not ironic or an act."

As you realize this truth, your constricting sense of loneliness will start to unravel, replaced by the divine peace that naturally radiates from your core. With the omnipotent powers of patience and compassion, you can break through the mental knot of loneliness that blocks your path to the awakened state of joy and love.

The Importance of Body Awareness

To further strengthen your relationships, you can practice honing your communication skills. This involves more than just speaking in the right tone. It is helpful to consider the nonverbal elements of a conversation, which include your posture, appearance, and behavior when engaging with others. By developing awareness of your body-language habits, you can learn to be a more effective communicator.

When engaging in conversation, it is essential to be mindful of your body gestures. Making eye contact with an open posture signals your attentiveness. In contrast, slouching, clenching your fists, or tensing your shoulders could signal disinterest or hostility. Before you communicate, ask yourself, "Am I at ease right now?" Releasing tension in your body and finding a calm posture will significantly improve the quality of your communication.

A good conversation requires that you listen attentively. Take time to fully absorb what the person is expressing to you, both verbally and nonverbally. You may have responses prepared in advance, but it is still important to be present in the moment and truly listen and value the words that are being spoken.

Being present and actively listening shows other people that you are genuinely interested in what they have to say. Failing to do this or rushing through a conversation to get to your point can end up damaging a relationship. "The greatest compliment that was ever paid me was when one asked me what I thought, and attended to my answer," Henry David Thoreau said.

Developing mindfulness before and during your interactions with others can be beneficial in many ways. It can help you remain composed when negative feelings arise during a discussion, recognize if you are talking incessantly, and realize when you are not paying attention.

Ask yourself, "Am I genuinely contributing to this conversation or simply talking for the sake of talking? Am I truly interested in listening or just waiting for my turn to speak?" By using your "observing mind" and noticing your tendencies, you will gain self-understanding and improve the quality of your dialogue and your relationship with others.

Anytime the DMN appears, you may lose focus as your mind wanders. During a conversation, this may cause you to tune out and lose the ability to listen, which can annoy and even anger others. You may start to ramble without purpose, leading to confusion. To avoid problems, notice that your mind has strayed and gently return to the present.

Body scan meditation is an effective way to improve your body awareness and communication skills. Practiced regularly, it will significantly increase presence and mindfulness, which will help you improve your connection with others.

Body Scan Exercise

Set aside fifteen to twenty minutes to relax and enter the now. Breathe deeply and feel the sights and sounds of your present environment. Carefully scan your body from head to toe, paying attention to each and every subtle sensation along the way. Notice the rising and falling of your chest, feelings in your back or abdomen, and pulsations in your legs and feet. Identify and release any tension that you detect.

Initially, you may only become aware of obvious sensations, such as a pounding headache or aching back. As you practice, learn to become aware of more subtle sensations, such as a twitch on your face or the thumping of your heart. Pay close attention to your shoulders, checking to see if they are relaxed or raised and tense. Notice if your fists are clenched or closed. Allow each part of your body to relax and be at ease. Continue to scan from your toes back to your head, and repeat the process.

During the body scan exercise, it is natural to be interrupted by thoughts and emotions. Respond to these internal disruptions with kindness and compassion, offering your "wandering mind" a warm smile. You can promote the "observing mind" by giving it affirmations of self-compassion and gratitude.

Breathing in, my mind clears.
I am grateful for this moment.

Body Awareness Strengthens Bonds with Others

At first, it may be difficult to maintain presence during a body scan, but with repeated practice your focus and concentration will improve. Your level of awareness will deepen, not just during the body scan but also in other daily activities. This will allow you to recognize physical tension and purposefully relax during your day, even when you are not practicing mindfulness.

Before a meeting or conversation, spend a few seconds to recognize and release any physical tension. Tightness often results from prolonged periods of stress, and during a dialogue it could signify hostility or disinterest. Simply noticing raised shoulders is enough to relax the area and calm your body. Similarly, check if your fists are clenched or closed, and allow your hands to be at ease.

Neck posture can also convey a variety of signals, such as confusion, aggression, or intimidation. Be aware if your head is tilted, raised, or lowered, and strive to maintain a relaxed, neutral position. Eye contact is also very expressive; it indicates your interest in the discussion, whereas looking away conveys a lack of interest or unease.

Good body posture is essential for effective communication. Standing tall and confident conveys interest, openness, and attentiveness. Conversely, a hunched or awkward posture can signify shyness, disinterest, or even an attempt to intimidate the speaker. Pay attention to your body language, so you can express yourself effectively and meaningfully.

You can practice the body scan exercise regularly in the morning and before an important discussion to help improve the overall experience. As you relax your posture, shoulders, and facial muscles, others will feel more comfortable around you, and the quality of the interaction will improve. When you are present and relaxed in your own skin, it is easier to focus on the person speaking and listen to what they are saying, rather than rushing them to respond with your ideas.

The more you practice body scan meditation and cultivate self-gratitude and compassion, the more this becomes an innate part of your verbal and nonverbal communication style. Take some time to reflect objectively on your interactions with others, whether at home, work, or social events. Doing so will help identify areas for improvement. This, in turn, will help strengthen your bond with others and reduce any loneliness you may have been feeling.

By setting an intention and nurturing your empathy and compassion, you can improve your relationships and cultivate health, happiness, inner peace, and wisdom. Confucius wrote, "To put the world in order, we must first put the nation in order; to put the nation in order, we must first put the family in order; to put the family in order, we must first cultivate our personal life; and to cultivate our personal life, we must first set our hearts right."

When Loneliness Turns into Depression

Depression and loneliness sometimes go hand in hand. Affecting over 16 million Americans, depression is a clinical disorder characterized by a persistently low mood and lack of interest in daily activities. Patients can suffer from significant impairments involving relationships, work performance, and personal health. Unfortunately, while treatments are available, the majority of people affected by this debilitating condition are undiagnosed and untreated.

Across the world, depression is a major source of morbidity (illness and disease), costing over $200 billion in the US each year. It can arise from stress, social situations, and a range of biological and psychological factors. Symptoms may include lack of interest in life, difficulty sleeping, loss of appetite, decreased energy, difficulty concentrating, suicidal thoughts, and a loss of self-esteem. Studies suggest that if an individual experiences one episode of depression (which typically lasts three to ten months), that individual has a 30 percent chance of recurrence within ten years. If two episodes occur, the likelihood of a third bout of depression is 80 percent.

Left untreated, depression can lead to significant long-term changes in brain function. Imaging studies of depressed patients have revealed an overactive default mode network, which contributes to excessive rumination and negative thought patterns that can worsen in a downward spiral. DMN malfunctioning is also found in other mental illnesses, such as autism and schizophrenia.

Depression is a medical condition requiring diagnosis and management by a healthcare professional. If you or someone you know suffers from depression, effective treatments are available. For example, selective serotonin reuptake inhibitors (SSRIs) can result in a 50 percent reduction in symptoms for the majority of patients.

Researchers are exploring new medications that may be effective. For example, in clinical studies, a single dose of psilocybin has been found to significantly reduce depression symptoms, even in patients who have exhausted all other therapeutic options. It works by directly inhibiting the DMN and offering a reprieve from negative thoughts. While the early data are encouraging, at the time of this writing psilocybin has not yet been approved by the FDA to manage this condition.

Many people with depression have benefitted from non-medication treatment options. As mentioned earlier, cognitive behavioral therapy involves working closely with a therapist to develop an understanding of your thought patterns. Many therapists use the RAIN technique, a feature of insight meditation presented in the chapter on addictive craving. The primary goal of cognitive behavioral therapy is to learn how to detach from negative thoughts, so you can live more comfortably with them.

Cognitive behavioral therapy and insight meditation share much in common, with a primary distinction that you can practice insight meditation yourself throughout the day. Studies have found that mindfulness-based therapy can be as effective as medication in reducing depressive symptoms and in preventing relapse.

An effective technique is to begin with a prayer or mindfulness practice focusing on your breath, sounds, or physical sensations. Once you are in the present moment, observe your thoughts from a place of acceptance, without judgment. You can apply the RAIN technique, detaching from persistent thoughts and watching them float by like clouds in a windy sky. By observing the quality of your thoughts, you will gain insight into what brings them on, how they affect you, and how to let them go.

Acknowledging your thoughts means not allowing them to overpower you. Rather than accepting false beliefs such as "I am worthless" or "no one will ever love me," you can observe these feelings from a distance, recognizing that they are merely transient and can be released if you choose to let them go. For example, rather than accepting the notion that "I am worthless," you can acknowledge that "I am just having a thought that I am worthless" and allow it to pass.

At first, it may be difficult to observe your thoughts without becoming consumed by them, as you may have developed strong attachments to them over time. However, with consistent practice, you will learn to change your relationship with your thought patterns and liberate yourself from their grasp. Gradually, their influence on your life will lessen, and you will find peace.

There is no one-size-fits-all solution for depression. Medication, cognitive behavioral therapy, and insight meditation may be helpful tools for you. Nevertheless, it is a good idea to manage the symptoms of this clinical disorder with the help of a healthcare professional.

Final Thoughts on Loneliness

Loneliness and depression are major public health issues, intertwined in many ways. In both conditions, you may build a wall between yourself and the outside world, creating an impenetrable barrier of isolation. The lonely journey may become increasingly difficult over time as your social needs remain unfulfilled. To make matters worse, you may suffer from an overactive default mode network that continually repeats negative thoughts, painful memories, fears, and doubts throughout your day.

Instead of seeking connection, you may respond to loneliness by retreating from others. This can create a vicious cycle of worsening negativity, causing you to further detach from others and lose your social skills. You may even start to enjoy your aloofness, despite your longing for meaningful relationships. As you get more entrenched in this mindset, it can become harder to break free and live in peace.

Your brain's default mode network, and the ego it sustains, may not only prolong your suffering but also act as a major impediment to connecting with others. Your biases may prevent you from gaining an understanding of the world, thereby limiting your wisdom.

Focusing only on yourself restricts your capacity for genuine connection. As you try to break free from old habits, the DMN often resurfaces and tries to drag you back to its ways. You should anticipate its presence on your journey and expect it to offer resistance.

Fortunately, you do not have to be held captive by your thoughts. Through techniques like insight meditation and cognitive behavioral therapy, you can develop a deeper understanding of your ruminations and find space between them and your true self. By allowing thoughts to pass without getting involved, you can find freedom. Extricating yourself from the storm of negative thoughts and emotions might be challenging, but it starts with an intention for a better life and a change in how you treat yourself and others.

The power of kindness, empathy, self-gratitude, and compassion will set you free. By consciously cultivating these attributes through affirmations, prayers, and mindfulness, you will break away from the dominance of your default mode network and stop the downward spiral of loneliness and depression. What emerges is the bliss of the awakened state. "Kindness is the golden chain by which society is bound together," wrote the German novelist and poet Johann Wolfgang von Goethe.

You can foster empathy and compassion in many ways. Wishing the best for others, giving your time and energy to your family and community, or donating to a charity are effective approaches. Mentoring a child or volunteering at a school, hospital, or elderly home can also be highly rewarding. Expressing gratitude for your relationships before you go to bed will reduce morning stress and improve your overall well-being. The act of giving or wanting to help someone shuts down the default mode network and grants a respite from self-absorbed suffering. Develop an intention to truly help others and notice the effect on your happiness level.

It may be difficult to genuinely give to others if you have not nurtured yourself. Practicing self-care, such as getting enough sleep, exercising, and eating well, are critical to maintain self-compassion. You must learn to be kind and generous to yourself before you can offer this to others. Performing self-gratitude will allow you to see the true value of your worth. "You are not a drop in the ocean," Rumi said. "You are the ocean in a drop."

During prayers and mindfulness practices, express gratitude for yourself and the air you breathe, never allowing feelings of worthlessness to dictate your life. When such thoughts arise, approach them with neutrality and a nonjudgmental attitude, recognizing the default mode network when it rears its head. You can also combat loneliness and negative thoughts with positive actions like calling a friend, messaging your family online, or taking a walk with your partner.

With focus and determination, the light of positive intent will extinguish the darkness of loneliness and depression, revealing the vast inner peace that radiates from your core to the world. "All the joy the world contains has come through wishing happiness for others," eighth-century Buddhist monk Shantideva said. "All the misery the world contains has come through wanting pleasure for oneself."

KNOT 5

NEGATIVITY—SHAKE OFF DOOM AND GLOOM

WE ARE CONDITIONED to make swift judgments of others in situations where we may not have all the facts. Our brain's inherent negativity bias leads us to assume the worst and blame others for our unpleasant experiences. This can trap us in a gloomy outlook of the world, preventing us from experiencing life's full splendor. Pessimistic thought patterns can be so detrimental to our relationships and health that they can contribute to breakups, serious diseases, and a shorter lifespan. Clearly, we are the victims of our own negativity.

If you suffer from negativity, there is hope. In this chapter, we will explore how this mental knot impacts health and well-being. With some simple adjustments, you can free yourself from doom and gloom and open the door to unconditional happiness in the present moment. A powerful remedy, equanimity, will give you the freedom to choose your destiny and the strength to fulfill it.

Negative Thoughts Cripple Our Health

Clinical studies have provided evidence that happiness has a positive effect on our health and longevity, while negative thought patterns are associated with disease and a shortened life span.

In a British study that tracked 11,000 people over fifty years old, participants with the most pessimistic moods had a 7.3 percent rate of death over five years. In contrast, those who experienced the greatest happiness had a lower rate of death (3.6 percent). After accounting for other possible causes of mortality such as age, wealth, education, health, substance use, physical activity, and other factors, the study found that the happiest people were 35 percent less likely to die within five years.

Our brains are wired to focus on the negative. It is why the nightly news starts with distressing stories, and why we tend to relive painful experiences. Our default mode network (DMN) wanders the mind away from the present, forcing us to experience the day's most painful emotions—anger, irritation, frustration, sadness, fear, or anxiety. As we watch the reruns of our life's stories, we become prisoners of the mind's internal broadcasts.

Due to its inherent negativity bias, our brain's DMN places greater focus on dismal experiences that have caused us hurt or embarrassment, far more than on the positive events that also may have occurred. We may not remember the times our teachers praised us, but the moments they expressed disappointment may remain vivid in our memories. Our DMN will persistently return to these painful memories, bringing with them the old heartache, anger, and other emotions.

Just one uncomfortable detail can ruin the positive memories of an event. We may be having a great day at work, receiving praise and adulation from colleagues for closing a long-awaited deal. We head home singing a happy tune with a smile on our face, only to be met by an angry partner demanding to know why we neglected an important household matter. In a split second, our positive vibes dissipate, and the takeaway from the day is the one dreary detail that overshadows the rest.

Also known as *positive-negative asymmetry*, negativity bias means our brains are naturally inclined to focus more on our bad memories than our good ones. This leads us to believe that our distressing moments are more significant than they actually are. Not surprisingly, bad impressions tend to linger, and our past traumas continue to nag at us despite our attempts to ignore them.

Our negative inclinations can express themselves in our posture, tone, and facial expression, and the energy shows itself to others. In the modern era, negativity is as harmful and contagious as a flu virus. We are the victims of the bitterness we receive from others, which can influence our mood, rob us of peace and happiness, and affect our health. It is critically important to be aware of how our pessimistic energy manifests and impacts not only ourselves but our family and community.

Negative Judgment in the Social Media Age

We human beings love to compare ourselves to others, and the digital age has magnified this tendency. We judge others and put ourselves on display to be judged. We record and share our everyday actions online, whether whimsical or mundane, with accompanying captions and soundtracks in the hopes of receiving likes, hearts, gifs, emojis, and comments. We continually check our devices, eagerly awaiting praise, often feeling defeated by a negative reaction or the lack of any reaction at all.

Social media can bring out the worst in us. Because of our mind's negativity bias, we are more likely to have cynical and derogatory impressions than positive ones. In a 2020 study, 64 percent of Americans surveyed said that social media had a negative impact on the country, while only 10 percent reported a positive influence. Both regular users and nonusers of social media maintained this trend. Nonetheless, 72 percent of US adults still reported being online with at least one social media platform.

Making snap judgments of others is nothing new. In previous generations, we based our opinions of others on their clothes, cars, or zip code. The element that distinguishes social media is its pervasiveness and instantaneous nature. Anything we say or do can be judged publicly by anyone. It is the perfect ammunition to feed our default mode network's obsessions.

At its core, social media (and other forms of digital entertainment) are designed to foster cycles of craving and aversion. We head to a restaurant because of a friend's post, only to be left frustrated when the experience fails to meet our inflated expectations. We compare our lives to others, resulting in pride, envy, or contempt. Mental overactivity heightens our stress level, while constantly shifting emotions distance us from the present moment. This can lead us to live unconsciously and disregard the pain and suffering we inflict on ourselves and others.

The cycle breeds unhappiness. We forget the world around us, the natural beauty that once filled us with awe, as our attention focuses on the next notification from our digital screens. Nature loses its color and vibrancy. We squander our appreciation for the present moment, as FOMO fuels the yearning to be elsewhere. It's a perfect recipe for long-term dissatisfaction and discontent.

We Are the Victims of Our Negativity

"Do not judge or you too will be judged," Jesus Christ warned. "For in the same way you judge others, you will be judged, and with the measure you use, it will be measured to you." Christ reminds us that our negative opinions of others do harm to us. There are several reasons why.

When we are quick to assume the worst, we often take false views without fully understanding a situation. Our ignorant viewpoints can garner ridicule and disdain from those around us. For instance, we roll our eyes at a customer at the grocery store who accidentally knocks over a display of soda cans, not knowing this person suffers physical challenges from multiple sclerosis. We tend to attribute blame without having all the facts, which can lead to new problems that didn't exist in the first place.

Another downside of negative judgment is that it restricts our ability to learn and develop. Our attitudes can become so confining that we shut our minds and ruin experiences before they have a chance to unfold. For instance, we are mowing the lawn when our neighbor pulls up in a brand-new BMW. We try in vain to conceal our envy, sarcastically asking ourselves, "Who did she sue to afford that?" Before the car is parked, we have judged our neighbor and closed off our mind to learning about her new business venture, something we might have benefited from had we engaged in an open conversation.

When we judge others, we limit our relationship with them and curtail a bond that could have been valuable and rewarding. For example, a friend sets us up on a blind date and, upon seeing the person walk through the door, we think, "They're dressed funny." Without giving him or her a chance to make it to the table, we have formed unfair opinions that can last for the rest of the date—or even our lives. We reject the opportunity to explore and get to know someone authentically, instead choosing to focus on our preconceptions.

Another major drawback of negative judgment is that it creates a cycle of blame. We often pin our difficult circumstances on others, such as our parents for pushing us too hard or not hard enough. We might blame external groups—political parties, ethnicities, the rich or poor—for our salary, title, or college admission. Rather than working hard to improve our situation, we breed blame, hatred, and envy, locking us in a prison of suffering that can be difficult to escape. "Do not overrate what you have received, nor envy others," Buddha said. "He who envies others does not obtain peace of mind."

Negative judgment also happens when we are in the middle of an experience but prefer something else. Rather than being present, we may wonder if this moment deserves to be highlighted on social media or whether it compares to our friend's recent post. In the midst of what should be an enjoyable experience with friends or family, our ruminating mind may question the quality of the time we are having due to unrealistic expectations for satisfaction. Unfortunately, this mentality takes away the joy and spontaneity of the moment.

Left unchecked, these forms of judgment foment a cycle of negativity that builds over time. Blame and dissatisfaction slowly give way to resentment and rage. For some, it can even lead to racism, sexism, and xenophobia. When we let darkness into our lives, it grows until it extinguishes our light of inner peace. We may not recognize the depths of our despair until our suffering becomes unbearable.

The brain's default mode network propels this vicious cycle forward. When the DMN switches on, our thoughts drift away from the present to the past or future. The moment that begins, our negative judgments start to come fast and furious, their intensity visible to anyone catching a glimpse of our scowling facial expression. We mentally snarl at everything from the young man standing on the street corner to the President's appearance on TV. If that weren't bad enough, the DMN also revives bitter memories of our rivals and ex-partners, unnecessarily causing us to fume with anger, regret, or irritation.

You do not have to live this way. If you choose to, you can free yourself from the prison of negativity and judgment. Put away your phone and join the conversation at the party. Be fully present at your kid or partner's events and make lasting memories. Instead of making premature accusations, tune into the truth of reality to learn and grow.

Keep in mind, your default mode network can form negative judgments unconsciously. When you become aware of this tendency with your "observing mind," you can end the vicious cycle in its tracks, even if this life-long habit was passed down to you. You have the capacity to permanently end your judgmental bias and find freedom from internal tensions, allowing you to savor the present moment without wanting to change it. This is the path to the enlightened state. To guide you along the way, the power of equanimity will help you break through the mental knot of negativity.

The Power of Equanimity

It may seem overwhelming or even impossible to break away from the ingrained habit of judgment and negativity. However, what feels natural to your mind is not always what is beneficial for you in the long term. For example, you may feel inclined to consume lots of sugar, sleep all the time, or view people around you as objects to use or avoid. But these habitual cravings run counter to a happy, healthy life.

You have the power to reverse the DMN's inherent mindset of negativity, opening the door to inner peace, happiness, and genuine connection with others. It begins with your intention for change. When you yearn for inner peace and set it as your daily intention, the process of positive transformation begins. As Henry David Thoreau wrote, "Go confidently in the direction of your dreams! Live the life you've imagined."

If your mind naturally gravitates toward doom and gloom, how can you reverse what might be a decades-old habit? Is change truly possible? The answer is yes, and it starts with simply letting things be. By acknowledging reality without forming an opinion about it, you will unravel the mental knot of negativity. This is the power of equanimity.

Equanimity means maintaining balance and composure, especially in difficult situations. It is a mental trait that you can train and empower yourself to experience. It involves recognizing that both positive and negative emotions will repeatedly occur, and there is no use in clinging to either of them. It means acknowledging that you will be fine with the circumstances of the present moment, whether favorable or not, by recognizing the DMN's tendency to crave, dislike, or gravitate toward the negative.

For example, if your teenager gets into a minor vehicle accident due to distracted driving, it is natural to feel angry that he damaged the car. But lashing out by calling him names and humiliating him in front of his friends will only make the situation worse, as it will damage your relationship and his self-esteem. With equanimity, you acknowledge the anger within while simultaneously not allowing raw emotions to drive your thoughts, words, and actions.

By choosing to engage your rational mind rather than the emotional one, you will better understand the situation and make the best set of decisions to repair the vehicle and educate the teen, deciding on the appropriate level of punishment with mental clarity and purpose. The goal of equanimity is not to absolve others of blame but to use rational understanding to make the best decisions.

Suppose one day at school you misunderstand the teacher and incorrectly complete a project, receiving a failing grade. Would it make sense to stand in front of a mirror to berate yourself and question your self-worth? Of course not. Blame and regret will exacerbate the pain. Instead, take advantage of the sorrow to motivate yourself to embrace constructive change. Confucius said, "Our greatest glory is not in never falling, but in rising every time we fall."

Equanimity does not mean simply having pleasant feelings and avoiding unpleasant ones. It means accepting the reality of the moment, whether it is good or bad, with clarity and an evenness of mind, especially under stress.

Be at ease with unease. When difficult emotions surface, acknowledge them as temporary states that will pass. Life is a state of constant flux, with good and bad times coming and going all the time. Developing equanimity means having an understanding of your emotions and how you relate to them. It is loud by its very silence, sending a powerful message of composure and strength to those around you.

Many religions prioritize this essential trait as a cornerstone of spirituality. In the *Torah*, it is referred to *hishtavut*, a state of balance that is a prerequisite for communicating with God. In Buddhism, it is one of the four great virtues that unlocks wisdom and happiness. Buddha taught that we are constantly caught in the push and pull of praise and blame, pleasure and pain, success and failure, gain and loss. The enlightened person accepts these states equally without approval or disapproval, guided by the "middle way."

When you learn to observe emotions without being impacted by them, freedom arises. You will replace negativity and judgment with presence and being. For instance, suppose during rush-hour traffic you are frustrated that the cars in the lane next to you seem to be going faster. Instead of weaving in and out of traffic and creating more stress for yourself (and other drivers), recognize your irritation as a fleeting feeling. Watch it from a distance and allow it to disappear, setting a purposeful intention to be patient. You may arrive at your destination slightly late, but you will have a composed, relaxed state of mind.

The more you learn to recognize emotions as they arise, the easier it is to understand and create distance from them. You will make decisions with your rational faculties rather than the emotional ones, leading to more success in the long run. "You have power over your mind—not outside events," Marcus Aurelius wrote. "Realize this, and you will find strength."

Cultivating equanimity allows you to break through negativity, revealing inner peace within. Instead of blaming people and passing judgment, you will take greater responsibility and better understand the actions of others. You will come to recognize the positive qualities of friends and family, regardless of their shortcomings. By refraining from assuming the worst, you will grow more appreciative of their presence.

Importantly, you should not ignore frustrations, annoyances, and other negative feelings but rather tune into them to learn their hidden meaning. For instance, if you've made a financial mistake that impacts your family, you should fully experience the regret of the moment, but do not wallow in it.

Instead of ignoring, medicating, or clinging to the pain, use the emotion as a driving force to learn and progress forward to a brighter day.

Looking in the mirror without judgment fosters self-compassion, making you more content with who you are in this moment, which opens the door to the higher self. It is ultimately your choice whether to feed your light of acceptance or the fire of negativity. By choosing to extinguish doom and gloom and cultivate equanimity, you can break through to the enlightened state.

The Cherokee tell an ancient tale of two wolves. In this tale, a grandfather shares a story with his grandson, explaining that within him resides two wolves constantly fighting. The first one has evil traits—anger, envy, greed, arrogance, resentment, lies, and false pride. The second wolf embodies all that is good—joy, peace, hope, love, humility, kindness, compassion, truth, and faith.

The grandfather explains that this fight is within everyone, including his grandson, with the two wolves competing to kill one another.

The grandson is fearful of the idea of two wolves, so terrifying and violent, living inside him. He asks, "Which one will win the fight, Grandfather?"

The sage replies, "The one you feed."

Change is a choice. You can choose to exemplify good behavior to those around you—children, family, colleagues, and friends—by rising above criticism, judgment, and habitual negativity. Belittling others will not help improve their conduct. Getting angry at friends may not encourage them to think differently. If you want to promote change, then you must set an example by first changing yourself.

Bayazid, a Sufi mystic, wrote of his youthful ambition to improve humanity: "When I was young, I thought and said to God in all my prayers, 'Give me the strength to change the whole world.'" As he reached middle age, he realized this was too much of a task and asked God to let him change his family instead. Finally, as he grew old, he understood that even this was too much, as he had not made the changes he desired in himself first. He finally realized that transforming himself was the key to unlocking growth in others around him.

Developing the Power of Equanimity

Equanimity meditation is an effective way to break free from negativity. By focusing attention on the breath or body sensations with the "observing mind," you learn to develop deeper awareness of your opinions, judgments, and biases as they arise. Understanding how you react to life's changing nature and developing an evenness of mind are the key steps to unlock health, happiness, and inner peace.

Equanimity Meditation Exercise

Start by spending a few minutes becoming aware of the present moment through a prayer or mindfulness exercise. This can involve focusing on your breath, body sensations, or sounds in the environment. Observe whatever state you are in—whether positive or negative—from a place of acceptance and neutrality. Then remind yourself of the intention of your practice.

Spend fifteen to twenty minutes taking notice of thoughts that arrive when your mind wanders and the default mode network switches on. Label these interruptions for what they are; for example, a recent memory or emotion. Observe objectively and notice how these thoughts and emotions make you feel. Do they lead to physical tension in your body? Are you reacting to them in some way? Watch and let go.

Pay close attention to emotional judgments—the negative reactions to your thoughts or environment. For example, you may suddenly recall the memory of an old conversation, which then triggers emotions like embarrassment or anger. Notice the uncomfortable feelings and how they manifest in your body. Ask yourself, "Am I excessively clinging to a particular thought?" The key is to recognize patterns and learn to let them disappear.

When you catch yourself in the act of judgment or blame, take note of the feelings and how they manifest. What happens when you detach from them and simply observe? After a few seconds, note how the emotions fade and lose their strength. Allow them to weaken and return to the present.

By labeling and letting go of these reactions, you cultivate equanimity. With repeated practice, you will gain insight into your thought patterns and find space from them, learning to recognize judgment and negativity during meditation and in regular life. William James wrote, "The greatest weapon against stress is our ability to choose one thought over another."

Equanimity Meditation Empowers Your "Observing Mind"

For people of faith, prayer effectively sets the intention of the practice and brings you into the present moment with God. It is a powerful way to shut down the judgmental mind (your default mode network) and awaken the "observing mind" (your central executive network). You can begin by expressing gratitude for life and the air you breathe, as you pray.

Lord God, the Infinite Unknown, the energy of the universe, I fill my lungs with Your grace. I breathe in Your benevolence, and I breathe out my negativity and my judgmental ways. I equally accept the good and the bad of life, and I trust that Your light will guide my way forward.

During equanimity meditation, body scans are particularly effective. Tune in with your "observing mind" and scan the body from head to toe, noticing areas of pain or tension. Become aware of not only the physical sensation but also your reaction to it. When you notice an aversion to pain, let it go and simply observe the discomfort for what it is.

After completing the body scan, take note of your mental state by asking yourself, "Am I at ease right now?" Search for any residual negativity or aversion in the mind and watch it from a place of neutrality and acceptance. By acknowledging it, you will find space from it. Lao Tzu said, "To the mind that is still, the whole universe surrenders."

In life, we tend to amplify our tensions by judging them as something bad that we must escape from or medicate. This actually makes them worse. By objectively observing your judgments, you can find freedom from them. As a result, you become more at ease with unease, and the intensity of your emotional pain will subside. This is the power of equanimity.

Initially, it may be difficult to break free from negative states. Painful thoughts may interrupt your meditation and overwhelm you, impacting your mood and well-being. But with consistent practice, the pressure from judgmental negativity will lessen as you learn to watch it like a passing cloud, understanding that it is a temporary state that does not require your involvement. As you become increasingly aware of your negative reactions, you realize that these thoughts do not actually improve anything but rather generate charged emotions that make life more difficult.

As you practice equanimity meditation, reflect on the differences between your "wandering mind" and the "observing mind." Notice the quality of their inner nature. The act of watching your mind turns on the central executive network (CEN), which is more insightful, free, and blissful than the ruminations of the default mode network (DMN).

You may notice that the hurtful opinions of yourself or others strengthen when your DMN shows up and makes your mind wander. However, when you become present once again and watch these judgments with the "observing mind," the negativity subsides. Through equanimity meditation, you can empower your "observing mind" and spend more time in the CEN, thereby reducing the DMN's judgmental negativity.

With training, you will also discover that the DMN tends to be more self-obsessive, negative, anxious, and fearful. In contrast, the CEN is more likely to be aware, calm, present, and focused. By looking closely and understanding these mental states, you will learn to recognize the DMN when it switches on, making it apparent that you are no longer ruled by your "wandering mind" and are now able to switch it off. As you learn to live in the present with deeper awareness, you will find space from the DMN and its judgmental ways. This is how you can break through the mental knot of negativity.

Keep in mind that success in meditation does not depend on whether you experience pleasant or unpleasant feelings. Having an uncomfortable sensation does not mean you are failing; on the contrary, it means you are developing a deeper awareness of yourself. In that moment of mindfulness, you are free from craving the pleasant and avoiding the unpleasant. When you can truly recognize your thoughts and emotions for what they are—temporary phenomena—you will find freedom.

With equanimity, you can recognize moments when you want to feel a certain way—perhaps frustrated, annoyed, or angry—and learn to let go. If you sense dissatisfaction with the present moment, you can greet it as a temporary feeling, sending it on its way. What emerges is a relaxed focus in the present moment that is blissful and serene.

As self-understanding deepens, wisdom arises. In this state, you are free of the internal opinions that interrupt priceless moments in life—enjoying children's performances, watching movies with a loved one, and holding meaningful conversations with friends. As you learn to accept the moments of life as they truly are—whether good and bad—inner peace shines. You replace doom and gloom with tranquility and euphoric presence. Seneca said, "True happiness is to enjoy the present, without anxious dependence upon the future."

Negativity from Chronic Pain

It can be challenging to maintain a positive outlook when you face chronic pain, an issue affecting millions of people. Roughly one in six Americans experience daily pain, with 40 million describing it as severe and 20 million unable to engage in normal activities. Chronic pain is a leading cause of disability in the US, with significant emotional, physical, and financial repercussions.

Physical pain is an unpleasant sensation that could signify actual or potential tissue damage. It might indicate an underlying medical condition that requires evaluation by a healthcare professional. In some cases, organ damage can cause referred pain to another area of the body; for example, an injured pancreas could cause back pain, and a heart attack may trigger sensations in the jaw or arm. Healthcare providers can recommend procedures to address chronic pain or prescribe medicines to treat specific types of pain, such as gabapentin for neuropathic pain or corticosteroid injections for arthritic pain.

However, in some cases pain may not be associated with internal injury and could instead have a psychological basis. For example, stress or anxiety can lead to real discomfort in the throat, chest, or back, which may be misinterpreted as a heart attack. In such cases, it is important to address the underlying psychological source of tension for pain relief to occur.

Rather than reacting negatively to physical pain or avoiding it, heed the signals from your body. During mindfulness exercises, when you tune into discomfort, listen to what your body is trying to tell you. If you sense tiredness, allow yourself some rest. If you notice strain in an elbow, avoid overexertion and allow it to heal. For stress-related pain, set a daily intention to take better care of yourself and ease your life pressures. Be mindful of your body's alert system and use it to ensure your well-being.

When you react to pain with dislike or aversion (for example, wishing it would go away), it tends to magnify and create even more distress than if you were to simply experience the sensation for what it is. Buddha taught that pain is the "first arrow," and the "second arrow" is the irritation, anger, resistance, and reaction that amplifies it. You can avoid the sting of the second arrow by changing how you perceive pain through equanimity meditation or cognitive behavioral therapy. This helps you recognize and separate the physical pain from your emotional reaction to it.

Acknowledging the second arrow lets you tolerate the condition you are in, so you can recover more quickly from stressors and avoid unhealthy coping behaviors, like consuming alcohol or inappropriate medication. Equanimity creates a healthier relationship with your discomfort, so you can learn to live with pain rather than treating it as an obstacle or annoyance. Acknowledging your chronic pain and committing to meet it with acceptance can help you lead a meaningful and satisfying life.

There are many healthy, effective ways to manage chronic pain. Breathing exercises, mindful relaxation, calm music, acupuncture, massage, stretching, and light exercise can significantly reduce stress-associated pain. Deep-breathing exercises trigger the relaxation response to calm jittery nerves and tight muscles. In case of injury, allowing your body to fully heal will significantly help. Your healthcare provider can provide tailored treatments to suit your specific condition.

In addition, take time to practice the mindfulness exercises in this book to manage your chronic pain. Clinical studies have found that mindfulness practices significantly improve pain severity, depression symptoms, and quality of life when practiced consistently. Cultivating mindfulness also improves mood and alleviates anxiety and depression. Prayer, a form of mindfulness practice, is also effective in improving psychological well-being.

Final Thoughts on Negativity

A famous Taoist fable personifies equanimity. A farmer works his crops for many decades. Aging and feeble, his neighbors regularly watch over him with concern. One day, his horse runs away. Upon hearing the news, his neighbors offer their sympathy and express concern for his bad luck.

"Maybe," the old farmer responds.

His neighbors are surprised and ask why he is not more upset. The old farmer explains that what they perceive as good luck or bad luck is all in the eye of the beholder. He is not sure if the horse's departure is good or bad, and he is not going to make that judgment. He will wait and let life play out and see what transpires.

The following morning, the farmer's horse reappears along with three other young, strong horses. His neighbors rejoice upon seeing this newfound fortune, praising the farmer's great luck.

He replies, "Maybe," and says nothing more.

The following week, the man's son attempts to ride one of the wild horses, only to be thrown down, breaking his leg. Later that afternoon, the neighbors returned to express sympathy for his son's misfortune, remarking on the father's recent spate of bad luck.

The farmer shrugs his shoulders. "Maybe."

A week later war breaks out, and the army arrives at the farm, demanding that the farmer offer up his son to fight. Upon seeing him hobbling on crutches, the officers deem him unfit for service and depart, leaving the farm in peace. The neighbors remark on the farmer's great fortune now that his son is safe.

"Maybe," the elder says.

What can we learn from this Taoist tale? Do not become too emotionally attached to life's ups and downs, and avoid letting your feelings dictate your decisions. The farmer remains stoic in the face of extreme circumstances, never acting rashly no matter how his day has unfolded. He controls his impulses rather than allowing them to control him.

Being relaxed in the present moment allows you to experience life as it is, not according to what you think it should be. Attempting to control situations to be the way you want them to be tends to cause frustration and suffering, as you have limited power over the impermanent nature of being. Resisting the present moment prevents you from learning and experiencing life to its fullest. When you let go, you can be present and adjust to change as it happens.

Happier people tend to thrive and lead more fulfilling lives, whereas those who succumb to negativity can find life passing them by. They may make snap judgments before understanding a situation, assigning blame with no evidence and often suffering with envy, self-loathing, and blame.

Unfortunately, negativity is a greater problem today than ever before due to the prevalence of instant information and social media. Our judgmental tendencies can be detrimental to relationships, health, and wisdom. They keep us from being present in the moment and getting to know those around us. By craving what we do not have, disliking what we have, forming opinions of people and events based on a sound bite, and using digital devices to talk *at* people (rather than *with* them), we find ourselves in a state of increasing unhappiness.

Remember, your default mode network amplifies the negative aspects of life's experiences. To cultivate equanimity, practice mindfulness and gratitude to move past your mind's negativity bias. To be at ease with unease means acknowledging life's ever-changing nature and not putting up resistance to what you dislike.

To have equanimity is to be proactive, open minded, and flexible. It does not mean avoiding negative emotions or letting people get away with bad behavior. Rather, it is the ability to recognize both good and bad emotions and not allow them to consume you or influence your decisions. By pushing past the gut reactions and knee-jerk behaviors, you create space for the rational mind to lead the way.

When you can truly accept life's situations without judgment, you unlock a deep inner peace that transcends the innate tendency to discriminate.

Equanimity meditation helps you recognize when you are being judgmental, allowing you to break free from old habits. You gain the upper hand over your emotions as they lose their control over you.

Equanimity frees your mind of bitterness, envy, and hate, replacing them with presence, peace, and compassion. To make lasting change, it is essential to set a daily intention and recognize if you have strayed from the path. Notice and cherish the positive effects of equanimity, using it as a guiding light for those around you who suffer from the darkness of negativity.

You have the choice to nourish your dual energies: to be Christ-like and do good or to be consumed by negativity and cause harm. As the Cherokee story reminds us, you can feed the good wolf inside you or the evil wolf.

Though you will experience conflicts and mistakes in life, you have the power to control your reactions to them. Feeding the instinctive doom-and-gloom tendencies can lead to suffering, but recognizing and letting go of negative biases helps you break through the mental knot of negativity to discover health, happiness, and inner peace. Equanimity gives you the freedom to choose your destiny and the strength to fulfill it.

KNOT 6

ANXIETY AND ANGER—RESOLVE YOUR SUFFERING

MANY OF US LIVE WITH PERSISTENT WORRY and uneasiness about the future. Anxiety is a common feature of our fast-paced society, manifesting as phobias, panic attacks, and generalized anxiety disorder. Anger, an extension of anxiety, can wreak havoc on our lives and damage our physical and mental health. This chapter will summarize the many faces of anxiety and how they take root as mental knots.

If you live at the mercy of these emotions, there is hope—a host of solutions can help you manage anxiety and anger. With the power of presence, you can resolve your suffering to discover health, happiness, and inner peace, awakening your higher self in the process.

Anxiety Is a Normal Human Emotion

Here is a scenario: It is Monday morning, and you get a somber email from your boss about an urgent meeting later that afternoon. Your heart races, and your palms grow sweaty as a feeling of dread takes hold. You wonder, "Am I in trouble? Are there layoffs coming?"

When anxiety takes hold, the natural tendency is to panic, which can manifest in many different ways—you may lose focus and become unproductive, or you may grow hypervigilant and spend the morning anxiously preparing for all possible scenarios. When the meeting time finally arrives and you find your boss's tone is calm and the topic is not critical, your heart rate returns to normal as the fears dissipate.

Anxiety is a natural human emotion that signals an impending danger or potential risk of harm. It is an anticipation that something unpleasant will occur. When that dreaded event occurs, the anxiety will either disappear or it will be replaced by fear or anger. On a rollercoaster, anxiety is the anticipation as you climb up the first lift hill and is replaced by fright when you plunge down the main drop.

Life is a state of constant unknowns. Healthy anxiety helps you adapt to life's obstacles by signaling that it's time to react to keep yourself safe. For instance, if you pull into your driveway and see your home's front door open, your apprehension escalates as you wonder if someone has broken in. Without hesitation, you use your smartphone to quickly check your security cameras for clues. As you get to the bottom of the situation, the unease will quickly dissipate (false alarm), or it will be replaced by the fight-or-flight response (intruder in the home).

However, many of us often ignore the messages coming from our worries because of inconvenience, insecurity, or disappointment. For example, we may fear that our partner is cheating on us, but we do not take any action due to the possibility of separation. Or we may avoid opening a child's report card or a letter from the IRS to prevent potential distress. Instead of facing the anxiety, we may choose to avoid it, medicate to forget it, or find a way to bury it.

Similarly, at times we may worry over circumstances that may not happen for years or even decades to come. We may be plagued with thoughts like these: "How will I afford a home? Will I ever get married? What if I lose my job? Will the economy collapse? Will my children succeed?" These long-term apprehensions can gradually develop into hardened mental knots of anxiety and overwhelm us, but only if we allow them to.

Left unchecked, anxiety will unleash stress hormones and harmful behaviors that can severely impact our health, work or school performance, relationships, and mental well-being. Anxiety can lead to high blood pressure, weight gain or loss, insomnia, and even arrhythmias (irregular heartbeat). It can also cause avoidance behaviors, where we try to escape or distract ourselves from difficult thoughts, feelings, and situations. For example, if we fear criticism, we may avoid work performance evaluations. This can have additional consequences, like falling productivity and poor life outcomes.

When worry spirals out of control, it can lead to a painful state of agitation that is difficult to escape. It is often characterized by irritability, where even minor events elicit strong reactions. We may try to convince ourselves that life will get better while simultaneously resisting change, thereby creating an internal conflict. For many people, anxiety is a constant companion that is unrelated to any single event or circumstance. Over time, it develops into a state of suffering that is difficult to manage.

The Many Faces of Anxiety

Anxiety disorders impact nearly 30 percent of adults at some point during their lives, affecting women more than men. They typically manifest during early adolescence or young adulthood but can emerge at any stage throughout one's life. To qualify as a clinical disorder, the fear and worry must be disproportionately greater than the issue of concern and hinder the ability to function normally.

To overcome anxiety, we must first learn to recognize it. Anxiety presents in many different ways, and the most common types include the following:

- ***Phobias***—This manifests as an excessive and persistent fear about a particular object, situation, or activity that is not inherently dangerous. Those affected often recognize that their fear is irrational but are unable to control its intensity. Common phobias include fear of flying, water, spiders, and public speaking—the latter of which is often ranked higher than fear of death. People suffering from agoraphobia experience intense fear in crowded spaces or unfamiliar places where escape is difficult. In some cases, fear can be so overwhelming it prevents people from leaving home.
- ***Social anxiety disorder***—This type of anxiety is the intense fear of being watched and judged by others. The condition can strain relationships and interfere with life activities, such as answering questions in class, dating, or interviewing for a job. In some cases, normal routines like using a public restroom, eating in front of others, or talking to a cashier can be challenging. Symptoms may include a rapid heart rate, difficulty speaking, inability to make eye contact, speaking too softly to be heard, blushing, sweating, or trembling in social situations.
- ***Panic disorder***—People with this disorder experience frequent panic attacks with symptoms that can include chest pain, elevated blood pressure, rapid heart rate, shortness of breath, dizziness, trembling, chills, and hot flashes. The episodes may be accompanied by feelings of detachment, loss of control, and fear of impending death. When it is severe, people believe they are experiencing a heart attack or other life-threatening illness, forcing them to go to the emergency room for treatment. When medical conditions are ruled out and the

patient is sent home, the disorder can worsen and lead to depression or other mental conditions.

- ***Generalized anxiety disorder***—This condition manifests as persistent and excessive worrying that impairs the ability to perform daily activities. Symptoms often last for more than six months and may include fatigue, restlessness, difficulty concentrating, irritability, muscle tension, and insomnia. Even simple tasks, like booking appointments or completing household chores, can be challenging for some people.
- ***Separation anxiety disorder***—People with this disorder experience intense fear of not being in the same physical space with a close contact. This may be a normal reaction for children when they first leave home to attend daycare or preschool, and their parents often suffer from it as well. People with this condition may refuse to leave the house or fall asleep if their family member, caregiver, or other close person is not around, resulting in high stress levels, nightmares, and night terrors.
- ***Obsessive-compulsive disorder***—People with this condition experience recurrent intrusive thoughts or ideas that lead to repetitive behaviors (or compulsions). Common obsessions include the need for order and cleanliness or the fear of losing something. Compulsive behaviors associated with these thoughts typically include repetitive handwashing, cleaning, arranging, checking locks and appliances, avoiding people or places, and other rituals.
- ***Post-traumatic stress disorder***—People experience PTSD due to severe anxiety associated with a traumatic event. Symptoms may include flashbacks, nightmares, and uncontrollable thoughts that can disrupt daily life.

The physical and emotional stress caused by these disorders can have a detrimental impact on long-term health. Effects on the nervous, cardiovascular, digestive, immune, and respiratory systems can range from heart disease, irritable bowel syndrome, weight gain, depression, migraines, memory loss, and recurrent infections caused by a weakened immune system. Anxiety is a medical condition that requires diagnosis and treatment by a healthcare professional.

In addition to its effect on our health, anxiety also gives rise to other emotional manifestations, including one in particular that can lead to devastation. Its presence signals a need for help.

The Root of Anger

It might surprise you to learn that anxiety and anger have a lot in common. Both can originate from our fearful thoughts and can intensify when we dwell on the past or future. When our rational control wears down, emotional eruptions can happen almost unconsciously. When anxious, we feel helpless to act on a threat that may or may not exist. When angry, we suddenly become overwhelmed that the threat is close at hand.

At its core, anger is a secondary emotion that arises from a primary source, such as anxiety, loss, or sadness. For instance, we may be worried about our family members' bad habits, like their tardiness or unhealthy eating. Instead of expressing our concerns directly, possibly out of fear that we may not be heard, we may vent our frustration with an angry outburst. Or when dealing with a breakup or the loss of a loved one, we may cope by releasing aggression.

Both anxiety and anger stimulate the stress hormones adrenaline and cortisol, leading to rapid heart rate, shallow breathing, sweating, and high blood pressure. Over time, stress wears us down, and if we do not find ways to manage our anxiety or anger, we can spiral out of control. Ultimately, we are the victims of our own emotions. Seneca said, "Anger, if not restrained, is frequently more hurtful to us than the injury that provokes it."

Because anxiety triggers the fight-or-flight response, it makes us more likely to develop anger. Our heightened anticipation of potential threats causes us to perceive them even when they are not actually there. This makes us react with hostility toward the changing circumstances of life.

For example, at work we may feel anxious about an upcoming project deadline, making us feel trapped. This may lead to a "fight" response where the frustration boils over into anger at home, catching our loved ones by surprise. Anxiety can cause us to be hyperreactive in situations where others would normally remain calm.

When we repeatedly experience anxiety or anger throughout the day, it is a sign of an overactive default mode network (DMN). When the DMN turns on, we ruminate on the past and future; unpleasant memories and potential future issues trigger uncomfortable emotions. It can lead to an exhausting cycle where thoughts arriving every two to six seconds take us on a rollercoaster of distress.

If we hold onto our negative emotions and do not resolve them, the DMN's persistent mind-wandering will further intensify them. For example, an employee develops growing anxiety over potential layoffs. It affects his sleep, productivity, and mood, causing him to become more withdrawn and reactive to criticism. He nags his coworkers and supervisor for reassurance, but their lack of concern makes him even more hostile and insecure.

Increasingly frustrated, he shuns collaboration and avoids the common area. One day a misunderstanding on a work project escalates to an angry outburst with a coworker, and he is referred to Human Resources for counseling and corrective behavior. Because his work quality, attitude, and productivity continue to decline, management is eventually forced to terminate his employment.

"Holding onto anger is like grasping a hot coal with the intent of throwing it at someone else," Buddha said. "You are the one who gets burned." When we allow the DMN to mind wander, our legitimate worries can turn into irrational thought patterns, opening the door to chronic anxiety and anger.

Walking Back from the Cliff's Edge

While a normally functioning DMN is important for self-reflection, memory processing, and decision-making, its hyperactivity can lead to excessive rumination and psychological distress.

When our DMN is chronically active, we find it difficult to stay present as our mind wanders excessively to the past or future, triggering anxiety or anger. The close association between the DMN and the limbic system creates a vicious cycle where recurrent thoughts trigger persistent turmoil.

Those of us suffering from chronic anxiety have a rewired neural circuitry that hijacks the brain without our awareness, trapping us in an endless cycle of pain and suffering. We become prisoners of our own minds, unable to break free even when loved ones urge us to "snap out of it," like an addict unable to resist the addictive craving. "Anxiety does not empty tomorrow of its sorrows, but only empties today of its strength," wrote Charles Spurgeon, a nineteenth-century English preacher.

For example, if a glass cup falls and shatters, a healthy brain may briefly experience some frustration in the heat of the moment. After we survey the damage and pick up the glass shards, we quickly return to a normal state. However, the anxious mind enters into a perilous abyss of concern or even anger. Compulsive actions may kick in, causing us to deep clean the area several times and then meticulously mop the floor, rearrange our glassware, and check the stove. Rather than recognizing our anxiety as irrational, we instead demand a state of unattainable perfection in order to return to peace.

Anxiety disorders reflect a mental imbalance of neurotransmitters in the brain, leading to an overactivation of key brain regions. Persistent thoughts and mood swings trigger high levels of glutamate, while GABA (the neurotransmitter responsible for sleep and relaxation) decreases. Key brain regions, such as the limbic system (the emotional processing center) come to dominate the brain and exert control over other regions, much like in addiction. This results in less neural connectivity and more rigidity within the brain.

For people suffering from anxiety, the overactivation of the DMN and growing mental imbalance can worsen into a downward spiral, leading to impairment of daily functioning and even suicidal ideation. If you suffer from this condition, there is good news—you can walk back from the cliff's edge and discover health, happiness, and inner peace. To stop anxiety in its tracks, you must turn off the DMN by harnessing a great power within.

The Power of Presence

One day in a small village, Buddha was giving a discourse about forgiveness and tolerance. "To be angry is to let others' mistakes punish yourself," he said to the crowd.

A man stood and pointed at Buddha, shouting, "I have never seen such a hypocritical beggar. You are spreading misleading lies. Are you not ashamed?"

Buddha did not react, remaining as calm as before. The man's anger intensified, and he spit on Buddha's face, then walked away. Buddha wiped his face and continued the speech with the villagers.

At home, the angry man could not stop thinking about his actions. As anger gave way to remorse, he felt a strong urge to repent. Hearing that Buddha had departed, the man panicked and ran to the neighboring village, finding him there a few hours later. He immediately grabbed Buddha's feet and wept, pleading for forgiveness.

"Who are you?" Buddha said.

"You don't recognize me?" the angry man asked. "I'm the one who misbehaved. I am here to apologize and ask for your forgiveness."

Seeing the man's deep concern, Buddha said, "Brother, what you are talking about has passed. I have already moved on, and I am present in this moment. You have already repented, so now leave the past behind and do good deeds here in this moment."

You can break through the mental knots of anxiety and anger by developing the power of presence. The key is to stop the recurrent thought loops that cycle endlessly when your mind wanders. Because the DMN (the "wandering mind") is the source of rumination, you must learn to switch it off and come back to the now. By training your mind to recognize these interruptions, you deactivate the DMN and empower your "observing mind," the central executive network.

While we are all born with the power of presence, many of us lose it as we age. If you have a hard time staying focused in the now, you are not alone; this is a problem that millions of people face. The good news is that just as you can build muscle with exercise, you can strengthen your ability to be present. To do so, identify those practices that best ground you in the present moment. Some of these might include:

- ***Music***—Whether you dance to a hit song, find nostalgia in an old tune, or attend a concert, music cuts through the web of anxiety and takes you to the present moment, as long as you disengage from the "wandering mind" and actively listen.
- ***Exercise***—A hike in nature, a stroll with your canine companion, yoga, sports, or other forms of exercise provide the right conditions for presence to thrive, particularly when you take time to appreciate the scenery, feel the breeze, and smell the air. Pay attention to your body and lungs as you walk, jog, swim, cycle, or lift weights.

- ***Creative arts***—From painting and drawing to sculpting, writing poetry, and coloring, art powerfully disengages the default mode network to soothe an anxious mind.
- ***Cooking***—Baking, grilling, or sauteing are effective ways to engage the senses and turn off your negative thought patterns. You cannot control the future, but by following a recipe, you can craft a delicious meal and provide satisfaction for yourself and your loved ones.
- ***Social connection***—Calling an old friend, dining with loved ones, and connecting with colleagues over coffee will brighten your spirits and grant reprieve from anxiety.
- ***Countless other possibilities***—Reading, gardening, watching the sunrise or sunset, and keeping a journal are just a few other ways to stay present in the moment.

The key is to make a conscious effort to identify those activities that best anchor you in the now. Take note of the state of your mind before and after each pursuit to rate its level of effectiveness, prioritizing those that work best. Consistent daily practice delivers the greatest benefit to reduce anxiety and prevent it from arising in the future.

During these activities, your presence can be further strengthened by purposefully steering your mind away from the DMN. For example, mindful relaxation helps you extend the feelings of peace and calm during a breathing exercise, hike, bath, yoga, meditation, or prayer. By intentionally extending the duration and intensity of relaxation, you weaken the DMN and the limbic system, finding respite from incessant thoughts and anxious feelings. The increase in GABA also helps improve sleep and overall mood.

As discussed previously, you can use concentration meditation to focus your attention on your breath, body sensations, or sounds in the environment. For instance, you can feel your chest or abdomen expand as you breathe, thereby anchoring you to the present moment. This allows you to recognize the default mode network when your mind wanders into thoughts of the past or future. By returning to the present moment and shutting off the rumination, you weaken the DMN and its cycle of anxiety.

In addition, insight meditation is a powerful tool to identify and manage sources of stress and anxiety. Remember to observe your mind—including thoughts and sensations—with curiosity and acceptance. Ask yourself, "What am I feeling? How does this change over time?" When you encounter anxiety or anger, closely examine it to identify its origins and assess if it's truly based in reality. This gives you a greater understanding of deep-rooted emotions and allows you to view them without judgment.

For example, if you suffer from fear of flying, you might react negatively to sudden jolts during a flight, perceiving them as signs of an impending crash. However, by observing the other passengers in the cabin who are relaxed, reading, or napping, you can recognize that your anxiety is internal and irrational. With insightful awareness, you can challenge your default mode network's narratives and recognize false perceptions, allowing them to dissipate. This enables you to uncover the roots of your anxiety, fear, and anger and resolve them permanently. You can use the light of your rational mind (your "observing mind") to dispel the darkness of irrational thinking.

Prayer is a mindfulness exercise where you communicate with the divine in an honest, intentional, and present manner. By quieting the DMN, praying can effectively reduce anxiety, fear, and anger. Faith has been a source of refuge and grace for millions of people struggling with mental distress, and many religions promote prayer, social connection, and community as effective means to combat anxiety.

In the Christian faith, the Bible points to the dangers of anxiety and encourages salvation in the kingdom of God. In Matthew 6:25-34, Jesus said:

- 6:25 Therefore I tell you, do not be anxious about your life, what you will eat or what you will drink, nor about your body, what you will put on. Is not life more than food, and the body more than clothing?

- 6:26 Look at the birds of the air: they neither sow nor reap nor gather into barns, and yet your heavenly Father feeds them. Are you not of more value than they?
- 6:27 And which of you by being anxious can add a single hour to his span of life?
- 6:28 And why are you anxious about clothing? Consider the lilies of the field, how they grow: they neither toil nor spin.
- 6:29 Yet I tell you, even Solomon in all his glory was not arrayed like one of these.
- 6:30 But if God so clothes the grass of the field, which today is alive and tomorrow is thrown into the oven, will he not much more clothe you, O you of little faith?
- 6:31 Therefore do not be anxious, saying, "What shall we eat?" or "What shall we drink?" or "What shall we wear?"
- 6:32 For the Gentiles seek after all these things, and your heavenly Father knows that you need them all.
- 6:33 But seek first the kingdom of God and His righteousness, and all these things will be added to you.
- 6:34 Therefore do not be anxious about tomorrow, for tomorrow will be anxious for itself. Sufficient for the day is its own trouble.

Regardless of your religious background, daily prayer to the higher power will ground you in the present moment and significantly reduce anxious thoughts. When you communicate honestly and with intention, mind-wandering stops in its tracks, and the power of presence grows. Find this freedom, as you pray.

Lord God, the Infinite Unknown, the energy of the universe, I fill my lungs with Your grace. I breathe in Your benevolence, and I breathe out my anxiety and anger. I have peace in this moment knowing that You guard my heart and mind.

Anxiety is not a permanent condition. Your mind is always changing and adapting to new conditions. Just like your teeth, which can be straightened with aligners even well into your adult years, your mind can be healed and purified at any age. Even if you have lived with anxiety for decades, you have the ability to conquer your negative thought patterns and find lasting peace.

Mindfulness practices such as prayer, concentration meditation, and insight meditation will shut off the mind-wandering that has imprisoned you for so long. The power of presence sprouts new neural pathways that will bring peace and serenity. Daily consistent practice along with the intention for health, happiness, and inner peace are the keys to lasting change.

Clinical researchers have established the effectiveness of mindfulness practice across a spectrum of mental health disorders. In a clinical trial involving 170 war veterans diagnosed with PTSD, transcendental meditation (a form of concentration meditation involving repetition of mantras, or short phrases) led to significant improvements in anxiety symptoms and sleep quality. In other studies, meditators and yoga practitioners had higher levels of GABA (relaxation), increased activity in the prefrontal cortex (executive function), and a thicker hippocampus and cerebral cortex (memory and cognition).

Initially in your journey to cultivate presence, you may encounter significant resistance. The DMN's influence will be strong, and it will prevent you from accessing the "here and now." You may find yourself unable to focus for more than a few seconds. If this happens, smile and do not give up. With repeated practice, you will eventually loosen the DMN's grip and find freedom from the thoughts and emotions of your "wandering mind." Confucius said, "It does not matter how slowly you go as long as you do not stop."

In your journey to cultivate presence, it is critical to uphold an *intention* to improve your life and consistently work toward better health. Every morning, remind yourself of your aspirations, pushing aside your fears and doubts to focus on what you want to achieve. Try repeating this simple (yet profound) intention.

May I have health, happiness, and peace.

Other Solutions for Anxiety and Anger

If anxiety or anger interferes with your daily life, consult a healthcare professional. A doctor, psychologist, or therapist can provide a range of treatment options, including medication, cognitive behavioral therapy, and support groups. If one form of treatment has side effects or does not improve your symptoms, you can try other solutions.

Cognitive behavioral therapy is an effective treatment in which a trained therapist can ease symptoms in as few as eight to ten sessions. This therapeutic approach uses a technique called *cognitive restructuring* to help you identify your anxious triggers at the root level. Similar to insight meditation, you will better understand your negative thought patterns—what triggers them and how they lead to harmful behaviors. For instance, you may come to recognize an innate fear of public speaking, social interaction, or flying as the source of your distress.

Once you have pinpointed the core underlying issue, the next step is to actively challenge these triggers to test their validity and usefulness. Ask yourself, "What are the chances that my deep fear will actually come true? Am I being rational or not?" Through affirmations and positive reinforcement, your therapist will help you replace these recurrent thought patterns with healthier ones.

Cognitive behavioral therapy also utilizes exposure therapy, where you actively confront your root stressors to overcome them. The technique starts gradually to build confidence and then slowly increases in intensity. For instance, treatment for arachnophobia (fear of spiders) could begin with insect-based animation films and then progress to pictures of spiders. Exposure therapy can help you break through old conditioning and permanently resolve deep-rooted sources of anxiety or anger.

Certain medications can relieve the symptoms of anxiety, which may include restlessness, rapid heart rate, and fear. These drugs are selective serotonin reuptake inhibitors, antipsychotic medications, tricyclic antidepressants, and benzodiazepines. However, these medicines may not cure the underlying disorder, and some of them could lead to addiction. To learn more, consult your healthcare provider.

As previously discussed, psychedelic drugs may be an effective way of silencing the DMN and managing anxiety, but they are not legally approved for medical use. Researchers are discovering their potential benefits in studies that may soon lead to FDA approvals.

In one study, cancer patients who were given a single dose of psilocybin (the psychedelic drug found in magic mushrooms) experienced a marked decrease in anxiety and depression that lasted for years. In other studies involving depressed patients, psychedelics reduced activity of the DMN, reversed anxious symptoms, and improved emotional health.

It is important to note that psychedelics come with potentially serious side effects. While these drugs effectively shut off the DMN and mind-wandering, they also connect parts of the brain that do not normally communicate. This can lead to drug-induced psychosis, resulting in long-term paranoia, changes in mood, visual disturbances, and other mental health issues. Because these drugs are not legally approved to treat anxiety disorders, you would need to approach psychedelic-assisted therapy with caution and under the supervision of a qualified healthcare professional.

Final Thoughts on Anxiety and Anger

The news grips our attention every night with tragic stories—earthquakes, economic collapse, and climate change. Despite the fearmongering, you do not have to live in a perpetual state of fear and worry. You have the power to break through anxiety and anger by developing your power of presence, reminding yourself that in this moment you are safe.

Your brain's default mode network is both a friend and an enemy; it loves the past and future, and it does not want you to be present. When it traps you in recurrent negative thought loops, you become its victim. And as you lose focus on the now, negative emotions like anxiety take hold. When this happens, time slips away, making it seem like you are aging faster.

Presence and time go hand in hand. Time is a concept encoded in the brain, and it changes over our lifetime. As we age, time can seem to speed up, even though each day has the same twenty-four hours as it did when we were children. Scientists believe this "acceleration of time" is related to our tendency to "check out" and group familiar experiences with old ones. We often tune out of routine activities and go into autopilot, ignoring life's details instead of savoring them. When our minds wander and we lose the present moment, new memories do not form. This results in a mental "time gap" where it can feel that we are aging more quickly.

For example, during the morning commute when you drop off the kids at school, you may zone out as you think about the upcoming day. Because you are not fully present, the car ride passes by almost instantaneously; any scant memories that form merge into a single blurred recollection. However, the children have a much deeper experience of the car ride, because they are more present. Each trip may have special memories of the songs on the radio or the views outside.

Just like in youth, you have the ability to be present and live completely in the moment, slowing the passage of time by savoring the familiar moments of life. Even during routine activities, you can experience the breathtaking beauty of the sky, a gentle breeze, and the sound of rain. When the clouds of anxiety lift, you can discover the inherent bliss of life. "To me, every hour of the day and night is an unspeakably perfect miracle," Walt Whitman said.

By developing presence through mindfulness exercises, you can maximize the joy of life's experiences, thereby forming new memories and slowing the passage of time. This in turn improves your short-term memory, allowing you to be more thoughtful and less prone to making errors. Greater connectivity between brain regions allows you to access your subconscious mind and glean insights to life's challenges.

Mindfulness exercises also significantly reduce stress, which may slow the aging process itself. At the cellular level, stress shortens DNA telomeres and accelerates a process known as *senescence*. Because presence powerfully reduces anxiety, it may also contribute to the deceleration of aging, which may explain why monks and priests tend to live longer than the general population.

Mindfulness exercises and prayer are powerful tools that keep you grounded in the present. It is important to practice in a comfortable setting where you can stay focused and free of distractions. Observe the breath, body sensations, and sounds with curiosity and awareness. When thoughts interrupt, approach them with gentleness and acceptance, returning to the present moment with a smile. Daily practice delivers the best results, allowing you to access mindfulness when you need it most throughout the course of the day. Setting an intention will guide you to your destination.

Presence can be cultivated in many ways. Whether it is through prayer, gardening, or a conversation with a friend, activities that ground you in the present moment will shut off your brain's default mode network (the "wandering mind") and grant a reprieve from negative thought processes. This in turn activates task-positive brain regions, such as the central executive network (the "observing mind"), helping you regain control of your life and discover the higher self.

Mindfulness and presence teach you to accept the ever-changing nature of life without trying to change it. Observing anxiety (without being consumed by it) allows you to find space. When you develop a deeper understanding of your thought patterns at the root level, you gradually discover freedom. This is how wisdom arises.

Self-understanding can arise in many other ways. With the help of a therapist, cognitive behavioral therapy will help you glean insights into the nature of your thoughts. If you prefer to work alone, insight meditation will achieve the same goal. In addition, you can find guidance and camaraderie from online resources and support groups where people with similar anxiety or anger issues exchange stories and healing techniques. A social safety net allows you to imagine a brighter future free from inner fears.

You can break through the mental knot of anxiety or anger by having the intention to do so. Acknowledging your condition and wanting happiness and peace is the first step toward a more fulfilling life. By being honest and recognizing the sources of your anxiety or anger without becoming overwhelmed by them, you can find the tools to overcome your worries.

As anxious moments recede, life regains its color and vibrancy. Your mind sharpens with more rapid access to facts, insights, and crucial information. This bolsters your working memory and communication skills, leading to greater success and productivity. The fog of anxiety is replaced with the sunshine of inner bliss.

KNOT 7

DISHONESTY AND DENIAL—UNLOCK YOUR TRUE POTENTIAL

ONE OF THE PRIMARY OBSTACLES to inner peace is the mental knot of dishonesty and denial, which prevents us from cultivating wisdom and self-understanding. The state of enlightenment requires complete honesty and acceptance—with ourselves and others. Unfortunately, we human beings tend to lie to each other and particularly to ourselves, which not only hinders our spiritual growth but can also impact our health and financial well-being.

In this chapter, we will explore the role of the default mode network (DMN) in sustaining dishonesty and denial. In some circumstances, the DMN can deceive you to promote an addiction, repress emotional pain from the past, or perpetuate anxious thoughts. Unfortunately, when you cling to these inner falsehoods, your deepest issues can remain unresolved, stifling you in pain. If you find yourself trapped in the mental knot of dishonesty and denial, with the right intention and practice you can free yourself and unlock your true potential. The remedy is simple yet profound—it is rooted in the power of integrity.

Lying Is Widespread

Researchers estimate that the average American lies 11 times a week—that's well over 500 lies per year. Even despite knowing the consequences of dishonesty, we still tend to speak untruths to others and especially to ourselves, making it difficult to see the truth of reality. We warn our children against lying but often fail to adhere to our own standards, a condition known as *hypocrisy*.

We bend the truth for a variety of reasons. About one-quarter of our lies are intended to protect ourselves and others. We also frequently fabricate to exaggerate our worth or to avoid certain people. Less commonly, we may lie to either benefit or hurt others. Most lies are told to friends, then followed by family members.

Our ego tries to convince us that deception is harmless, but in reality it can cause substantial damage. In 2021, there was $6 billion in fraud attributed to lies, a number that fails to capture the untold conflicts, breakups, and emotional devastation attached to them. Some lies are so heinous they become part of our collective memory, haunting people for many generations.

We have seen it in sports. In 1919, the Chicago White Sox won the American League and faced the Cincinnati Reds in the World Series. Boasting some of the greatest talent in baseball, including "Shoeless" Joe Jackson, the White Sox had won eighty-eight games that season. However, something suspicious began to unfold during the final matchup against the Reds.

Early in the series, the White Sox suddenly appeared to be unable to hit the ball and appeared stymied on the field, struggling to play the game. The scandal soon unraveled as it became clear that eight players were paid to play poorly on purpose. The White Sox lost the World Series, and as their fraud was exposed the consequences were severe. The eight players involved were permanently banned from baseball, leaving the team and their fans devastated. The franchise would not claim the World Series title until 2005 after an eighty-eight-year drought.

Financial fraud has infected capitalism since the beginning of recorded history, with crimes like blackmail, bribery, corruption, and embezzlement causing irreparable loss and suffering. Swindlers like Bernie Madoff have used Ponzi schemes to steal billions of dollars from unsuspecting investors. More recently, cybercrime has taken hold with nearly 800,000 offenses in 2022 and losses totaling over $10 billion.

Scientific fraud can be highly damaging. In 2006, scientists published a paper in *Nature* claiming to have identified the cause of Alzheimer's disease (a protein called *amyloid beta 56*). Over the next decade, pharmaceutical companies and others invested more than $1 billion in amyloid-related research, and medical researchers opened clinical trials with the hope of helping Alzheimer's patients, but many of the studies failed to show any therapeutic benefit. It was later found that the authors of the *Nature* article had falsified images and data.

Sometimes, those we trust most turn out to be the biggest liars. This was the case when *The Washington Post* inquired about five men breaking into the Democratic National Committee headquarters at the Watergate Hotel in Washington DC. Then-President Richard Nixon denied any involvement in the incident and was reelected that same year. However, when two reporters from the *Post* persisted in their investigation, they eventually linked Nixon to the break-in and subsequent cover-up. Nixon's infamous phrase, "I am not a crook!" is still remembered today. Eventually, in August 1974, he became the first and only US president to resign the office.

While we may admire Honest Abe Lincoln for telling it like it is, many of us act more like Nixon in our daily lives. Studies suggest that 95 percent of us cannot go a week without telling a lie. We claim that these minor falsehoods are harmless. Unfortunately, even our best-intentioned "little white lies" may hinder us from reaching our full potential.

The Nature of "White Lies"

Coined in a 1741 article in *The Gentleman's Magazine*, the so-called white lie was meant to satisfy the "itch of amusing people by telling them wonderful stories." It referred to "entertaining tales" that were passed down across generations, such as during Christmas Eve when we rush our children to bed because Santa Claus is on his way, when in reality we are hurriedly wrapping presents.

Sometimes we find it socially acceptable to omit the truth rather than offend or hurt someone. On a terrible first date, we may resort to the white lie of pretending to be sick and needing to leave, rather than simply saying, "I don't think we are a match, and I don't want to spend any more time with you." Or we may pretend to enjoy our partner's cooking to avoid their embarrassment.

Several features distinguish a white lie from a harmful one. Among them are intent and impact. Harmful lies are meant to hurt someone else or benefit the liar, and they can have far-reaching consequences. On the other hand, white lies are supposed to be inconsequential and have a minimal impact, but often this is not the case.

A third distinguishing feature is the beneficiary—a harmful lie is designed to benefit the liar by avoiding trouble or gaining an advantage, while the beneficiary of a white lie is usually the person being lied to. We may fabricate to prevent others from experiencing pain. However, what we believe is a white lie may be considered harmful by others, resulting in distress that we had not anticipated. There is often no clear line between a "good" and "bad" lie.

For example, rather than telling certain colleagues that they are not invited to a party, we may invent a false excuse to avoid their emotional discomfort. However, when those colleagues discover the truth, it could unintentionally lead to turmoil. In another example, someone forgets to pick up an important package and blames it on needing to care for an ill family member, which is a lie. This can cause a backlash when the truth is revealed. In these scenarios, the liars may have convinced themselves of their harmless intentions, but in actuality they may have been trying to avoid guilt or responsibility.

The knot of dishonesty is toughest to untangle when we commit harmful lies, particularly when we deceive for personal gain. Cheating at school or work, lying on taxes, or taking advantage of someone's naivety for our own benefit all have repercussions and deprive us of the development and knowledge that comes with truth and hard work. In the end, the harmful lie takes away far more than it grants.

What about white lies? Do they impact our well-being? It turns out that all forms of dishonesty and denial can impede our long-term growth. When we avoid the high road of integrity, we prevent ourselves from fully comprehending reality as it is. To gain insight into our negative emotions and discover the roots of our anxieties and addictions, we must be unconditionally honest with ourselves. Only then can we delve deep into our psyche and discover what we are feeling and why.

On the journey to enlightenment, self-deception is a major barrier that blocks us from reaching the pinnacle. The awakened state is attainable only with truthful self-observation and acceptance. Lying to ourselves, even in the most muted and well-intentioned manner, prevents us from recognizing subtle cravings and aversions, making it impossible to access our "observing mind" and see the road to inner peace. To forsake enlightenment in the name of trivial lies and self-deception is perhaps the biggest tragedy in our lives.

Lies Damage Our Health

When we engage in deception, our body reacts with physical signals that can be detected with a polygraph test, which is 90 percent effective in detecting lies. The act of lying triggers the stress response, leading to a rapid heartbeat, elevated blood pressure, and cortisol release. The physical and psychological strain of dishonesty can have dire consequences on our well-being, contributing to serious illnesses like cancer and heart disease.

Researchers at the University of Notre Dame conducted a study to determine whether truth-telling impacts health. They studied a group of adults and college students, half of whom were instructed not to lie for ten weeks, whereas the other half were not given any instructions about lying. Both groups included people from diverse ethnic and socioeconomic backgrounds.

For ten weeks, the participants received medical and emotional evaluations, with those in the "no lie" group receiving regular polygraph tests. Astonishingly, individuals who told fewer lies experienced better health and relationship quality. Those in the "no lie" group who told less than three white lies a week had the fewest physical and mental health complaints. Committing fewer lies (whether harmful or not) led to a better quality of life.

When we are honest, we don't have anything to hide from ourselves or others, giving us peace of mind. On the other hand, lying leads to a state of anxiety where we fear being exposed. This subtle tension disrupts our ability to be mindful and present, taking away our priceless inner peace.

Dishonesty—whether it is with ourselves or others—is a slippery slope that ultimately leads to hypocrisy, a state where we claim to ourselves and others that we have high moral standards when our behavior says otherwise. It is a state of instability that can lead to a lifetime of suffering. One lie necessitates many more to keep the original intact, and eventually the house of cards collapses. "No man has a good enough memory to be a successful liar," President Abraham Lincoln said.

For example, let's say you plan a trip with family but don't have vacation days to cover it, so you call in "sick" without considering the consequences. Upon returning to work, your boss may ask questions about your symptoms and why social media pictures show you and your family on the beach. This can impact your credibility and work performance. In the end, the short-term benefits of a white lie are not worth the long-term risks.

A study of 1,200 American adults revealed that those who lived their lives with high moral standards had significantly better physical health and a substantially lower risk of depression and other mental illnesses. A separate study of 9,800 adults found that upholding honesty and integrity was associated with lower risk of depression, lung disease, immobility, and dependence on others during daily activities. When you prioritize the truth, you can improve your health and happiness.

You have the ability to overcome dishonesty and denial and discover the light of enlightenment. To get there, you can rely on a profound force that underpins religious and spiritual practice.

The Power of Integrity

Integrity is more than just being honest. It is a commitment to adhere to strong ethical standards to determine what is right and wrong. We use a moral compass to guide our decisions, actions, and judgments, prioritizing virtue and conduct at all times, regardless of who is around. Having character means doing the right thing, even if our friends and neighbors do otherwise. Whether we are in a crowded office or alone in our home, we remain committed to following our deep-rooted principles.

Integrity means encouraging wholesome actions that benefit the peace and well-being of others. It means recognizing and letting go of unwholesome actions that harm the peace and well-being of others. Wholesome behaviors cultivate a calm, focused mind that is capable of breaking through to the enlightened state. On the other hand, unwholesome behaviors agitate the mind and prevent enlightenment from taking hold.

If you want to awaken lasting inner peace and happiness, integrity must be at the forefront of your intentions. Prayer and insight meditation are effective only when you are fully honest with yourself; otherwise, your efforts will be futile. If you delude yourself with lies—denying or concealing the truth from yourself—there will be no chance to attain enlightenment. Wisdom is born from an honest and impartial comprehension of your thoughts and actions.

Unfortunately, the mental knot of dishonesty and denial prevents wisdom from taking hold. In many cases, the default mode network (the ego) plays a key role through its fabrication of a separate self. The DMN can hold on to delusional, self-rooted thoughts and deceive you into believing the lies are beneficial for survival. For example, addicts may tell themselves their cravings are good for their health. This can end up magnifying negative emotional states like anxiety or anger.

When the DMN hides the truth, you are unable to acknowledge your true condition. Without the capacity to be forthright with yourself, you can remain in a state of perpetual tension. By quieting the DMN through prayer, meditation, and other mindfulness exercises described earlier, you can access the truth within.

Breaking through the mental knot of dishonesty and denial is a prerequisite for reaching enlightenment. It begins by fully accepting and being aware of the present moment, regardless of its positive or negative nature. You cannot lie when you are in the now, as there is no other way to experience this moment other than as it is. With complete honesty and acceptance, you can become aware of the sounds and sensations around you and ask yourself, "Am I at ease? What are the qualities of my thoughts?"

When you step back and observe your feelings and sensations from a distance, you can begin to look deeply into your soul with genuine acceptance. Watch your cravings or fears and recognize them as temporary states that do not require your time or engagement. Take note if your ego bends the truth or engages in delusional thoughts. Acknowledge and return to the present. By looking within, you can separate yourself from self-deception and awaken your higher self.

The practice of integrity makes life easier and more natural. The burden of self-doubt and worry is lifted, freeing you to live in the moment. Guided by your soul's light, you can sail toward your ambitions and intentions without resistance, reaching your goal for health, happiness, and inner peace with ease.

The more you exercise integrity, the more effortless it becomes. Doors that were once shut will open with welcome. Your honesty and openness will draw others to you, making you a more desirable friend, partner, and leader. When you uphold virtue, others will more comfortably share their feelings and ideas with you. "Always do right," American writer and humorist Mark Twain quipped. "This will gratify some people and astonish the rest."

The greatest leaders in history were guided by strong moral principles. No one questioned their motivation, because they personified honor and conduct, addressing challenges with transparency and ease. Marcus Aurelius, the Roman emperor, advocated for a good life based on "right speech," which must be "truthful, not hurtful."

The Greek Stoics (who believed in the philosophy of Stoicism) viewed supreme happiness as attainable only through the pursuit of integrity and honesty. This was a stark contrast to the hedonistic lifestyle of their contemporaries who sought to force their own needs, wants, and desires upon the present moment.

Stoics believed wealth and pleasure were not inherently good or bad but that virtue held the highest reward. They reasoned that negative emotions like jealousy or fear stem from "errors of judgment" and that we can overcome them by understanding the rules of the natural order rather than by trying to impose our own. Worrying about things and lying to change reality is counterproductive. Truth and integrity represent the greatest ambitions of all. "The happiness of your life depends upon the quality of your thoughts," Marcus Aurelius said.

Integrity Is the Gateway to the Soul

Virtue lies at the heart of the world's religious institutions. High moral standards are the hallmark of our greatest leaders — Abraham Lincoln, Martin Luther King Jr., Mother Teresa, Nelson Mandela, and Mahatma Gandhi—as well as our most revered saints, rabbis, bodhisattvas, and imams. Integrity is the light that radiates from our spiritual essence, and our civilization has prospered due to this desire to uphold and fulfill righteousness. "Whatever satisfies the soul is truth," Walt Whitman wrote.

In modern society, it may seem challenging to maintain high moral standards, but doing so opens up possibilities you may have deemed improbable. People who uphold integrity in their family, profession, or house of worship are often chosen to lead the way forward. Power and wealth are entrusted to the virtuous, and a life of honesty guides you to health and happiness, as science is now demonstrating.

Researchers have discovered that integrity is an intrinsic human trait, embedded in our genes from birth. As babies, we are guided by moral tendencies, and it is later in life that we learn behaviors like lying, stealing, and cheating. These unethical actions run counter to our core values, causing disruption and instability in our lives. When we abandon immorality and embrace integrity, our lives become more harmonious and rewarding.

This truth has been spoken since ancient times. One of the oldest stories ever written was the tale of Gilgamesh from ancient Sumer, the civilization that invented writing, mathematics, and irrigation. Written nearly 4,000 years ago, the fable tells of an ancient Sumerian king who subjugated his people in a search for immortality.

During his violent journey to discover the secret of eternal life, King Gilgamesh is humbled by the death of a friend and the scorn of the gods. Learning that death is inevitable, he undergoes a transformation where he abandons his old, malevolent ways and develops compassion toward his people. The profound importance of virtue and justice becomes apparent to the king, who eventually earns the respect of his people.

Integrity is a cornerstone of religion. In the Judeo-Christian tradition, the Ten Commandments encourage us to "not bear false witness." To lie to a man is to lie to God. Jesus taught in the Sermon on the Mount: "Blessed are those who hunger and thirst for righteousness, for they shall be satisfied."

In Buddhism, the Five Precepts form the cardinal system of morality. They forbid lying, stealing, killing, sexual misconduct, and intoxication. A study of 644 Thai adults found that those who followed these precepts had lower rates of stress-related depression.

In Islam, lying is condemned as a cardinal sin. The *Koran* teaches that dishonesty is a disease of the heart that will worsen over time if left uncorrected.

Modern science is beginning to validate the importance of these core religious tenets. A meta-analysis of 8,946 clinical studies provided strong evidence for the positive health benefits of spirituality and spiritual values. The published report recommended that hospitals and clinics implement spiritual care in the treatment of serious illnesses and include specialty practitioners of spiritual care in healthcare teams. The report's authors also advised healthcare providers to receive spiritual care education.

To break through the mental knot of dishonesty and denial and awaken inner peace and happiness within, it is essential to set a daily intention to live a life with high ethical standards. Practice mindfulness exercises—especially insight and concentration meditations with a focus on equanimity and compassion—to help you stay on the path to your higher self. Practice with complete self-honesty and acceptance, regardless of your mental or emotional state on that day.

When you have strayed, take notice with empathy, and make adjustments to get back on track. Your higher power will provide refuge and guidance in times of need, as you pray.

Lord God, the Infinite Unknown, the energy of the universe, I fill my lungs with Your grace. I breathe in Your benevolence, and I breathe out my dishonesty and denial. Taking refuge in Your presence during these times, I strive to lead a life of virtue and integrity.

Final Thoughts on Dishonesty and Denial

In your daily routine, you may find it tempting to bend the truth to lessen your workload or avoid uncomfortable situations, but you are ultimately the victim of your own deception. When you welcome dishonesty and denial into your life, it becomes impossible to cultivate present-moment awareness and see reality for what it is. Your inner pain intensifies. Immorality conditions your mind to turn away from the truth, forcing you to live in a state of suffering.

Remember, your brain's default mode network (the ego) will deceive you to sustain an addiction, repress emotional pain from the past, or mask your loneliness. It is easier to hide from the truth than to face it. Unfortunately, when you cling to these inner falsehoods, your deepest mental knots remain unresolved. The cycle of unhappiness perpetuates as you try to cover up guilt, worry, or responsibility, and instead of truthful healing you may instead deflect this pain to your friends and family.

Thankfully, you can permanently end this state of tension by setting an intention to break through the mental knot of dishonesty and denial, cultivating virtue and integrity. Maintaining complete honesty with yourself is key; when you observe and accept your inner thought patterns and behaviors for what they are, you take one step closer to enlightenment. "Honesty is the first chapter in the book of wisdom," President Thomas Jefferson said.

To get there, you can harness the power of integrity. This means acknowledging a set of moral principles in your life, whether in the company of others or in solitude. Although this may seem challenging, the bliss of enlightenment will be worth any short-term inconvenience. Honesty and integrity are vital for achieving health, happiness, and inner peace.

There is something natural and effortless about knowing that when you go to work, attend family gatherings, or socialize with friends, you are not deceiving anyone in any way. Integrity awakens the unbridled joy of the soul, unlocking self-esteem and improving stress and physical health. It is a natural cure for anxiety and depression, one that will also reduce risks for serious illnesses.

Living with high moral standards has immense long-term benefits, from improved health and success to greater love and happiness. It is a strong magnet for trust and companionship, fulfilling your deepest aspirations and awakening inner peace. "Happiness and moral duty are inseparably connected," American Founding Father George Washington wrote.

KNOT 8

INACTION—SHARPEN YOUR FOCUS

FINDING INNER PEACE takes effort. Whether it's setting your intention, developing mindfulness, or honing your integrity and wisdom, the results of your practice depend on the time and energy you invest. Unfortunately, even with the purest motivations, it may be challenging to consistently take action toward your goals.

Recently, science has revealed how the brain focuses, providing new insights on how you can break through the mental knot of inaction. The remedy is based on a concept known as *relaxed effort*. Through techniques that can help you improve your focus and concentration, you can put an end to procrastination and access the energy needed to reach the peace and bliss of the enlightened state.

When the Day Gets Away

We have all experienced procrastination. Let's say you wake up excited about the day, bursting with the desire to fulfill your goal to look and feel better. You eat a nutritious breakfast and head to work, but as you reach your desk you find it hard to concentrate.

Staring at your emails and assignments, you suffer a mental block that prevents you from getting started. Frustrated, you check your favorite social media platform to find a clip of a dog reuniting with a soldier returning from war. You watch it three times with joy, sharing it with your close contacts.

You notice a playlist of similar pet videos, so you spend another ten minutes watching them with glee. Before long, you're exploring the local animal shelter website, browsing pictures of dogs that need homes and reading the instructions on how to adopt one. You glance at the time and realize that nearly an hour has passed. You finally put down the smartphone and look again at your work tasks in dismay, deciding that a cup of coffee may help you focus.

Making your way to the break room, you chat with a few colleagues about their upcoming vacation plans. You discover a hidden gem off the coast of Mexico and make a mental note of it. You grab some coffee and return to your workspace, spending a few hours looking up tropical getaways and planning your next vacation.

By the end of the day, your mind feels exhausted, not from the effort you have placed in your tasks but from the constant distractions and lack of focus. You have been mentally active but not productive. You have let the day slip away and never regained control of it. It is an all too familiar cycle of frustration, exhaustion, and confusion.

Why can't you focus? What are you doing wrong?

If you suffer from forgetfulness, inaction, or procrastination, you are not alone. Like millions of people, your brain may have become conditioned to wander off rather than stay focused on the activity at hand. It's easy to blame smartphones and social media for this tendency, but they are not forcing themselves upon you. The problem lies within.

Thankfully, inaction is a mental knot that you can overcome. To sharpen your focus, you can identify the underlying causes of procrastination and take the necessary steps to bring about lasting change. The way to overcome inaction is to cultivate a "relaxed effort" that combines intention, commitment, and practice. Performing tasks with relaxed effort means you should not be overly strenuous or rigid but rather have a calm and consistent focus. However, when unwholesome thoughts or emotions take hold, there should be an urgency to return to a balanced state.

If you want to achieve relaxed effort, start by setting it as your aspiration and commit to it daily with a resolute intention. Remind yourself of the advantages of being "in the zone," the state of flow where you can realize accomplishments more effortlessly. Abraham Lincoln said, "Always bear in mind that your own resolution to succeed is more important than any other."

No one is born with perfect concentration; it is a skill you can develop with training, similar to building physical strength with exercise. Just as regular workouts will help you achieve a desired physique, focus techniques will help you build concentration and mental stamina. In both cases, the occasional burst of activity will not lead to consistent improvement. After a few days of inactivity, you will find yourself right back where you started.

You should not expect results merely by deeming it a good idea; instead, real growth will only come from steady implementation. Only consistent effort can bring about lasting change. The process takes time and energy.

Before describing focus techniques, let's take a closer look at the inner workings of the mind.

How the Brain Focuses

You can train your biceps to lift more weight and strengthen your legs to travel farther when jogging. On the tennis court, you can improve your reaction time to an incoming serve. Through commitment and consistent repetition, you can improve your body's abilities to execute tasks, and the same applies to your brain. Focus is a trainable skill.

Most sensory information (like sights and sounds) pass by without your direct awareness, and your brain chooses what to focus on. It can take 300 milliseconds to become consciously aware of incoming information. With practice, you can learn to focus more deeply on the world around you, coaching yourself to be more present and aware.

At first it may be difficult to pay attention for long periods as distractions pull you away. However, with some simple exercises, focusing for longer periods becomes an easier and more natural thing to do, helping you achieve more at home and work. "Concentration is the secret of strength," Ralph Waldo Emerson said.

This process can begin as early as one year of age. In a British study, twenty-one babies were taught to focus on various images on a computer screen. During the fifteen-day study, the infants learned to sustain attention on specific objects of interest and improve their reaction times. They were even able to learn complex patterns and demonstrate rational thinking.

The focusing ability of the brain lies in the locus coeruleus, also known as the *blue spot*. Located deep in the brainstem, it is a tiny cluster of neurons that connects with over one hundred brain regions. It reacts to incoming information by releasing noradrenaline, a key neurotransmitter that helps direct your attention. The blue spot determines how attentive the brain is to specific information, depending on the situation.

When your brain is in a state of inactivity, neural activity slows to a frequency of ten hertz and forms a pattern known as *alpha waves*. This filters out incoming information, allowing you to effectively ignore the outside world. But in response to certain triggers, such as seeing an animal on the highway while driving, the blue spot releases noradrenaline and turns on parts of the brain involved in sensory perception, memory, and attention.

The blue spot can quickly wake you from inattention and trigger concentration when the moment deserves it. For instance, it can increase the size of your pupils and strengthen visual acuity. When your pupils grow larger, more light enters the eyes, and you can see more in your environment. Alpha waves disappear as the brain awakens from a state of inactivity.

For example, during a road trip from Houston to Los Angeles, you pass San Antonio, and the landscape turns to desert. With little to hold your attention, the brain drifts off and enters a rhythm state of alpha waves. Suddenly, blue-and-white flashing lights in your rearview mirror alert you to an approaching police car, prompting the blue spot to release a surge of noradrenaline. This sharpens your focus and activates your brain's central executive network (CEN), sending you into a flurry of actions—slowing the car, scanning the environment, and searching for an excuse to explain why you were driving ninety-seven miles per hour in a seventy-mph zone.

You can hone your blue spot's focusing ability, so it shines like a powerful high beam rather than a dim candle. With practice, your deepening concentration can turn into a state of flow, allowing you to be totally present and impervious to distraction. In this state, the blue spot is synchronized with the brain's task-positive networks (like the CEN), empowering you to act without doubt, hesitation, or fear. When you are "in the zone," you are wholly absorbed in the moment, capable of accomplishing anything you set your mind to.

Developing focus isn't only for better work performance. It also helps strengthen your spiritual power—boosting the effectiveness of mindfulness exercises and prayer, gaining greater awareness of the world, and ultimately acquiring wisdom. This enables you to break through your mental knots and generate insights about your true condition, unlocking the enlightened state.

The blue spot focuses your attention, but other parts of the brain divert your focus from the present to elsewhere. Notably, the default mode network (your ego) plays a significant role in the mind's movements, directing the brain to drift off when incoming data information does not directly relate to yourself. Let's take a closer look at this process.

How the Brain Loses Focus

It can be challenging to stay "in the zone," especially if you suffer from self-doubt or nagging negativity. As you know, the default mode network (DMN) is to blame for this tendency of the mind to wander. The DMN is the polar opposite of the blue spot—as one gains momentum the other sees a decline. The two forces vie for control of your attention.

When you struggle to stay focused on a task, it may be because your blue spot and the DMN are in opposition. Even when the blue spot is fully engaged in concentration, the DMN may remain active in the background, creating a battle between the urge to finish a task and the desire to do something else. It can feel like a strong magnet pulling you toward distraction. This is especially prominent in people with attention-deficit/hyperactivity disorder (ADHD).

When the DMN turns on, the mind can drift in unhealthy directions, revisiting moments of worry, confusion, guilt, or shame. The DMN draws your attention away from the present, trapping you in a cycle of idleness. When the tendency to wander becomes stronger than the will to focus, procrastination develops. It can be an exhausting cycle where your energy is spent on useless thoughts and worries.

The DMN may pull you into a state of inaction and prevent you from executing your tasks for several underlying reasons. Reasons for procrastination include:

- Anxiety (for example, fear of criticism)
- Perfectionism
- Low energy (for example, lack of sleep)
- Task aversiveness (for example, boredom)
- Feeling overwhelmed or confused
- Poor mood
- Conflict with authority
- Underlying condition (for example, depression)

The DMN can be an internal stressor that traps you and makes even the simplest tasks seem like climbing Mount Everest. To avoid being overwhelmed with negative emotions, simply become aware of the DMN, and name the feelings for what they are—fear, anxiety, depression, shame, and so on. Once you have identified these feelings with your "observing mind," they will lose some of their power.

In addition to the DMN, you may have other sources of distraction that take away your focus. These can include a noisy environment, unwholesome acquaintances, constant notifications from digital devices, and the list goes on. Identify them, and try to cast them aside or manage them to the best of your ability. Exercising restraint is not easy; if it were, it wouldn't conjure up images of handcuffs. Distractions are inherently difficult to avoid and find space from. We have become so accustomed to checking apps or websites that it becomes second nature when we power on our devices.

In the modern era, many jobs require digital communication and device usage, and it's easy to lose focus. A recent study found that American workers waste three hours of their workday not doing their jobs. Internet usage was the biggest excuse, followed by socializing with coworkers. Other distractions included "spacing out" and "applying for other jobs."

One particularly sinister practice that some employers encourage is multitasking, where we impart less attention to two or more tasks instead of dedicating our full attention to one task. When the brain switches back and forth between activities, we waste more energy and become less efficient, making mistakes more likely. You should avoid multitasking due to its negative effects on your focus and attention.

The growing prevalence of on-demand information has led to a new behavior known as *media multitasking*, where you interact with multiple streams of information while also engaging in other activities. Studies have shown that American youths spend about ten hours per day using technology, with nearly one-third of that time engaged in media multitasking. This can lead to a decline in focus and social skills, along with growing isolation.

When we allow devices to take over our lives, it impacts how we interact in social situations, such as making small talk at a party or going on a first date. We may be so distracted that we are unable to comprehend what the other person is saying, struggling even to recall names after a few moments of conversation. No machine is more important than the person in front of us. The latest notification on our smartphone may seem urgent, but ignoring the people around us (known as *phubbing*) can be damaging to our relationships and mental health.

Identifying and limiting distractions will greatly improve your attentiveness and productivity. To further boost focus and concentration, you can tip the scales in favor of the blue spot by practicing exercises that will strengthen its power while reducing the impact of the DMN. There are a number of ways to do this.

Three Exercises to Improve Focus

Some pharmaceutical drugs will enhance attention and concentration. For example, medications for ADHD include stimulants, such as amphetamines and methylphenidate, and nonstimulants, such as clonidine. These compounds work by increasing the levels of neurotransmitters (like noradrenaline) that the brain uses to focus. Though effective, they may not cure the underlying issues and can lead to a dependency on the medication.

The preferred approach is to silence the DMN with techniques that prevent it from distracting you. Focus exercises are useful in quieting the DMN while at the same time strengthening the blue spot. Developing a daily routine, especially during the morning, will empower your blue spot and gradually improve your ability to focus.

For example, morning meditation has been proven to increase concentration throughout the day. Before beginning the day's activities, take fifteen to twenty minutes to observe your breathing, thoughts, sounds, and sensations. This practice calms the DMN (your "wandering mind") and strengthens the blue spot and CEN (your "observing mind"), keeping negative emotions at bay. It also allows you to process old information, so you can start the day fresh.

If you find yourself struggling to stay productive during the day, take five to ten minutes to practice one of the following three focus exercises, which will help you regain and strengthen your concentration.

Quick Focus Exercise

Start with three deep breaths and become aware of the present moment, noticing its sounds, sensations, rhythm, and depth. Listen for five sounds in your environment. Next, look around and name five objects in your view, taking a few seconds to notice each one. Now count five body sensations, such as the tension in your neck or back. What do you smell and taste?

To improve body energy, stretch the neck, roll the shoulders, rotate the wrists, and flex the arms. By stretching and taking time to fully engage your five senses, you will receive a boost of focus.

Breath Focus Exercise

Spend a minute becoming aware of your breath, noticing the temperature and flow of air entering and leaving your nostrils and throat. Pay attention to your chest and abdomen rising and falling. Consciously relax your head, neck, and shoulders. Then count your breaths from one to five at the end of each exhalation. Anytime you lose focus, start again at the count of one. After five to ten minutes, notice the state of your mind as it relaxes back to baseline.

Focus Training

Relax into the present moment and tune into your "observing mind." Prepare to become aware of five distractions that turn on your "wandering mind." As each one occurs, count it, and note how much time passes between each distraction. Train your mind in this way to stay focused for longer periods of time.

Another approach is to set a timer and repeat a short phrase every ten seconds, such as "thank you for focus." Whenever you become distracted, take note and refocus. You can practice this during physical exercise, like on a treadmill or elliptical machine. Over time, you will train your mind to concentrate for longer periods with less effort.

More Tips to Improve Focus

The three focus exercises are designed to shut off the DMN and activate the CEN, giving you an instant jolt of concentration while providing a break from repetitive thoughts. A mindful prayer achieves the same thing—a momentary escape from mental chatter and full presence in the now, giving you a surge of focus.

Lord God, the Infinite Unknown, the energy of the universe, I fill my lungs with Your grace. I breathe in Your benevolence and breathe out my distractions. Taking refuge, I strive for greater focus and concentration in this moment.

It is important to practice these exercises consistently every day. Consider each opportunity as an investment to incrementally improve your overall focus, so it is available when you need it. This keeps the DMN in check and helps you stay increasingly attentive.

As noted, it is helpful to begin each day with a mindfulness exercise. In addition, it is helpful to establish a midday prayer or mindfulness routine to retain your focus throughout the day, which may require finding a quiet spot free from distractions. Place your phone on silent, and allow your mind to completely rest. To avoid losing focus, sit in an upright posture; slouching or lying down can make you drowsy. If that happens, straighten your back, and keep your eyes open.

Be kind to yourself. If you lose focus, do not fume or pout. Simply acknowledge the distracted state and remind yourself that focus will one day come. When it does, be thankful for its arrival. In other words, cherish the positive moments and take note of the negative ones, responding to them not with criticism or anger but with affirmations.

I will get through this difficult period. I will regain focus. My time will come.

During moments of inattention, ask yourself, "What are the triggers for my mindlessness?" Pay close attention to how you feel during the day, particularly when focus starts to wane. You may find that the DMN (your "wandering mind") appears during mundane tasks, like brushing your teeth or washing dishes. Experiment with switching to your "observing mind" to be fully focused in the moment. Observe what happens before, during, and after these activities when you intentionally stay present.

While it may seem insignificant to remain mindful for a few minutes while brushing your teeth or washing dishes, these moments of clarity help to quiet the DMN, allowing for greater focus later on. The next time you find yourself in a "mindless" activity, try repeating a prayer or affirmation to focus your mind and then see how it impacts your day.

Maintaining attentiveness in the digital era can be difficult. We are constantly bombarded with notifications, messages, and news bytes that vie for our attention. Ask yourself if your latest digital obsession is causing a drain in concentration. If so, exercise restraint, limit your screen time, and delete any apps or notifications that do not bring value to your life. Inconvenient as it may be in the short term, removing these distractions is well worth a future state of crystal-clear focus.

Final Thoughts on Inaction

It is natural—and frustrating—to lose focus during inopportune moments, such as public speaking or virtual meetings. Multitasking and our digital apps are perfect catalysts for distraction. You may find that you do your best work in the mornings, but by afternoon it can be difficult to stay focused.

Inaction is the opposite of focus. For example, you may wake up one morning with a flurry of unresolved memories and emotions from the previous day. This fluttered state can persist throughout the day, impeding your ability to focus. When your DMN turns on, it diverts your attention away from your goals and tasks, hindering your long-term ambitions and the satisfaction that comes with achieving them.

Rather than reacting negatively to this lack of attentiveness, simply observe the fog and take preventive measures to reduce the likelihood of it occurring again. By understanding when and how you lose focus, you can glean insights into the nature of your distracted state. With this knowledge, you can then train your mind to develop greater concentration, helping you accomplish more in less time. This brings freedom from distraction and greater health, happiness, and inner peace, which will flow from you to your family and friends.

The time you invest in focus exercises, mindfulness, and prayer will return to you tenfold. It is not a quick process but one that develops gradually with training. It is important to celebrate each and every success along the way, which will motivate you to practice more.

It can be challenging to find momentary focus and inner peace and then watch it disappear. It might feel like panning for gold and seeing a big nugget, only to reach down and find it has fallen back into the riverbed. In that moment, acknowledging your state and setting an intention to regain attentiveness is the best course of action. Rather than getting upset, remind yourself that focus will return at some point.

When it does, express gratitude! In this way, your mind will understand that clarity is a top priority. Consistent mindfulness exercises, prayer, and focus techniques will improve your energy and ambition over time. It is important to maintain a relaxed effort, being careful not to overexert yourself. Laughter, lightheartedness, joy, and empathy are important. To remain resilient and driven, be conscious of rigidity and use your energy in a tranquil way. Remain calm and judicious in your exertion; this relaxed effort will enable you to maintain focus without becoming fatigued.

As mentioned earlier, the concept of right effort is cardinal in many religions, particularly Buddhism, where it refers to prioritizing wholesome qualities while pushing aside unwholesome ones. Observing your actions and their effects will help you more purposefully avoid unwholesome behaviors, guided by the endgame of enlightenment.

For example, consuming a lot of nicotine or caffeine products may seem tempting on a difficult day, but it's important to note any discomfort or fatigue that follows. At first, these side effects may not become apparent until the next day, but with greater awareness you will anticipate them during the act of consumption. It will become clear that using these substances as crutches during hard times only serves to pull you down. Connecting your current emotions to past behaviors helps you gain wisdom on the journey to your higher self.

If something is taking away your peace, take time to acknowledge it. When you have identified it, exercise restraint and limit its power over you. The path to enlightenment involves strengthening your ability to focus and concentrate while also casting aside the unwholesome forces of distraction. Like a snowball rolling downhill, the process gains momentum on its own as long as you set it as your intention. You may have been conditioned to live life in an unconscious state, but through the power of effort and focus, you can awaken to your full potential. This is the journey to your higher self.

KNOT 9

DISSATISFACTION—SEE THE BIG PICTURE

EVEN IF YOU HAVE OVERCOME addictive craving, emotional pain, or anxiety, you will not reach your true potential until you have broken through the mental knot of dissatisfaction. This subtle emotion may not be apparent to those around you, but it can be disruptive and all-consuming when you experience it. When you look within, try to recognize this knot's ability to take away your peace and happiness. By understanding the root causes of dissatisfaction, you can fully awaken to the glory of reality and make progress toward the enlightened state.

In this section, you will learn how dissatisfaction is rooted in cravings for something new or better. Instead of enjoying the moment as it truly is, your default mode network can prevent you from seeing the magnificent nature of life. By silencing the DMN, you can truly fathom the awe of the present moment on this remarkable planet.

It Starts with Expectations

It's your birthday, and your partner has surprised you with a trip to your favorite seafood restaurant. It's Saturday night, and the atmosphere inside is impeccable. Beaming with a cocktail in hand, you peruse the menu and spot your favorite dish—lobster tail. When the waiter takes your order, you point to it and excitedly ask for it by name, only to be met with a disappointed look. Turns out they just ran out of it, and they're ever-so-sorry, but you must pick something else.

You shrug it off and smile at your partner. Soon you find good spirits as the appetizers arrive. But then it happens. You head to the restroom and, on your way back, you spot him—the guy who ordered the last lobster tail. He's devouring it as if there's no tomorrow!

Now in a foul mood, you stomp back to the table as your partner asks, "What's wrong?" You fling your hand in the air like a kindergartner whose favorite toy has been taken away. Your meal arrives—grilled fish and vegetables. Unfortunately, it's not your preferred dish; that went to some clown who happened to arrive fifteen minutes ahead of you. You will have to make do with your second choice, which is not fair as it's your birthday, and you had high hopes for the evening.

Angrily slicing into the fish, you question why your partner even chose this restaurant in the first place. Overpriced and overrated, it apparently can't even stock a full kitchen for a Saturday night. You spend your birthday meal fuming in regret, wondering why the world has failed you on this important day.

In an instant, the joy of the occasion melts like ice cream in the summer sun. If you could be present in the moment, you would recognize the effort your partner has placed in the evening and its potential to become a fond memory. Sadly, your dissatisfaction has taken away your ability to enjoy the evening; it has pulled you out of the present moment, preventing you from appreciating the warm ambiance of the restaurant and your partner's affection.

Dissatisfaction arises when our expectations of the present moment are not fulfilled, which causes unhappiness when fate takes an unexpected turn. This can manifest as restlessness, where we need life to happen in a certain way. Plain existence seems boring and needs to be "brightened" with music, beverages, or entertainment.

For example, you see a friend's social media post about an exciting new theme park, and you have high hopes for a memorable day of family fun. But the intense heat, greasy fair food, and long lines leave you feeling dissatisfied. In some ways, the present moment has become a prison of expectation.

At its core, dissatisfaction arises from cycles of craving for something new and better and aversion toward the less-than-perfect moments in life. These cravings and aversions are often subtle and unconscious. When we yearn for something and it does not appear, our hopes can turn to loathing. Our default mode network exacerbates this intense dislike by ruminating and intensifying it further. When we view our lives through the lens of these negative narratives, we might grow convinced the world is against us.

Driving past a certain place or hearing a familiar song can activate our DMN, which brings back our uncomfortable memories and plunges us into dissatisfaction. This is a realm far removed from peace, focus, and mindfulness. In this state, we find nothing satisfactory. Even if our wildest wishes were granted, we would find something to complain about. This dissatisfaction can ultimately lead to intense suffering, a phenomenon Buddha discovered 2,500 years ago.

The Four Noble Truths

Life is impermanent. Change happens every second of every day, whether or not we are aware of it. The default mode network (our ego) ignores this fact, falsely believing that our lives are constant and exempt from the laws of the universe.

The DMN has a tendency to cling to the past and future, demanding that the present moment conforms to its terms. With good intentions, the DMN seeks to ensure our survival by attempting to control how life unfolds, a feat that is inherently impossible to achieve.

When the ego is in charge, it tries to dictate reality based on conditions of the past and expectations of the future. Instead of allowing you to be present and fully exist within the present moment, the DMN tries to govern existence. This illusion leads to a state of dissatisfaction, a concept Buddha described in his teachings of the Four Noble Truths.

1. ***Dukkha***—Dissatisfaction is an innate characteristic of our human existence.
2. ***Samudaya***—The cause of this dissatisfaction is our own craving or attachment.
3. ***Nirodha***—The letting go of craving and attachment can bring an end to dissatisfaction.
4. ***Marga***—There is a path from craving and dissatisfaction to the awakened state of nirvana.

Despite lacking an advanced knowledge of medicine or neuroscience at the time, Buddha's insights into the workings of the human mind were remarkable. He recognized two distinct modes of living that depended on the qualities of our mind. The first is an existence led by the DMN, which has a tendency to crave and cling to things, leading to samsara, the repetitive cycle of highs and lows. This process can leave us wandering aimlessly without an end.

Rather than engaging with reality as it is, the DMN creates opinions, concepts, desires, and aversions to it. Scientists estimate it takes milliseconds for us to form an opinion of whether we like something. When the DMN leads our lives, we spend our time shifting back and forth between wanting and disliking things as we work, play, and eat. This state of unfocused distraction is an exhausting chase that leads to only temporary fulfillment.

One powerful force propels the DMN's rollercoaster ride. When we pull back the villain's mask, we reveal its identity as ignorance. Every negative thought, craving, aversion, bad opinion, and mean-spirited judgment originates from a lack of understanding of reality's true nature. Ignorance leads us to believe we are separate from and superior to other people or that our happiness depends on external forces like politics, money, or romantic love.

Buddha recognized a second mode of living—an awakened state where we are fully grounded in the miracle of the present moment. This higher self is guided by an understanding that transcends our cravings and aversions. Freed from the DMN's trappings, our higher self comprehends the ever-changing nature of reality, the ebb and flow of emotions, and the impermanence of life. This leads to the liberation from ignorance where we can be unconditionally happy, regardless of external forces.

For example, stormy weather outside prevents you from going on your morning walk, souring your mood on what otherwise would be a cheerful day. You experience the rain negatively because of your ego's preconceived ideas, reacting to the gloominess with quick fixes—coffee and donuts. Thanks to your DMN, you are in a constant battle between your craving (desire to exercise outside) and aversion (dislike of the weather).

Your higher self perceives the storm differently. When you are in the second mode of living—the awakened state—you tune into the moment to experience the sights and sounds, recognizing the rain's critical sustenance for living things. You acknowledge the minor setback of not being able to walk outdoors, but you move on with little impact to your mood. You observe your negative thoughts for what they are, releasing them but remaining engaged with the here and now, regardless of the circumstances.

Buddha recognized that these two modes of living were not predetermined or permanent. *You* have the power to choose how you want to experience life. If you are not content with the current state, you can tap into your higher self and awaken to its blissful nature, guided by its innate peace and satisfaction. To do so, Buddha outlined an Eightfold Path that serves as a guide to the awakened state:

1. ***Right view***—A true understanding of reality (that is, wisdom)
2. ***Right intention***—The aspiration to act with compassion and loving-kindness
3. ***Right speech***—Abstaining from lying, divisive/abusive speech, or idle chatter
4. ***Right action***—Upholding virtue and avoiding immorality while exercising patience and restraint
5. ***Right livelihood***—Advocating for ethics and honesty
6. ***Right effort***—Endeavoring for wholesome thoughts, words, and deeds while renouncing unwholesome ones
7. ***Right mindfulness***—Developing awareness of mind, emotions, and behaviors
8. ***Right concentration***—Practicing skillful meditation and developing the mind's focus

"He who walks in the Noble Eightfold Path with unswerving determination is sure to reach nirvana," declared Buddha. This does not mean dreaming of sunshine and rainbows; rather, it involves experiencing the dark aspects of life, recognizing and eliminating their root causes, and replacing them with positive seeds. Enlightenment is the process of replacing darkness with light.

The key to breaking through the mental knot of dissatisfaction and reaching the awakened state is developing an accurate understanding of reality. It is the light of knowledge that unlocks the powerful energy deep in the fabric of your soul. Without the "right view" of wisdom, the DMN will prevent you from awakening and keep you locked in a state of suffering.

You cannot achieve wisdom by shushing the DMN like an unruly child or getting angry when it disrupts you. Anytime you feel dissatisfied with the present moment and demand a quick fix for relief, you are succumbing to the DMN's power over your thoughts and emotions. The answer to your restlessness is not on your phone, on your TV, or in your refrigerator. The remedy for dissatisfaction—and the ignorance that causes it—lies inside and all around you at this precise moment.

Awakening to Reality

What is reality? Let's start with the facts. You are one of nearly 8 billion people on a planet that is infinitesimally small compared to the known universe. To understand your existence, you must acknowledge the miracle of being alive and conscious at all, given the origin of the cosmos. But before delving into the cells and constituents that make you up, let's reflect on what has come before you in time.

As your DMN (the ego) tries to convince you of your uniqueness on this planet, let's frame your place on it. Earth is located in the Milky Way galaxy, which contains about 100 billion stars and at least 100 billion planets. Our galaxy spans 100,000 light-years from end to end.

A single light-year is the distance light travels in one year, which is equivalent to 6 trillion miles. The Earth's circumference at its widest point, the equator, is roughly 25,000 miles. Therefore, one light-year is equal to 240 million trips around the Earth. Multiplying this by the length of the Milky Way galaxy is equivalent to 24 trillion trips around the Earth, which is quite literally astronomical.

You may think the Milky Way takes up most of the known universe, but you'd be wrong. The Andromeda galaxy, our nearest neighbor located 2.5 million light-years away, is more than double the size of the Milky Way. In about 5 billion years, our two galaxies are expected to collide. By then, our sun will already have become a red giant and will have engulfed Mercury, Venus, and Earth.

Based on what the Webb Space Telescope has shown us, the known universe contains at least 100 billion galaxies and spans about 90 billion light-years. Astronomers estimate that the universe contains 100 quintillion planets; for context, 1 quintillion seconds equate to about 32 billion years. Our diminutive presence in the grand scheme of things is undeniable.

Now consider the origins of the atoms that make up your body. Most of them (like carbon, oxygen, and nitrogen) were formed in the fiery interior of stars that have since exploded and released their contents into space (also known as *supernova events*). The hydrogen atoms in your body originated in the Big Bang some 14 billion years ago. Therefore, you are not a drop in the universe but quite literally the universe in a drop.

We humans have existed for only 0.002 percent of the time since the Big Bang. Our species (*Homo sapiens*) has been around for about 300,000 years, a mere fraction of the 165 million years that dinosaurs roamed the planet. In fact, our most notable inventions, such as technology and culture, have emerged only in the last 50,000 years. While we might have created the internet, automatic transmission, and fried chicken, we cannot claim any real longevity when it comes to our time on Earth.

If you were to compare the entire history of time on planet Earth to a 24-hour period, modern humans would not appear until the very last second before midnight, 11:59:59 p.m. This means the entirety of humankind's existence is equivalent to a single second in a day. On the grand scale of the cosmos, we have just arrived.

That frames your existence in the context of the universe, but you then need to consider the sheer miracle of your life on this planet. Your body is composed of about 100 trillion cells, which is the number of stars in 1,000 galaxies the size of the Milky Way. These cells come in 475 distinct varieties, each carrying out specific functions to sustain your life and enable you to grow. Additionally, you are home to over 2,000 bacterial species, mainly in the gastrointestinal tract, that help you digest food and defend against harmful microbes.

The instruction code for all your cells is found in your genetic code, consisting of 25,000 genes encoded in 3 billion base pairs of DNA. This code is present in all plants and creatures—from flowers and insects to lions, tigers, and blue whales. All these life forms carry out seven essential processes—movement, reproduction, sensation, nutrition, excretion, respiration, and growth—using the same DNA blueprint and many of the same cellular structures.

We are all connected in a wondrous, intricate system where every living being has a great deal in common. Your lungs and alveoli are structurally similar to the branches and leaves of trees. Your organs, such as kidneys, lungs, and blood vessels, form through a process known as *branching morphogenesis*, which is directed by similar developmental pathways in plants, fish, and mammals. The same sets of gene families, such as the Wnt, Hedgehog, and Notch pathways, drive embryonic development across many species.

All living beings experience the same life cycle and need the same essentials for survival, and one of the defining characteristics of life is perpetual change. At the cellular level, one percent of the cells in your body are replaced on a daily basis. Within 300 days, all your cells will have been renewed, essentially creating a new you.

Although transformation is all around us, our DMN fiercely opposes it. Our ego wants us to ignore or postpone changes in our bodies with surgery, medications, and "fountain of youth" ointments, adamantly refusing to let us modify our habits and accept our bodies' changes. But no matter how hard we resist, life is never permanent.

If you accept that change is an inevitable part of life, it can be deeply liberating. Recognizing your part in the greater whole, rather than as a solitary entity existing outside of life's boundaries, can lead to a greater appreciation of existence and the role you play in this intricate system. All of us should be grateful for the astonishing sequence of events that have resulted in us being here at this exact moment. Life is a miraculous gift that deserves to be cherished.

"The universe is wider than our views of it," Henry David Thoreau said. When you come to understand how extraordinary it is that you are alive and consciously aware in this moment, no words can adequately describe the swell of wonderment that arises. No concept, belief, or thought can express the magnificent magnitude of the universe and your existence in it. This awe is so strong and empowering that it can effectively quell the ego and directly awaken your higher self. Twenty-five centuries ago, Buddha recognized the power of awe as an essential step on the journey to enlightenment.

The Power of Awe

Some moments in life can render us speechless, silencing the DMN and awakening a selflessness that illuminates the light within. The birth of a child or the passing of a loved one can move us in ways that defy words and concepts. In these reverential moments, our ego's preoccupations vanish, and we become one with the glory of the present.

My most memorable experience in medical school happened when I met an elderly patient who had suffered a heart attack. A team of doctors, nurses, and technicians worked tirelessly in the ICU to stabilize her condition as her grandson anxiously sat at her bedside. The team stabilized her and transferred her to a medical ward where she seemed to be improving.

Suddenly, her breathing pattern began to change. Seconds of alarm turned into a peaceful stillness that enveloped everyone in the room. As her grandson's feverish cries quieted, I placed my arm around his shoulder, and we watched her pass away as a warm smile radiated from her face. "She's gone," her grandson whispered. We stood in silence for several minutes, so wonderstruck by the peace that we forgot about the preoccupations of the moment.

Buddha referred to this profound awe as "emptiness." Reality is so miraculous that it surpasses our capacity to conceptualize or define it. The universe is so immense that it cannot be contained in our minds. The only way to fully experience it is to quiet the DMN by cultivating a complete presence in the now and peering into its infinitely complex, ever-evolving nature in admiration.

The key to breaking through the mental knot of dissatisfaction is to awaken to reality—to see life as it truly is. To do this, you must set aside the false preconception that you are the center of the universe. You must remove the filters that block you from seeing the truth and discard opinions that are rooted in ignorance. Doing so will allow you to discover an enlightened state of seeing and being. Regularly practicing this oneness meditation will help you release concepts about "me" and "mine."

Oneness Meditation Exercise

Take a few deep breaths and become aware of your breath, sounds, and sensations. When thoughts of craving, aversion, or delusion interrupt you, label them and come back to the now. When feelings arise, observe them as temporary states that are commingling with your true essence. Allow them to pass and not bear influence on your present-moment awareness.

When your DMN is silenced, take time to observe the living things around you. Notice each one, feeling its shared character and quality. Become aware of the interconnectedness of life, its constant passing and renewal. Observe without naming or conceptualizing, becoming one with your environment. "Learn how to see," the Renaissance artist and scientist Leonardo da Vinci said. "Realize that everything connects to everything else."

When the light of inner peace starts to shine, notice how you view the world in this moment. Take note of how your "observing mind" perceives reality compared to the DMN's "wandering mind." How would you describe your level of satisfaction, resistance, and energy level when you are fully immersed in the present?

This exercise features two important elements. The first is to recognize and release concepts such as "me" and "mine" when they arise. The DMN will do everything in its power to stop you from being mindful. Its fabrication of a distinct "self" falsely claims that you are separate from the world, preventing you from appreciating the beauty of the present moment. "By letting it go, it all gets done," Lao Tzu wrote. "The world is won by those who let it go."

The second is to identify and label the hallmarks of the DMN when they appear. By learning to recognize them, you will strengthen your central executive network (CEN) and fully awaken to reality. As you learned in the insight meditation exercise in a previous chapter, these include:

- Craving (desiring more of a good experience)
- Aversion (disliking, avoiding, or denying bad experiences)
- Delusion (rationalizing ignorance, denying the truth, and mind-wandering)

Meister Eckhart, a thirteen-century German theologian said, "God is not found in the soul by adding anything but by subtracting."

Oneness Replaces Selfishness

When you rise above the DMN so that the "observing mind" becomes stronger than the "wandering mind," you free yourself from the ego and its cynicism and selfishness. This liberates you from its frantic obsessions, allowing you to fully experience the miracle of living. The wisdom and understanding of your CEN will silence the DMN, and you will overcome suffering and ignorance.

Meditating in this state of oneness can be challenging at first. It requires patience, dedication, concentration, and the ability to let go of emotions, thoughts, and other attachments as they arise. It is like being on a boat in the middle of a storm, riding the waves and waiting for the clouds to clear. Even as the waves crash, you should remain composed, knowing with certainty that the cyclone will eventually pass.

When and how you awaken to reality is unique to you. You may receive instruction from the most gifted religious leaders and gurus but still struggle to find meaning from spoken words. Your own journey and the experiences in it will guide you to the inner peace in the fabric of your soul.

Having a flexible mindset and an openness to new ideas and perspectives is essential for growth. Even if you are an advanced theologian or meditator, maintain the attitude of a beginner and let go of preconceptions and rigid beliefs. Practice the philosophy of shoshin, the Buddhist concept of the beginner's mind. Avoid skepticism and embrace an eagerness to learn and question, so you can reach your ultimate potential.

This can be an arduous struggle. Be patient and recognize that the journey may take time. Celebrate each learning experience along the way, and appreciate the effort and dedication you have placed into your spiritual growth. As your wisdom grows, it will become easier to expand upon, and eventually the progress will become self-sustaining.

You can overcome any roadblocks that arise with a daily prayer or affirmation to help you stay on the path. Setting an intention with focus and resolve will help you ultimately overcome the mental knot of dissatisfaction.

Lord God, the Infinite Unknown, the energy of the universe, I thank you for this moment of being. As I quiet my ego, I fill my lungs with Your infinite grace, being a part of the miracle of life. I strive to continue down the road to the awakened state, so I may experience the peace and serenity that drives the universe.

Final Thoughts on Dissatisfaction

An ancient Sufi fable serves as a compass on the path to the higher self. One day, the Sun and Cave conversed, each marveling at the other's existence. Sun was puzzled at Cave's description of its home as dark and dank, while Cave, engulfed in darkness, could not fathom terms like light and clarity.

After a few hours of confusion, the two decided the best way to understand each other would be to exchange positions. Cave levitated upward and marveled at the scenery as it rose into the sky. "This is amazing!" he exclaimed. "I see it all so clearly now. The colors and lights are brighter than I ever imagined!"

Sun smiled. "Thank you for the kind words, Cave. Now let me see your home."

Cave wondered if Sun would have the same wondrous reaction he did. He led Sun down from the sky into the depths, but as they entered the low passages, Sun's rays were so bright that they lit the cavern like a warm, summer day. "I don't see anything different down here," Sun said in confusion.

When you awaken to the brilliance of reality, you have the power to shine that light anywhere, even in the darkest of caves. During times of hardship, your higher self will reassure you that brighter days will come. When you awaken this mighty force from deep within, the light of wisdom and confidence will dispel the darkness of fear, anxiety, and dissatisfaction.

Dissatisfaction is a subtle mental knot that modern medicine and psychiatry do not recognize as a problem. Caused by your own unrealistic expectations of how things should be, it ruins the present moment and keeps you from enjoying life's splendor. It may or may not lead to misery and suffering, but it will block you from awakening your higher self.

Consider this common example. You may complain that the temperature is too cold when you rise in the morning, not warm enough when you want to exercise outdoors, and too hot when you try to garden or mow the lawn in the afternoon. In all these circumstances, the current weather is the cause of your dissatisfaction. While the weather certainly changes, it is your *attitude* that triggers discontentment toward the weather.

When our desires and distastes don't align with reality, we often become upset and point the finger at the external world. Seneca wisely observed, "We suffer more often in imagination than in reality."

You can rise above dissatisfaction to discover natural joy. As you awaken to reality and observe your thoughts for what they are, you will recognize the early onset of craving and its potential to cause future dissatisfaction. Rather than succumbing to the yearning, you can choose to let it go and engage with the present moment, preventing negative states from arising. There is nothing inherently wrong with craving, and you cannot stop it from arising, but through deeper self-understanding you can avoid its trappings.

Developing the ability to choose how to respond to your thoughts and emotions is the key to wisdom. When knowledge and mindfulness join forces, they bring about freedom. The chains are broken from the underlying causes of suffering—ruminations on past and future, cravings and aversions, dissatisfaction and discontent. As the power of the DMN diminishes, reality reveals its full glory, and you will bask in its light.

Inner peace begins to shine, leaving you wondering how you ever managed without it. You feel connected to the universe and the cosmic forces guiding your destiny on Earth. Your higher self emerges, granting you the wisdom to do what is right and decide whether or not to react to your current life situation.

Wisdom is not something you can learn in a class or webinar. Rather, it is a deep understanding of how things work. Acquiring wisdom is only possible through direct experience. Studies have shown that wisdom is encoded into the prefrontal cortex, home to the central executive network (CEN). While the DMN is rigid and self-centered, the CEN is more adaptable, expansive, and selfless.

As you gain wisdom, your perspective shifts from "me" and "mine" to one that is more compassionate and collaborative. Breaking out of samsara (the repetitive cycle of highs and lows) and releasing yourself from unhealthy attachments, you can develop a healthier self capable of observing cravings and aversions without becoming enslaved by them. This leads to a deeper happiness that does not rely on external factors to sustain it.

It is never too late to strive for the best version of yourself. No matter your age, you can always learn something new, recognizing that solutions may have been in front of you all along. Start now to make lasting change—be mindful, enjoy life, discover new joys, form new relationships, and set ambitious goals. The past is gone, and the future is yet to come; focus on the here and now.

You will never fully eliminate stress, anger, fear, or pain. Nor should you, for they are all part of the human experience. But when you linger in these negative emotions, they will cause great harm and pain, ultimately consuming you in the process and preventing you from living to the fullest.

By awakening to reality and harnessing your wisdom, you can minimize dissatisfaction and reduce its impact on your thoughts and actions. As negative states become more fleeting and lose their weight, peace and happiness naturally rebound. A state of enlightenment arises where you are in love with life as it is now without any preconditions or judgments.

KNOT 10

POOR LIFESTYLE—IMPROVE YOUR DIET, SLEEP, AND EXERCISE

THE ESSENTIAL BENEFITS of diet, sleep, and exercise have been known for many years, but finding the right balance of these lifestyle elements can be difficult. Sadly, the vast majority of diet programs fail and less than one-quarter of Americans get enough exercise during the week. The primary challenge is that mental knots prevent you from making healthy choices. But as you resolve conditions like stress, emotional pain, addictive craving, loneliness, negativity, and anxiety, it becomes much easier to develop a healthful lifestyle.

This chapter presents science-backed insights to help you achieve and maintain your ideal diet, sleep, and exercise routines, allowing you to reach the physical, mental, and spiritual energy level of your dreams.

The Dangers of Overeating

Our brain sends signals telling us when to eat (hunger) and when to stop (fullness). After we start a meal, it takes about twenty minutes for our stomachs to feel full. Unfortunately, we often ignore our body's natural signals and overeat, a dangerous habit that can lead to illnesses.

When we eat, we activate the body's rest and digest response (also known as the *parasympathetic pathway*), which diverts blood and energy from other organs to our stomach and intestines. Eating too much forces our body to work harder to process food, sapping our strength and making us feel drowsy and sluggish. Our body needs extra hormones, acids, and enzymes to break down the excess food, potentially leading to heartburn and ulcers.

In addition, overeating gives rise to long-term consequences. The excessive consumption of fat, carbohydrates, and cholesterol carries a higher risk of heart attack, diabetes, stroke, and cancer. Moreover, our bodies convert the food that is not used for energy to fat, putting additional strain on our heart and lungs. This can also disrupt our circadian rhythm, making it harder to fall asleep and stay asleep at night.

We overeat for a variety of reasons. Many of us turn to food when feeling stressed or anxious. These conditions trigger the hormone cortisol, which in turn makes us crave sugary, fatty, and salty foods. This explains why a tub of ice cream or a bag of chips can feel so satisfying after an overwhelming day. For many people, overeating is a form of self-soothing therapy, a way to cope with challenging emotions.

Depression, loneliness, and dissatisfaction can also lead to overeating. Consuming chocolate, pizza, and processed foods releases endorphins in the brain, providing temporary relief from negative emotions. The default mode network (DMN) can fuel this cycle by ruminating on our problems and intensifying them, making us seek out unhealthy foods as a misguided attempt to alleviate our distress.

When we use food to cope with stress or depression, it can lead to uncontrollable cravings and addictive behavior. Dieting may result in temporary weight loss, but our DMN (the ego) eventually takes over and breaks our will, causing us to look for excuses or blame others, fall back into old habits, and regain the weight, rendering any dieting attempts ineffective. This is a primary reason why the majority of diets fail.

Overeating is not always related to mental conditions like stress or anxiety. Eating too quickly can lead to weight gain, because the brain does not have enough time to process the "fullness" signal. Certain medications can also cause food cravings. Additionally, some people may be predisposed to overeat due to genetic factors beyond their control.

With its many causes and predispositions, obesity is a serious global health crisis. According to the Centers for Disease Control and Prevention, obesity rates in the US rose from 31 percent in 2000 to 42 percent in 2020. Severe obesity (defined a body mass index higher than forty) almost doubled in this period, from 4.7 percent to 9.2 percent.

Neglecting our diet sets us up to suffer from serious illnesses, not only affecting us but also the people we love. As noted, being overweight can lead to heart disease, stroke, diabetes, and cancer, with an estimated annual medical cost of $170 billion in the US. On average, the medical bills for someone with obesity are $1,800 higher per year than those of someone with a normal weight.

Adding to the obesity epidemic is the increasing abuse of tobacco and alcohol, which are both classified as carcinogens that can lead to cancer. Acetaldehyde, the primary breakdown product of alcohol, can permanently damage DNA and cells. The Dietary Guidelines for Americans recommends no more than two drinks per day for men and one drink per day for women. For optimal health, it is best to abstain from alcohol completely.

Healthy Eating Starts in the Mind

The difficulties you may face in losing weight and eating a balanced diet highlight the DMN's influence on your lifestyle habits. Due to the DMN's self-serving focus, it can inadvertently encourage unhealthy decisions that can reduce your life expectancy. Thankfully, you have the power to make lasting changes to your health by silencing the DMN and breaking through the mental knots that cause you to overeat. In this way, you can reverse and prevent the complications of an unhealthy lifestyle.

If you do not resolve your mental knots, those short-term diet programs could end in failure. This is a pitfall that diet gurus and nutritionists ignore and allow their clients to stumble into again and again. None of the many fads, supplements, or medications will have a lasting effect if you don't first alter your thought patterns.

You can break the cycle of unhealthy eating. The change you desire begins in your mind. To tackle this obstacle, you must work from the inside out to resolve the mental knots that cause you to overeat—stress, emotional pain, addictive craving, loneliness, or anxiety. When you do, a healthy lifestyle comes almost naturally.

Through insight meditation or cognitive behavioral therapy, you can pinpoint why you overeat and identify those foods that contribute most to your weight gain. You can learn to listen to your body, recognizing when you are overeating and exercising restraint when cravings urge you to eat more.

Presence, focus, concentration, mindfulness, virtue, and restraint all help to foster the right diet. Resolving your mental knots makes it nearly effortless to lose weight, to say no to junk food and highly processed foods, and to abstain from alcohol and tobacco. With the right mindset, you can lead a balanced, healthy lifestyle into old age.

What Does a Healthy Diet Look Like?

The phrase "you are what you eat" begs the question: What exactly *is* the right diet? With the multitude of dieting options out there, which one is the most beneficial for weight loss, well-being, and longevity?

For weight loss, a diet low in carbohydrates is thought to be the gold standard. However, recent studies suggest there may not be a major difference between a low-carbohydrate diet and one that is low in fat. A clinical trial of 600 participants found that, after one year, those on a low-fat diet lost 11.7 pounds on average, while those on the low-carb diet lost 13.2 pounds. This 1.5-pound difference over 12 months was not significant, suggesting that limiting either carbohydrates or fats can be beneficial for weight loss.

For disease prevention and a long life, a number of popular diets are beneficial. One of them is the longevity diet found in the so-called Blue Zones, which are various locations in the world where people tend to live the longest. This diet is rich in fruits, vegetables, nuts, seeds, whole grains, beans, olive oil, and fish, while limiting red meat and processed foods.

The longevity diet recommends vegetable fats found in nuts, avocados, and olive oil. Refined carbohydrates and sugars are limited (with the exception of occasional dark chocolate), and white meat (chicken or turkey) is consumed in moderation.

The Mediterranean diet is another popular option that focuses on a high intake of vegetables, fruits, legumes, nuts, and whole grains along with low consumption of meat products (like poultry), moderate-to-high intake of fish, and a low intake of dairy (except for yogurt and cheese). Alcoholic beverages are allowed in moderation (such as a glass of wine during meals).

The Harvard diet combines many of these elements and simplifies the process of healthy eating. Half of your plate should consist of fruits and vegetables (potatoes excluded). A quarter of your plate should be whole grains, like brown rice, whole wheat bread, barley, or oatmeal. The remaining quarter of your plate should contain healthy proteins, such as fish, chicken, beans, and nuts. Following the Harvard diet, you would avoid red meat and processed meats, such as bacon and sausage; use healthy plant oils, such as olive, sunflower, or canola; and limit sugary drinks and dairy products.

For vegetarians and vegans, healthy proteins can come from plant sources, such as peas, beans, lentils, chickpeas, seeds, nuts, soy products, and whole grains. Vegan diets, which lack any animal products (including dairy and eggs), may require vitamin B12 supplementation. Several large clinical studies have found that plant-based diets significantly reduce the risk of diabetes and cancer.

No matter which diet you follow, to maximize your nutrition it is important to consume a variety of whole fruits and vegetables of differing colors, particularly greens, reds, and oranges. Incorporate legumes like beans and peas into your diet. Choose dairy items (milk, cheese, and yogurt) that are fat-free or low fat and meats that are lean (seafood and poultry). Limit your intake of saturated fats, trans fats, and processed foods.

Sugar and caffeine may provide a burst of energy, but they can make you feel sluggish in the long term. For sustained energy opt for nuts, seeds, fruits, and lean protein. Stay hydrated by keeping a bottle of water close to you throughout the day—and drink it!

Transitioning to a healthy diet can require some education and effort. Is it worth it? Studies have shown that transitioning from a diet rich in red meat and processed foods to one based on fruits and vegetables, grains, nuts, fish, and white meat can add up to thirteen years to your life expectancy.

When you consume food is also important. Eating within a twelve-hour window, such as from 7:00 a.m. to 7:00 p.m., is optimal for health. In addition, fasting for limited periods can bring many health benefits, such as allowing the digestive system to rest and reducing food cravings. Ultimately, when and what you eat is essential for your overall well-being.

Intermittent fasting has gained immense popularity in recent years with studies showing that it can improve heart and brain health. The most popular version is to consume food for eight hours in the day (for example, 8:00 a.m.

to 4:00 p.m.) and abstain from eating outside of that period, which may mean skipping a meal. Others prefer to eat only one meal on a given day every week.

During intermittent fasting, the body burns through its sugar stores and starts to burn fat, a process known as *metabolic switching*. Several randomized clinical trials have found that this process results in myriad health benefits, including reductions in body weight, fat mass, glucose, cholesterol, and blood pressure.

If you choose to fast, you are in esteemed company—Jesus, Buddha, and Muhammed all fasted. Doing so gives your digestive organs (stomach, pancreas, gallbladder, liver, and intestines) time to rest and heal. "Everyone has a physician inside them," said Hippocrates, a Greek physician who is considered the father of modern medicine. "The natural healing force within each one of us is the greatest force in getting well . . . to eat when you are sick is to feed your sickness."

How you eat is also important. Applying mindfulness to eating can help you make healthier food choices and can lead to weight loss in a sustainable and enjoyable way. This means paying attention to what you are eating and focusing on the experience—savoring each bite and being aware of sensations that arise. Take time to appreciate the taste, texture, and smell of food, as well as how it makes you feel. This allows you to be aware of fullness signals and to stop eating when you are satisfied.

Eating can be a delightful experience if you stay present and enjoy each bite. Put away your phone and turn off the TV, and take time to appreciate the flavors before swallowing. Eating quickly can lead to overeating, so it's essential to slow down and give your brain the twenty minutes it needs to make you feel full. Pay attention to your body's signals and practice restraint when you feel the urge to overeat.

After your meal, notice how you feel. Use your "observing mind" to sense whether you feel content and energized or bloated and sluggish. Reflect on how the type and quantity of food contributes to your emotional state. Avoid foods that adversely affect your sleep or mood.

The best diet should make you feel healthy and energetic. By being mindful of your body's sensations, you can learn to make adjustments and develop the right eating habits.

The Importance of Quality Sleep

Sleep is essential for our well-being. We often take it for granted, finding ways to power through our fatigue. Rather than seeking help, we may instead suffer through or medicate our sleeplessness, forgetting how great it feels to get a good night's rest.

When we don't get enough sleep, our body and mind suffer. Wounds and aches don't heal as effectively, preventing our organs from recovering from the stress of the day. Our brain cannot process its memories and properly reset, making it difficult to focus, learn, and stay present in the moment.

How much sleep is enough? As babies, we need to sleep about 75 percent of the time, which amounts to 16 to 18 hours per day. As children and teenagers, we need 9 to 10 hours of sleep, while for adults the recommendation is 7 to 9 hours.

Unsurprisingly, the average American sleeps 6.8 hours per night, while the majority of US teenagers get less than 9 hours. As our lives have become increasingly busy, our commitment to quality rest has suffered. In 1942 more than 80 percent of people were sleeping 7 to 9 hours per night, but since 1985 the number of people sleeping less than 6 hours per night has increased by 41 percent.

When we don't get enough sleep, harmful consequences arise. Roughly 50 to 70 million Americans suffer from a sleep disorder, resulting in an annual $411 billion loss in productivity to the US economy. Chronic sleeplessness can contribute to diabetes, heart disease, obesity, hypertension, increased susceptibility to mood disorders, and a reduced life expectancy.

To develop better sleep habits, it is important to understand the science of sleep and the conditions that will deepen it.

The Science of Sleep

Our brain signals its fatigue by releasing chemical messages that prepare the body for sleep. A key neurotransmitter is GABA, which relaxes our eyelids, limbs, and neck and diminishes our attention and arousal. Simply allowing GABA to put us to sleep will help us get the rest we need. Instead, we often fight these natural prompts and disrupt our body's normal wake-sleep cycle.

Our capacity to override the brain's sleep-promoting machinery is surprisingly powerful. The DMN, in particular, can hijack our brains into staying alert and active, even when our internal signals point toward needing rest. Like an annoying sportscaster, it encourages us to ruminate about the past, worry about forthcoming events, and recall our recent embarrassing, unfortunate, or negative experiences.

So begins the painful process of losing sleep and playing catch-up. During the day, we doze off for a few minutes, then jolt back awake with the help of caffeine or digital stimulation. We may regain some semblance of alertness, but when it's time to actually unwind, our minds struggle to detach, and we find it hard to snooze. As our sleep cycle (circadian rhythm) becomes disturbed, our fatigue intensifies, making it difficult to stay focused and relaxed.

Sleep is an intricate process that requires various brain regions to work together in unison. First, our circadian rhythm—the pattern of wakefulness and sleep—guides our daily lives. The hypothalamus largely controls this tempo based on the amount of light hitting our eyes during the day.

Prior to the modern era, this light pattern was based on the sun's daily rhythm of rising and setting, thus being regular and predictable. These days, artificial light from phones, TVs, and computers can disrupt our circadian rhythm, making it difficult to fall asleep and remain asleep. Therefore, it is essential to limit exposure to these devices for at least an hour before bedtime.

As it switches to night mode, our hypothalamus communicates with the brain stem to prepare the body for sleep. This is largely driven by the GABA neurotransmitter, which softens muscles and reduces brain activity. To help GABA do its job, it is important to turn off electronics, quiet the mind, and practice the mindful relaxation exercises described earlier.

Shortly before sleep, we start to tune out the external world. This is facilitated by our thalamus, a relay point that sends sensory information to our cognitive areas. During sleep, it filters out most sights and sounds (except for potentially threatening ones), allowing us to doze off. Later, during the deepest portion of sleep, it turns on again and communicates the images, sounds, and sensations that make up our dreams. To help the thalamus, choose a comfortable sleeping environment that is quiet and dark. Turn off notifications on all electronic devices, and use eye shades or ear plugs if necessary.

Other brain regions are also critical for falling asleep. The pineal gland, located between the two hemispheres of the brain, produces melatonin during the night phase of our circadian rhythm. This hormone plays important roles in setting our sleep cycle and maintaining our metabolic and reproductive health. If our circadian rhythm is disrupted (for example, from jet lag or stress), melatonin levels—and our health and sleep quality—can become disrupted.

Another region of the brain, the basal forebrain, releases a sleep-inducing chemical known as *adenosine*. Caffeine blocks adenosine and prevents the brain from naturally falling asleep. To ensure an adequate amount of sleep, it is important to avoid stimulants such as caffeine for several hours before bedtime.

Now let's address the act of waking, which is controlled by the ascending reticular activating system (ARAS). Like a car ignition, arousing from sleep involves a sudden release of energy. We get this influx of energy from different brain regions and neurotransmitters. A spike in cortisol gets the heart rate and energy going for the day. However, if an excess of cortisol is present due to chronic stress, emotional pain, or overwork, it can lead to premature or frequent waking.

For example, if you are suffering from high stress or anxiety, you may wake up early at dawn with rapid heart rate, headache, and emotional pain. Known as the *cortisol awakening response*, this state of morning tension can be challenging to shake off. Rather than getting angry at your body, acknowledge it as a sign to quiet the DMN and resolve the stress or anxiety leading to your condition.

The delicate interplay between these brain regions is essential for a night of deep sleep. Disruptions to any portion from too much artificial light, sounds, caffeine, or an overactive DMN can lead to insomnia—a condition where people have difficulty falling asleep or staying asleep.

Insomniacs can suffer from daytime sleepiness, irritability, increased risk of injury, and a lack of energy. More severe symptoms can include fatigue, an inability to concentrate, and a decline in health. The condition may last for a few days, weeks, or even longer; it can occur on its own or in combination with other medical issues. Left untreated, insomnia can have a significant impact on your well-being.

It's not just the quantity of sleep that matters but also its overall quality. The deepest and most important portion of sleep occurs when there's rapid eye movement (REM). REM sleep is important for dreaming, memory consolidation (deciding which memories to keep versus discard), and healthy brain development. REM sleep also activates the amygdala, which provides feelings to your dreams and helps you process the day's emotions.

Numerous substances and medications can disrupt REM sleep, such as alcohol, nicotine, benzodiazepines (found in some sleeping pills), opiates, and antidepressants. A study of 4,000 adults found a correlation between reduced REM sleep duration and higher risk of cardiovascular disease and early death. Other research has demonstrated that inadequate REM sleep can lead to cognitive deficits like poor focus and memory loss.

If you're having difficulty mastering the art of mindfulness, it might be related to insufficient sleep. Without the right quantity and quality of rest, it is difficult to maintain focus, concentration, and patience. Poor sleep affects your ability to recall information, find the right words, and be productive at work. A study of 833 adults found that daily alertness is a modifiable trait that is driven by the quality and quantity of sleep, exercise, and morning diet.

Maintaining good sleep hygiene is essential for unlocking your highest potential. Without adequate rest, even simple tasks can become challenging. By improving your sleep, you will see improvements in work and school performance, better social engagements, and progress on the journey to health, happiness, and peace of mind.

Tips for Good Sleep Hygiene

Developing a reliable sleeping pattern requires practice and commitment, just as it does for the other mental knots. It is important to set a daily intention for improved sleep and remind yourself during prayer and meditation. Maintain a log or diary of your sleep patterns, noting which changes work best for you.

Rather than sleeping little on workdays and oversleeping on weekends, it is essential to maintain a consistent bedtime throughout the week. A dark, quiet room is also critical for good sleep; avoid using the bed for any other purpose, such as working on your laptop, watching TV, or surfing the internet. Train your body to recognize that when you lie in bed, it's time to snooze.

Regular exposure to sunlight helps your brain establish a circadian rhythm. It's important to go outdoors and be with nature every day (unless the weather is particularly foul). "In every walk with nature, one receives far more than he seeks," said John Muir, an environment advocate and philosopher. Exercising during the day also readies your mind for rest later that night, improving the length and depth of sleep.

However, do not exercise too close to bedtime, as your body may have difficulty relaxing. Set a strict cutoff of one to four hours prior to bedtime to avoid exercise and the other major sleep disruptors: caffeine, nicotine, alcohol, and artificial light from TVs, smartphones, and computers. To stimulate GABA, consider playing soft music, practicing deep breathing, or meditating, taking a bath, and engaging in mindful relaxation.

Give your mind some time to transition from wakefulness to sleep mode.

Think about your morning routine: you do not usually wake up at 6:30 a.m., jump in the car at 6:31 a.m., and start working at 6:32 a.m. In the same way that you have a gradual process for waking up, you should also create a routine for falling asleep. This means patiently allowing your mind and body to wind down, tune out, and relax.

The DMN (your "wandering mind") is a major obstacle to quality sleep. It draws energy as it meanders around the mind, ruminating on the past and worrying about the future, generating feelings of fear, anxiety, and anger that stimulate glutamate and prevent GABA from forming. To enjoy a good night's rest, quiet the DMN by practicing mindfulness exercises such as prayer and meditation. This helps you tune into your body's natural sleep signals, making it more effortless to fall asleep.

Several studies have shown that mindfulness exercises can help people suffering from sleep disorders. In one randomized study, patients with chronic insomnia experienced significant improvement in falling asleep and staying asleep after eight weeks of mindfulness-based therapies. In another study, at-risk elementary school children who participated in a mindfulness curriculum gained more than an hour of sleep per night.

Going to bed feeling angry, anxious, sad, or tense can disrupt your sleep quality and impact your morning mood. When these feelings persist, observe them with your watching mind. Practice compassion or equanimity meditation, repeat a prayer, or talk to a friend or loved one about the issues. Acknowledge your emotions and find peace in them to ensure a good night's rest.

If sleep problems persist, consult a healthcare professional. Many medical conditions, such as sleep apnea, hyperthyroidism, heartburn, restless leg syndrome, and menopause can trigger insomnia. Certain medications may interfere with the process of falling, staying, or waking from sleep. To help your doctor better understand your sleep habits, keep a log of your bedtime habits and how you feel each morning.

As you resolve your mental knots and improve your sleep, you will gain focus and concentration. This enables you to tune into your mind and body with the confidence needed to reach the enlightened state.

The Importance of Exercise

Physical exercise has countless benefits for your mind and body. It helps reduce stress, improve sleep, and reduce the risk of major illnesses like heart disease, diabetes, and stroke. According to the Centers for Disease Control and Prevention, adults should aim for 150 minutes of physical activity a week. Exercising 2.5 hours a week may seem daunting, but when broken down into 5 daily sessions it amounts to 30 minutes per day. If you stay active while tuning into an audio book or podcast, that should meet the minimum guidelines.

For optimal health, spend this time engaging in both aerobic and strength training exercises. Examples of aerobic activities include speed walking, hiking, jogging, swimming, and cycling where you experience a moderate increase in heart rate and breathing rate. Strength training programs involving weights or resistance bands are designed to build strength and improve muscle tone.

A morning or early afternoon workout is most beneficial, as it releases a healthy dose of endorphins, allowing you to feel relaxed and better prepared for sleep later in the evening. Exercising at night can make it difficult to fall asleep.

You don't have to be an exercise fanatic to benefit from physical activity. A study following over 100,000 people for 20 years found that either moderate or high-intensity training were both effective in reducing the risk of death from cardiovascular disease (by up to 30 percent). As a general guideline, your heart rate during exercise should not exceed 220 minus your current age. For instance, if you're 49 years old, your maximum heart rate should be less than 171 beats per minute (220 - 49 = 171).

However, if you feel dizzy, lightheaded, or weak or have chest pains while working out, stop immediately and consult a healthcare professional. If you have health conditions such as heart disease or obesity or if you are older than fifty, you should ask your doctor about the right exercise program for you.

It is often our ego, the DMN, that keeps us from reaping the many benefits of exercise. Our "wandering mind" would much rather have us reminiscing on the past or worrying about the future than jogging in the park and taking in the beauty of the sky and nature. Thankfully, you have the power to silence the mental chatter by engaging in prayer and mindfulness exercises and switching on your "observing mind," making it easier to do what is best for your body.

Consistent physical activity benefits your health in many ways. Not only does it relieve stress and anxiety, it also helps improve mood and alertness. It creates the need for muscles to rest, which makes it easier to sleep at night. Improved natural energy reduces the reliance on sugary food and caffeine, which makes you happier, healthier, and more productive.

This positive feedback loop propels you toward your higher self. As you consume healthier foods, your body burns more calories, turning the tide against overeating and weight gain. This in turn reduces the strain on your heart, muscles, joints, and digestive tract. Your improved sleep and lowered stress provide greater energy, focus, and concentration, which deepens your mindfulness practice.

Exercise Mindfully

Practicing mindfulness during a workout can improve focus and endurance, significantly enhancing its overall effectiveness. This is because your DMN's tendency to wander creates resistance and self-doubt, diminishing your effort and energy level. Mindfulness silences the DMN, allowing you to remain alert and focused while exercising.

Some tips for mindful exercise include:

- Feel your muscles tense and relax while you stretch.
- Tune into your breath during exercise.
- Feel body sensations as they arise—your legs while you jog, air passing through your nose, and any sights and sounds.
- Time your body movements with your breath or pulse.
- Acknowledge any negative thoughts and let them go, focusing firmly on your workout.
- Consider activities that are designed to promote mindfulness, such as tai chi, yoga, and Pilates.

When you synchronize your mind and body and intentionally focus on the act of exercising, you experience greater satisfaction. You will maximize the benefits of a workout by getting "in the zone" and staying present as your body releases sweat and endorphins. A study found that applying mindfulness meditation during an exercise routine resulted in improved movement and weight reduction. Other studies have demonstrated additional health benefits such as improved mental peace, sleep quality, and cardiovascular health, all of which can help boost energy and focus.

Endorphins released during exercise can help you naturally alleviate aches and pains, helping you break through mental knots. Mindfulness encourages you to appreciate the warmth of the sun's rays on your skin and the freshness of the air you breathe, aiding you on the journey to health and enlightenment.

Final Thoughts on Poor Lifestyle

When you lead an unhealthy lifestyle, it makes tackling your mental knots even more challenging. The lack of energy makes it hard to maintain focus, restraint, and mindfulness. Similarly, building a long-term diet or exercise routine can be tough if your mentality is not in the right place. As the DMN drives you to distraction, dissatisfaction, and anxiety, it becomes harder to implement lasting change.

For example, when sleep-deprived or lacking energy, you may be more susceptible to stress. Rather than acknowledging the roots of the tension as coming from an unhealthy lifestyle, the DMN may blame others and opt for rapid relief from alcohol, binge eating, or digital distractions.

These quick fixes may provide short-term happiness, but they don't address the core problems and end up compounding your distress. For instance, booze and overeating can lead to acid reflux and sleeplessness, making you feel sluggish and fatigued the following day. As a result, you may forgo your morning workout and substitute a breakfast of sugary foods and caffeinated drinks to make it through the day, creating a vicious cycle that can be difficult to escape.

Countless diets, fads, medications, and routines promise a healthier you in a few weeks. However, these short-term solutions may not be effective in the long term if you are struggling with stress, emotional pain, addictive craving, loneliness, or anxiety. To make a lasting impact on your lifestyle, it is important to also address these underlying issues and foster your intention, presence, mindfulness, focus, and concentration.

When you resolve your mental knots and learn to be mindful in the now, you will feel invigorated to look and feel your best. Your higher self will take root, allowing you to work toward your goals with greater ease and satisfaction. Inner peace encourages you to maintain the diet, sleep, and exercise regimens that best align with your aspirations. This is in stark contrast with the resistance and self-doubt espoused by an unhealthy DMN.

When you fully awaken to reality and realize the precious miracle that is the human body, it feels unnatural to put it through the hardships of inactivity, poor nutrition, and inadequate rest. Fortunately, you have the opportunity to undo the harm caused by a poor lifestyle. It is never too late to start making healthier decisions to live a better life.

You may roll your eyes and argue that our health outcomes are predetermined by our genes, and there is some truth to that. Scientists have discovered a cluster of genes that influence our longevity, placing some aspects of our health beyond our control.

The good news is that your health largely remains in your own hands. To unlock your higher self (one that is fit and energetic), you will want to master three pillars—quality sleep, a nutritious and balanced diet, and regular physical exercise. Finding the right balance of these lifestyle elements will significantly improve your emotional and psychological well-being, enabling you to face life's challenges with greater ease.

"To keep the body in good health is a duty," Buddha said. "Otherwise, we shall not be able to keep the mind strong and clear."

KNOT 11

RESISTANCE TO CHANGE—ADAPT AND BLOSSOM

LIFE IS CONSTANTLY CHANGING—a fact understood across science and religion. Buddha named impermanence as a hallmark of life, while scientists like Antoine Lavoisier and Albert Einstein found that transformation of energy and matter continually occurs at the subatomic level. Unfortunately, our default mode network (DMN) demands that our life conditions stay permanent, leaving us stubborn, complacent, and unprepared for our challenges. Thankfully, by tapping into your power of resilience, you can welcome change as an opportunity to adapt and blossom.

Nothing Is Permanent

Change is a natural part of life, and although it may bring sadness or pain it also provides us with the opportunity to grow, learn, and discover new experiences. If we become upset every time life throws a curveball, we will live in a perpetual state of stress, fear, and heartbreak. But by embracing change and staying positive when it arises, we will create a better future for ourselves and those around us.

A somber Buddhist parable tells of a young woman who marries a powerful member of her community. She soon becomes pregnant with their child, and the village rejoices with the birth of the baby boy. Unfortunately, shortly after his first birthday, he suddenly falls ill and dies within days.

The woman is grief-stricken, unable to comprehend how this could have happened. Given her husband's wealth and standing in the village, she is determined to find a remedy that can revive her baby. Wrapping him up, she roams from house to house, desperately inquiring if anyone has a cure that can restore her son to life.

Eventually, the woman encounters a Buddhist who instructs her to visit Buddha; maybe he has the answer. She hastens to him and presents her deceased son. Buddha listens with empathy and says, "There's only one way to resolve your dilemma: find me four or five mustard seeds from a family that has never encountered death."

Thrilled to have a solution, the woman quickly scurries around the village. Everyone she visits has mustard seeds to spare; however, every time she inquires about the passing of a loved one the answer is the same. Regardless of their social status or wealth, all the village families have a sorrowful tale of death and bereavement to relate.

Eventually, the woman realizes that her situation is not unique. She is not the only one who has endured the loss of a child; in fact, grief of death is commonplace. It is a natural part of life, with no way to escape its finality. Coming to terms, she is able to accept the loss, bury the child, and find ways to move past the pain.

While somber, the Buddhist fable illustrates the point that change is a natural part of life, manifesting as continuous transformation. Spill a cup of water on the kitchen floor and by tomorrow it will be gone. If we cut ourselves while shaving, a few days later the skin will have healed. Our cells constantly grow, die, age, and renew, making us different from yesterday. Johann Wolfgang von Goethe said, "Life belongs to the living, and he who lives must be prepared for changes."

We typically react to change with negativity. We may feel apprehensive when a new leader emerges, skeptical when a popular trend arises, or resistant when our ingrained habits are challenged. Loss of our job, friends, or loved ones can lead to deep sorrow and the five stages of grief—denial, anger, bargaining, depression, and acceptance. Expecting permanence leads to disappointment and suffering. We must embrace the fact that hardship will inevitably arise in our lives; otherwise, it may be difficult to cope when it does.

Our stubbornness to change is driven largely by our DMN—the part of our mind that seeks to control the present moment based on past occurrences and future expectations. When events occur that are different from the DMN's forecast, it responds with displeasure and puts up a fight, making it harder to adapt to new conditions.

For example, at work you may feel dread when a new boss replaces your trusted mentor. Fearful of uncertainty, you may find faults in the new hire and resist opening up to this new leader, clinging to your old attachments. The stubbornness of your DMN prevents you from connecting with your new boss, ultimately hurting your work performance.

By recognizing the DMN as the source of this inflexibility, you can learn to look past it and embrace the ever-changing nature of life. This helps you to approach new circumstances with an open mind and find new opportunities amid the shifting landscape. Adopting a positive perspective allows you to welcome these new possibilities with enthusiasm and optimism.

In other examples, you may cling to possessions you no longer need or refuse to move out of living accommodations that are too small for your growing family. You may not want to leave a safe job that doesn't provide real value or see a doctor for worrisome physical symptoms. Perhaps you mistakenly think that as long as nothing changes, nothing will go wrong. This false view, driven by the DMN, hinders you from growing and reaching your true potential.

Fortunately, you can rise above the DMN and tap into a powerful energy that is central to the world's religions. This force not only allows you to greet change with openness, but it has been proven to foster physical, spiritual, and professional growth.

The Power of Resilience

Resilience is the ability to adapt to life's changing circumstances. It is the capacity to rebound in the face of adversity, whether it's physical or emotional hardships, such as illness, divorce, bankruptcy, or the passing of a loved one.

Those who possess resilience are able to accept roadblocks as a natural part of life. They anticipate and acknowledge new developments, assess the impact, and then adjust accordingly. Rather than responding to change with judgment or negativity, resilient people view it as a challenge to be embraced and an opportunity for growth. Regardless of its source, pain is recognized as a valuable fuel to deepen spiritual practice.

Even if you were to break through all mental knots and reach a state of enlightenment, no one can guarantee you will have a drama-free future. Resilience is the power that keeps you in the awakened state, so no worldly events can disturb your inner peace. Without it, a major health or financial setback could drag you back into the darkness of depression, anxiety, or addiction.

Studies have shown that people with resilience enjoy greater health outcomes and life satisfaction. A study of 3,000 older adults with diabetes found that those with psychological tenacity experienced better quality of life and physical functioning with fewer bouts of depression or hospitalization.

Cancer patients with resilience can more easily adapt to the side effects of life-saving treatments. A prostate cancer study found that hope and fortitude were vital to maximize the positive effects of social support. The most resilient patients had the greatest benefit from the resources available to them and experienced the best quality of life.

Studies of breast cancer patients have found that higher levels of resilience were associated with lower anxiety and depression and improved sleep, leading to greater physical, emotional, cognitive, and social quality of life. Those who were resistant to change reported more severe side effects from therapy and had poorer outcomes. Resilient patients actively cope with change as it occurs rather than attempting to minimize or avoid it.

It is clear that stubbornness to change can adversely impact your health and well-being when life hands you a difficult situation. To sustain the inner peace you have worked hard to attain, you must foster your power of resilience. You can choose from several ways to do so.

Developing Your Resilience

Resilience is a mental quality you can cultivate and empower. Regular practice allows you to better manage unexpected situations and recover more quickly from them. The most effective catalysts to develop resilience include:

- Spirituality
- Mindfulness
- Positive thinking
- Social support
- Problem-solving skills
- Physical activity

A study of over 600 cancer patients found that spirituality significantly bolstered psychological resilience and enhanced subjective well-being. Deepening your relationship with a higher power lets you live with a greater purpose, one that is less concerned with day-to-day inconveniences. By communicating with the Infinite Unknown through prayer, you free yourself from the DMN's focus on the past and build presence in the now, liberating yourself from the negativity and anxiety that comes from stubbornness to change. As described in the Book of Proverbs, "Though the righteous fall seven times, they rise again, but the wicked stumble when calamity strikes."

Mindfulness techniques like meditation and yoga can cultivate resilience by increasing awareness and emotional regulation. Similarly, positive thinking and smiling can help foster an optimistic outlook despite aches and pains. Practicing problem-solving skills (like brainstorming) can help you find ways to adapt, while physical activities like hiking, jogging, or swimming will reduce resistance and improve your will.

Resilience meditation is an effective tool to prepare you for life's challenges. Practicing consistently, especially in the mornings, helps to maintain the connection with your higher self.

Resilience Meditation

Take a few slow, deep breaths and relax into the now. Feel your chest and abdomen expand with each inhale. As you breathe in, remind yourself, "Breathing in, I clear my mind." On the out-breath, affirm, "Breathing out, I relax my body." Feel the waves of peace and relaxation and express gratitude for this moment of life.

Remind yourself of your intentions and affirmations, repeating, "In this moment, I am safe." If any thoughts or emotions arise, observe them without judgment and return your focus to the present moment. Pay close attention to tension or discomfort when it appears, allowing it to subside naturally. Allow your DMN to fade as you focus on the present moment.

Imagine yourself walking down a road, looking ahead as it disappears at the horizon. Remind yourself that no matter what happens in life, whether positive or negative, you will stay on this path to the awakened state. Express your determination to remain on the journey, regardless of challenges or obstacles that may appear. Repeat to yourself with resolve, "I will walk forward toward the awakened state of enlightenment."

Additional Steps to Build Resilience

Some moments in life will shake you to your core—natural disasters, vehicle accidents, divorce, bankruptcy, or a serious illness. When you accept that such events may happen but that you will learn to cope and move on, you are building your capacity for resilience. You can reinforce this power with a smile and a prayer.

Lord God, the Infinite Unknown, the energy of the universe, I thank you for this moment of being. I trust that You will guide me through this difficult period. No matter what the future has in store, as long as I accept Your grace, I will thrive.

Accept and acknowledge in your prayers and meditations that change will come, often when you least expect it. Further build your resilience with these steps:

- ***Value your relationships like gold***—Ensure the people close to you are aware that you care for them, and maintain close ties with those who are compassionate and dependable. Put in the work needed to maintain your relationships so that in hard times you will have supportive people close to you who can help.
- ***Always have an aspiration***—Keep a bucket list of intentions and goals for the next two to three years and visualize the big picture of your life. Plan your next vacation or family getaway, start working on that long-awaited hobby, and strive toward your dreams rather than living in a future of regret.
- ***Join a social circle***—Nothing compares to the joy of being surrounded by people who share your interests. It's a chance to build strong relationships and discover the world in new ways. Reconnect with old friends or explore groups online. Find the social circles that are most meaningful for you.
- ***Find ways to help others***—Whether it is volunteering for a shelter, working at a school or church, contributing to a charity, or simply helping family or neighbors, giving rewards you with joy, karma, and satisfaction that no amount of money can provide.
- ***Be proactive***—Now is the perfect time to tackle that long-awaited home project, search for a new job opportunity, or start a family. Don't let the fear of change hold you back. Seize the moment and start making a difference in your life.
- ***Stay positive***—Become aware when your mind goes negative, as it is wired to do, and actively maintain a bright outlook. Enjoy the little things like watching the sunrise, feeling the breeze on your face, or sharing a cup of tea with a friend.
- ***Be mindful of your mental state***—Take time to observe how you feel. Whether you are happy or sad, remind yourself that feelings are temporary states. When life throws a curveball and turmoil arises, be aware of your needs—take a day off, prioritize sleep, call friends

and family, or seek professional help. It's okay to feel pain, sorrow, or distress, but don't let it take over your life.

Final Thoughts on Resistance to Change

Change is a normal part of life. The DMN resists this fundamental truth, clinging to the familiar and predictable. It goes to great lengths to resist new developments, perceiving they will bring trouble or misery. It would rather ignore warning signs of looming disasters to maintain the status quo, urging you to overlook health checks, hold onto outdated possessions, and ignore potential risks. It stubbornly refuses to admit that life is impermanent.

Whether we like it or not, change is inevitable and affects us all. Ignoring or resisting it only makes it harder to recover from the curveballs. But acknowledging and preparing for difficult times gives you a better chance of coping with even the most overwhelming events. Charles Darwin, the nineteenth-century naturalist, said, "In the struggle for survival, the fittest win out at the expense of their rivals, because they succeed in adapting themselves best to their environment."

You can adapt and blossom by developing your resilience, which is the ability to anticipate that life will present you with challenges that are disguised opportunities for personal and spiritual growth. This encourages you to test and hone your skills, take on unfamiliar tasks, connect with diverse people, build tolerance for pain, and lighten your load by releasing long-held burdens.

The DMN believes that if you can prevent change, you will avoid suffering. However, if you look back at every challenging turning point in your life, you may recognize those moments of hardship as the defining points that brought you to where you are today. For example, if you had never lost a partner or friend, you may have never realized the true value of love. Without knowing the suffering of loss, you might take for granted that life is precious, not appreciating the importance of expressing gratitude for family and friends. Rather than avoiding pain, experience it for what it is and try to recognize the benefits that will arise when you overcome it.

Resilience is a virtue you must develop and nurture, so it can be available during times of need. At some point in the future, you may suffer from a serious illness, the loss of a loved one, or a layoff. Start cultivating resilience through prayer and meditation now, as this will provide a strong foundation that will help you cope with uncertainty and loss. Through its power, you can more quickly restore your health and quality of life.

The power of resilience sustains your soul and higher self during challenging times, which are integral to the human experience. Without the regular and often drastic changes that have occurred since the dawn of humanity, you would not be here today. Confucius said, "The gem cannot be polished without friction, nor man perfected without trials."

FINDING THE WAY HOME

A HEALTHY DEFAULT MODE NETWORK (DMN) plays a critically important role in your life, enabling you to be productive and successful. It wanders your mind away from the present in order to process old memories and emotions and prepare for the future. However, when overactive, your "wandering mind" can ruminate on negative past events and future possibilities, triggering harmful conditions like depression, anxiety, and addictive craving. Fortunately, you have the power to transcend these states of suffering and live in unconditional happiness and serenity.

The goal is not to eradicate your thoughts and memories but to foster a healthy relationship with them. Your mind will continue to drift off, but you can smile as you return to the present moment, acknowledging that your DMN is doing its job to keep you safe and sound. Gratitude and fulfillment replace negativity, judgment, and anxiety.

This journey to the higher self has taken place for millennia. It is the taming of the internal fires that originated when we lived in the wild, the ascension to the fountain of wisdom that is our namesake—*Homo sapiens* (wise human being). The road to get there can be bumpy and difficult, but sometimes our most painful experiences are the best opportunities to gain wisdom.

As you resolve the mental knots that your DMN has fomented, you will start to access the divine inner love and peace that is already within you. Having a more balanced relationship with your DMN will help you live joyfully in the present, make healthy decisions, and avoid troublesome people and places. Your deepening self-understanding will help you prevent painful knots from forming again in the future.

The key to this process is awakening your "observing mind" and the power of your central executive network (CEN). As you journey to your higher self, track your progress by periodically asking yourself, "How am I feeling? Am I at ease?" Tune into any feelings of craving, aversion, anger, anxiety, jealousy, judgment, and negativity. Note their pull, intensity, and duration. If you observe that these knots are weakening, you are well on your way to your higher self.

Being at peace and in the moment is the state where your mind performs most optimally, guiding you to the best outcomes. While harmful substances or people will abound, inner peace will steer you away from them toward natural contentment and gratitude. The more inner peace you cultivate, the greater its power will be.

Described in many religions as *supreme happiness*, inner peace is awakened when you free yourself from the pull of worldly attachments like greed, envy, and craving for pleasure. In Judaism, Christianity, and Islam, this bliss is rooted in virtue, wisdom, and a connection with God, as described in the Book of Psalms: "Blessed is the man who walks not in the counsel of the wicked, nor stands in the way of sinners, nor sits in the seat of scoffers; but his delight is in the law of the Lord, and on His law he meditates day and night."

In the Judeo-Christian tradition, finding peace means resting in the Lord, a spiritual respite from worry, stress, and confusion. It is a break from the internal and external enemies of our soul. In the Buddhist tradition, peace is the dharma (the truth of reality) and the attainment of nirvana, a spiritual awakening where we are freed from the flames of desire, anger, hatred, and jealousy.

Suffering is the fuel that helps you finally break through to the enlightened state and attain parami, a state of wholesomeness consisting of ten ideal virtues—generosity, morality, renunciation, wisdom, energy, patience, truthfulness, resolve, loving-kindness, and equanimity. These same qualities are at the heart of every major religion, highlighting the commonality between all of us and the core force driving spirituality.

Those of us without religious backgrounds may find solace in the emergence of science and medicine into the spiritual realm. Clinical studies have shown the healing nature of inner peace and the health benefits of compassion and positive thinking. This provides a fresh credence and a new dimension of support for the journey. Like scientists, we can approach our practice with healthy skepticism and curiosity while exercising patience and conviction for the truth.

Breaking through the eleven mental knots takes time and effort; change may start to occur in several weeks, but the process may last months or years. Some knots, such as negativity or loneliness, may be deeply ingrained and challenging to undo. And it may seem nearly impossible to escape the gravitational pull of addictive craving, anxiety, or emotional pain.

In the Allegory of the Cave, Plato describes a group of people who have been chained in a cave, forced to watch puppet shadows cast onto a wall. One of the prisoners escapes outside, only to face the blinding light of the sun. Despite the pain, he battles through and marches forward. As his eyes adjust, he experiences the breathtaking beauty of nature, giving him a newfound understanding of the world. He rushes back inside to share his knowledge with his friends, but they ridicule him for leaving the comforts of the cave.

On your journey, it may feel overwhelming or frightening to embrace the truth of reality, and it may be tempting to return to the old ways, back to the comforts of your "cave." Stand tall when your DMN (the ego) poses resistance and allow your mind to adjust to the sunshine of the CEN (the higher self). Continue to strive forward in a proactive way with commitment and set daily intentions. The more time and effort you give to breaking through your mental knots, the greater the likelihood that you will discover the serenity of inner peace. "Very little is needed to make a happy life," Marcus Aurelius said. "It is all within yourself, in your way of thinking."

In the enlightened state, you will recognize the interconnectedness of all living beings and the insignificance of terms such as "me" and "mine." The question, "What is the meaning of life?" becomes moot as life's profound, glorious nature cannot be conceptualized or described in words. Daily problems do not loom so large, and you will be able to approach situations with greater calm. This makes it easier to manage stress and anxiety, allowing you to welcome insights and stay resilient in a changing world.

As you awaken your higher self, the light of your presence shines bright and becomes a beacon to those around you. Like a mother consoling her crying child, your presence gives hope to those still suffering, allowing them to sense the possibility of freedom. By improving yourself, you are actually improving others and changing the world.

Friends, family, and colleagues are naturally drawn to your light. They recognize in you what they aspire to be—a free soul who is liberated from stress and anxiety, not weighed down by judgment and negativity, and able to stay focused on the present moment rather than be held back by the pain of the past or the worries of tomorrow.

Cultivating the qualities of the enlightened state, you will become an inspiration to those around you without even realizing it. Buddha described this as a bodhisattva, one who leads with great wisdom and compassion for the benefit of others. Whether you are a leader at work, the head of a household, or simply part of a circle of friends, your energy will help others overcome their frustrations, fears, troubles, and concerns.

Finding the bliss in present-moment reality and the inner peace in your soul awakens your higher self. It is your Christ-like, inner Buddha that is connected to all living beings and the universe itself. It is not that you have "fixed" yourself or attained something new, but rather you have found the way home to the serenity and bliss that was there all along.

Suffering exists because you are unaware of the wealth already within. The sun shines, the Earth nourishes, and the grace of inner peace is there for you to accept and embrace. You are worthy of divine inner love and happiness simply because you are a glorious being. Embark on the path within and remember that it is the journey that counts. Rumi said, "What you seek is seeking you."

The Source of Inner Peace

As you awaken your higher self, you will become aware of a healing power guiding you, a benevolent force distinct from your material wants and needs. Your eyes open to the universe and a question naturally arises: "What is the source of this energy?"

You know it exists because you can feel it, but it is hard to conceptualize or describe to others. You may call it God, the Infinite Unknown, or Pure Energy—the power that drives the universe and gives rise to the moral fabric encoded in your DNA. This vital force can be described as righteous, just, merciful, and compassionate. It delivers grace—the spontaneous, unmerited gift of purification and regeneration. Some may question its existence, but it is nonetheless available to anyone in need.

Regardless of our name for it, it is evident that a wholesome power has been with humanity during its tumultuous history amid upheavals, starvation, plague, and natural disasters. Around 74,000 years ago, the Toba supervolcano erupted in present-day Indonesia, propelling gigatons of ash into the atmosphere and causing a harsh volcanic winter that lasted ten years. Severe drought and death of vegetation led to mass starvation.

Our ancestors struggled to survive as the entire human population fell to several thousand. Because human babies depend entirely on their parents, it was only through unconditional altruism and devotion to their children that our predecessors survived. We are alive today because of the love and benevolence of our forefathers and mothers. Without that deep commitment, we would not be alive today.

The compassion that your ancestors relied on for survival still lives within you, though you may not realize it. One day, this truth will be revealed, whether it is at the end of life or before that time. When you come to this understanding, you will find comfort in an everlasting energy that radiates like the sun.

Regardless of your sins or flaws, this grace becomes accessible when you awaken inner peace. You have inherited positive karma from your ancestors, and you will find tremendous fulfillment in creating a better world for future generations. *You* can be the source of grace for those to come, providing them with the same level of support that has enabled your own existence.

Ultimately, the source of inner peace cannot be described but must be experienced firsthand. Life is profoundly beautiful, and it would be tragic not to realize this until your last breaths. Even if you have spent a lifetime focused on materialistic pursuits, it is never too late to look within and awaken your soul to experience the breathtaking beauty of the universe.

When you come home to your soul, you can fully savor God's grace, a Biblical term that also translates as *loving-kindness*. His gracious gift of purification and renewal can awaken freedom and profound bliss, as expressed in the popular hymn, *Amazing Grace*:

Amazing grace, how sweet the sound,
That saved a wretch like me,
I once was lost, but now I'm found,
Was blind, but now I see.

Imagine Your Future

Breakthroughs in medicine and neuroscience are just beginning to show their potential, offering humanity the opportunity to shine brighter than ever before. The development of new, effective therapies for cancer and other diseases, as well as increasing access to them, will improve the quality of life for all.

Human consciousness will also continue to flourish as the gap between science and religion narrows. The universe started with hydrogen and over time produced beings capable of reflecting on its profound nature. Our journey is not yet complete, and there is hope for a collective spiritual enlightenment that will bring out the best in our species. Science can be a source of spirituality.

To get there, we must break through our mental knots and nurture the hopes and dreams in our hearts. When you accomplish this, you are helping humanity on its quest. You can manifest anything you strive for, provided you stay connected to your higher power—your subconscious mind, the Infinite Unknown, Almighty God. As you tune in and listen, the path forward will be revealed. "Ask, and it shall be given to you," Jesus said. "Seek, and you will find; knock, and the door will be opened."

With aspiration and commitment, you will achieve the glory of peace within. Stay on your journey by reiterating your intentions daily. Express gratitude when peace shows up, and be accepting when it does not. Most importantly, strive for wisdom and compassion, and be a source of inspiration to others.

Recognize when you have strayed and reclaim the road forward. In difficult times, take refuge in your higher power. Across all faiths, the shared belief is that attaining an awakened state means overcoming our limited material desires—the perpetual hankering for money and pleasure, the fixation with "me" and "mine."

A visualization meditation and prayer can help you stay on the path to the enlightened state.

Visualization Meditation

Take a few minutes to become aware of your breath. Notice the temperature and flow of air as you inhale and exhale through your nostrils and mouth. Pay attention to your chest and abdomen rising and falling. Relax your head, neck, and shoulders. If thoughts come up, greet them with a smile and return your focus to the present moment.

Imagine yourself in a lush garden with a blue sky above, birds chirping in the trees, and a river flowing beside you. Take a few minutes to take in the fresh air and the soothing sounds. Feel the serenity of the landscape and bask in its glory.

In front of you lies a plot of soil. Choose the type of seeds you wish to grow and imagine yourself planting the seeds and tending to your garden. Every day, come back to this visualization and imagine your seeds sprouting to become plants and beautiful flowers.

Lord God, the Infinite Unknown, the energy of the universe, I stay on the path to the enlightened state, choosing to lead with compassion, wisdom, patience, and kindness. For as long as I am connected to Your infinite grace, I am complete with the inner peace that fills my soul.

With inner peace, there is no limit to what lies ahead. Divine inner love can bloom like a flower for you. All you have to do is nourish it, tend to it, and watch it thrive.

May you be happy.

May you be healthy.

May you have peace.

SPECIAL BONUS FOR READERS

WOULD YOU LIKE ADDITIONAL MATERIALS to support your journey? Visit the *Break Through* website to share your experiences and to access downloadable meditation guides, lifestyle tips, and other tools to guide you on your journey.

May you find health, happiness, and inner peace along the way!
www.YourDefaultMode.com

NOTES

Chapter 1

Tindle, HA, et al. (2009). "Optimism, Cynical Hostility, and Incident Coronary Heart Disease and Mortality in the Women's Health Initiative." *Circulation*, 120(8): 656–62.

Chapter 2

Dai, S, et al. (2020). "Chronic Stress Promotes Cancer Development." *Frontiers in Oncology*, 10: doi:10.3389/fonc.2020.01492.

Killingsworth, MA, and Gilbert, DT (2010). "A Wandering Mind Is an Unhappy Mind." *Science*, 330(6006), 932–932.

Stahl, JE, et al. (2015). "Relaxation Response and Resiliency Training and Its Effect on Healthcare Resource Utilization." *PLOS ONE*, 10(10): e0140212.

Hoge, EA, et al. (2023). "Mindfulness-Based Stress Reduction vs. Escitalopram for the Treatment of Adults with Anxiety Disorders: A Randomized Clinical Trial." *JAMA Psychiatry*, 80(1):13–21.

Bauer, CCC, et al. (2019). "From State-to-Trait Meditation: Reconfiguration of Central Executive and Default Mode Networks." *eNeuro*, 6(6): ENEURO.0335-18.2019.

Kirste, I, et al. (2015). "Is Silence Golden? Effects of Auditory Stimuli and Their Absence on Adult Hippocampal Neurogenesis." *Brain Structure and Function,* 220(2):1221–8.

Samaha, M, and Hawi, NS. (2016). "Relationships among Smartphone Addiction, Stress, Academic Performance, and Satisfaction with Life." *Computers in Human Behavior*, 57, 321–325.

Rathakrishnan, B, et al. (2021). "Smartphone Addiction and Sleep Quality on Academic Performance of University Students: An Exploratory Research." *International Journal of Environmental Research and Public Health*, 18: 8291.

Misra, S, et al. (2016). "The iPhone Effect: The Quality of In-Person Social Interactions in the Presence of Mobile Devices." *Environment and Behavior*, 48(2), 275–298.

Bhasin, MK, et al. (2018). "Specific Transcriptome Changes Associated with Blood Pressure Reduction in Hypertensive Patients after Relaxation Response Training." *The Journal of Alternative and Complementary Medicine,* 24(5):486–504.

Chapter 3

Chen, BK, et al. (2019). "Artificially Enhancing and Suppressing Hippocampus-Mediated Memories." *Current Biology*, 29(11): 1885–1894.e4.

Giotakos, O. (2020). "Neurobiology of Emotional Trauma." *Psychiatriki*, 31(2):162-171.

Ho, MY. (2023). "International REACH Forgiveness Intervention: A Multi-Site Randomized Controlled Trial." doi:10.31219/osf.io/8qzgw.

Chapter 4

Oswald, LM, et al. (2005). "Relationships among Ventral Striatal Dopamine Release, Cortisol Secretion, and Subjective Responses to Amphetamine." *Neuropsychopharmacology*, 30(4): pp.821–832.

Jebb, AT, et al. (2018). "Happiness, Income Satisfaction and Turning Points around the World." *Nature Human Behaviour*, 2(1):33–38.

Volkow, ND, et al. (2019). "The Neuroscience of Drug Reward and Addiction." *Physiological Reviews*, 99(4): 2115–2140.

Buck, SA, et al. (2021). "Roles of Dopamine and Glutamate Co-release in the Nucleus Accumbens in Mediating the Actions of Drugs of Abuse." *The FEBS Journal*, 288: 1462–1474.

Bogenschutz, MP, et al. (2022). "Percentage of Heavy Drinking Days Following Psilocybin-Assisted Psychotherapy vs. Placebo in the Treatment of Adult Patients with Alcohol Use Disorder: A Randomized Clinical Trial." *JAMA Psychiatry*, 79(10):953–962.

Costandi, M. (2012). "Psychedelic Chemical Subdues Brain Activity." *Nature*, doi.org/10.1038/nature.2012.9878.

Chapter 5

Cacioppo, S, et al. (2014). "Toward a Neurology of Loneliness." *Psychological Bulletin*, 140(6): 1464–1504.

Waldinger, RJ, et al. (2010). "What's Love Got to Do with It? Social Functioning, Perceived Health, and Daily Happiness in Married Octogenarians." *Psychology and Aging*, 25(2):422–31.

Waldinger, RJ, et al. (2015). "Security of Attachment to Spouses in Late Life: Concurrent and Prospective Links with Cognitive and Emotional Well-Being." *Clinical Psychological Science*, 3(4): 516–529.

Landes, SD, et al. (2014). "Childhood Adversity, Midlife Generativity, and Later Life Well-Being." *The Journals of Gerontology*, 69 (6): 942–952.

Bzdok, D. et al. (2022). "Social Isolation and the Brain in the Pandemic Era." *Nature Human Behaviour*, 6(10), 1333–1343.

Adam, EK, et al. (2006). "Day-to-Day Dynamics of Experience-Cortisol Associations in a Population-Based Sample of Older Adults." *Proceedings of the National Academy of Sciences*, 103(45), 17058–17063.

Cacioppo, JT, et al. (2009). "In the Eye of the Beholder: Individual Differences in Perceived Social Isolation Predict Regional Brain Activation to Social Stimuli." *Journal of Cognitive Neuroscience*, 21(1): 83–92.

Engert, V, et al. (2017). "Specific Reduction in Cortisol Stress Reactivity after Social but not Attention-Based Mental Training." *Science Advances*, 3(10): e1700495.

Desbordes, G, et al. (2012). "Effects of Mindful-Attention and Compassion Meditation Training on Amygdala Response to Emotional Stimuli in an Ordinary, Non-meditative State." *Frontiers in Human Neuroscience,* 6:292.

Chapter 6

Song, CF, et al. (2023). "Happy People Live Longer Because They Are Healthy People." *BMC Geriatrics,* 23: 440.

Steptoe, A, et al. (2011). "Positive Affect Measured Using Ecological Momentary Assessment and Survival in Older Men and Women." *Proceedings of the National Academy of Sciences*, 108(45): 18244–18248.

Chei, C, et al. (2018). "Happy Older People Live Longer." *Age and Ageing*, 47 (6): 860–866.

Auxier, B. (2021). "64% of Americans Say Social Media Have a Mostly Negative Effect on the Way Things Are Going in the US Today." Pew Research Center.

National Pain Advocacy Center. (2023). "Fast Facts About Pain." Nationalpain.org

Hilton, L, et al. (2016). "Mindfulness Meditation for Chronic Pain: Systematic Review and Meta-Analysis." *Annals of Behavioral Medicine*, 51(2):199–213.

Chapter 7

Bormann, JE, et al. (2018). "Individual Treatment of Post-Traumatic Stress Disorder Using Mantram Repetition: A Randomized Clinical Trial." 175 (10): 979–988.

Krishnakumar, D, et al. (2015). "Meditation and Yoga Can Modulate Brain Mechanisms that Affect Behavior and Anxiety—A Modern Scientific Perspective." *Ancient Science of Life,* 2(1):13–19.

Gothe, NP, et al. (2019). "Yoga Effects on Brain Health: A Systematic Review of the Current Literature." *Brain Plasticity,* 5(1):105–122.

de Gouw, HW, et al. (1995). "Decreased Mortality among Contemplative Monks in The Netherlands." *American Journal of Epidemiology*, 141(8):771–5.

Epel, E, et al. (2009). "Can Meditation Slow Rate of Cellular Aging? Cognitive Stress, Mindfulness, and Telomeres." *Annals of the New York Academy of Sciences*, 1172:34–53.

Goodwin, GM, et al. (2002). "Single-Dose Psilocybin for a Treatment-Resistant Episode of Major Depression." *New England Journal of Medicine*, 387:1637–1648.

Chapter 8

Kelly, AE. (2012). "A Life Without Lies: How Living Honestly Can Affect Health." American Psychological Association's annual meeting.

Brinke, LT, et al. (2015). "The Physiology of (Dis)honesty: Does It Impact Health?" *Current Opinion in Psychology*, 6: 177–182.

Serota, KB, et al. (2022). "Unpacking Variation in Lie Prevalence: Prolific Liars, Bad Lie Days, or Both?" *Communication Monographs*, 89:3, 307–331.

Federal Trade Commission (2021). "New Data Shows FTC Received 2.8 Million Fraud Reports from Consumers in 2021." *Consumer Sentinel Network Data Book.*

Weziak-Bialowolska, D, et al. (2021). "Being Good, Doing Good: The Role of Honesty and Integrity for Health." *Social Science & Medicine*, 291: 114494.

Weziak-Bialowolska, D, et al. (2023). "Prospective Associations between Strengths of Moral Character and Health: Longitudinal Evidence from Survey and Insurance Claims Data." *Social Psychiatry and Psychiatric Epidemiology*, 58: 163–176.

Wongpakaran, N, et al. (2022). "Moderating Role of Observing the Five Precepts of Buddhism on Neuroticism, Perceived Stress, and Depressive Symptoms." *PLOS ONE*, 17(11): e0277351.

Balboni, TA, et al. (2022). "Spirituality in Serious Illness and Health." *JAMA*, 328(2):184–197.

Chapter 9

Ehret, G, et al. (2022). "Awareness and Consciousness in Humans and Animals—Neural and Behavioral Correlates in an Evolutionary Perspective." *Frontiers in Systems Neuroscience,* 16: 941534.

Wass, S, et al. (2011). "Training Attentional Control in Infancy." *Current Biology,* 21(18): 1543–7.

Dahl, MJ, et al. (2022). "Noradrenergic Modulation of Rhythmic Neural Activity Shapes Selective Attention." *Trends in Cognitive Sciences,* 26(1): 38.

Herman, L (2020). "How Much Time Do We Waste at Work?" *The Muse,* themuse.com.

Matthews, N, et al. (2022). "Media-Multitasking and Cognitive Control Across the Lifespan." *Scientific Reports,* 12: 4349.

Chapter 10

Lindgaard, G, et al. (2006). "Attention Web Designers: You Have 50 Milliseconds to Make a Good First Impression!" *Behaviour & Information Technology,* 25:2: 115–126.

Schiller, B, et al. (2016). "Clocking the Social Mind by Identifying Mental Processes in the IAT with Electrical Neuroimaging." *Proceedings of the National Academy of Sciences,* 113(10):2786–91.

Longrich, NR. (2020). "When Did We Become Fully Human? What Fossils and DNA Tell Us about the Evolution of Modern Intelligence." *The Conversation,* theconversation.com.

The Tabula Sapiens Consortium (2022). "The Tabula Sapiens: A Multiple-Organ, Single-cell Transcriptomic Atlas of Humans." *Science,* 376(6594): eabl4896.

Sender, R, and Milo, R (2021). "The Distribution of Cellular Turnover in the Human Body." *Nature Medicine,* 27(1):45–48.

Fischetti, M, et al. (2021). "A New You in 80 Days." *Scientific American,* 324(4): 76.

Meeks, TW, et al. (2009). "Neurobiology of Wisdom." *General Psychiatry,* 66(4): 355.

Chapter 11

Adult Obesity Facts (2021). Centers for Disease Control and Prevention, Overweight & Obesity: Data & Statistics, www.cdc.gov.

US Department of Agriculture and US Department of Health and Human Services (2020). Dietary Guidelines for Americans: 2020–2025, dietaryGuidelines.gov.

Gardner, CD, et al. (2018). "Effect of Low-Fat vs. Low-Carbohydrate Diet on 12-Month Weight Loss in Overweight Adults and the Association with Genotype Pattern or Insulin Secretion: The DIETFITS Randomized Clinical Trial." *JAMA*, 319(7): 667–679.

Longo, VD, et al. (2022). "Nutrition, Longevity, and Disease: From Molecular Mechanisms to Interventions." *Cell*, 185(9), 1455–1470.

Fadnes, LT, et al. (2022). "Estimating Impact of Food Choices on Life Expectancy: A Modeling Study." *PLOS Medicine* 19(2): e1003889.

Shah, UA, et al. (2022). "Plant-Based and Ketogenic Diets as Diverging Paths to Address Cancer: A Review." *JAMA Oncology*, 8(8):1201–1208.

Tantamango-Bartley, Y, et al. "Are Strict Vegetarians Protected against Prostate Cancer?" (2016). *The American Journal of Clinical Nutrition,* 103(1):153–60.

Qian, F, et al. "Association Between Plant-Based Dietary Patterns and Risk of Type 2 Diabetes: A Systematic Review and Meta-Analysis." *JAMA Internal Medicine,* 179(10):1335–1344.

de Cabo R, et al. (2019). "Effects of Intermittent Fasting on Health, Aging, and Disease." *The New England Journal of Medicine*, 381(26):2541–2551.

Patikorn, C, et al. (2021). "Intermittent Fasting and Obesity-Related Health Outcomes: An Umbrella Review of Meta-Analyses of Randomized Clinical Trials." *JAMA Network Open,* 4(12):e2139558.

Gu, L, et al. (2022). "Effects of Intermittent Fasting in Human Compared to a Non-intervention Diet and Caloric Restriction: A Meta-Analysis of Randomized Controlled Trials." *Frontiers in Nutrition,* 9:871682.

Sleep and Sleep Disorders (2023). "Are You Getting Enough Sleep?" Centers for Disease Control and Prevention, Sleep, www.cdc.gov.

Hartmann, ME, et al. (2018). "Calculating the Contribution of Sleep Problems to Undergraduates' Academic Success." *Sleep Health*, 4(5):463–471.

Comondore, VR, et al. (2008). "The Impact of Sleep Deprivation in Resident Physicians on Physician and Patient Safety: Is It Time for a Wake-up Call?" *British Columbia Medical Journal*, 50(10): 560–564.

Leary, EB, et al. (2020). "Association of Rapid Eye Movement Sleep With Mortality in Middle-Aged and Older Adults." *JAMA Neurology*, 77(10):1241–1251.

Drazdowski, TK, et al. (2021). "College Students' Using Marijuana to Sleep Relates to Frequency, Problematic Use, and Sleep Problems." *Journal of American College Health*, 69(1):103–112.

Rusch, HL, et al. (2019). "The Effect of Mindfulness Meditation on Sleep Quality: A Systematic Review and Meta-Analysis of Randomized Controlled Trials." *Annals of the New York Academy of Sciences*, 1445(1):5–16.

Troxel, WM, et al. (2021). "Longitudinal Associations of Sleep Problems with Alcohol and Cannabis Use from Adolescence to Emerging Adulthood." *Sleep*, 44(10):zsab102.

Ong, JC, et al. (2014). "A Randomized Controlled Trial of Mindfulness Meditation for Chronic Insomnia." *Sleep*, 37(9): 1553–63.

Chick, CF, et al. (2022). "A School-Based Health and Mindfulness Curriculum Improves Children's Objectively Measured Sleep: A Prospective Observational Cohort Study." *Journal of Clinical Sleep Medicine*, 18(9): 2261–2271.

Piercy, KL, et al. (2018). "The Physical Activity Guidelines for Americans." *JAMA*, 320(19): 2020–2028.

Lee, DH. (2022). "Long-Term Leisure-Time Physical Activity Intensity and All-Cause and Cause-Specific Mortality: A Prospective Cohort of US Adults." *Circulation*, 146:523–534.

de Bruin, EI, et al. (2017). "Mindful2Work: Effects of Combined Physical Exercise, Yoga, and Mindfulness Meditations for Stress Relief in Employees." A Proof of Concept Study. *Mindfulness*, 8, 204–217.

Loucks, EB, et al. (2015). "Positive Associations of Dispositional Mindfulness with Cardiovascular Health: The New England Family Study." *International Journal of Behavioral Medicine,* 22, 540–550.

Tang, YY. (2020). "Long-Term Physical Exercise and Mindfulness Practice in an Aging Population." *Frontiers in Psychology,* 11(358): 1–10.

Stults-Kolehmainen, MA, et al. (2014). "The Effects of Stress on Physical Activity and Exercise." *Sports Medicine,* 44(1): 81–121.

Yang, CH, et al. (2018). "Momentary Negative Affect Is Lower during Mindful Movement than While Sitting: An Experience Sampling Study." *Psychology of Sport and Exercise,* 37:109–116.

Kennedy, A, et al. (2015). "Mindfulness and Physical Activity." *American Journal of Lifestyle Medicine,* 9(3):221–3.

Roberts, K, et al. (2010). "Mindfulness and Health Behaviors: Is Paying Attention Good for You?" *Journal of American College Health,* 59(3):165–73.

Ulmer, C, et al. (2010). "Mindfulness and Acceptance Are Associated with Exercise Maintenance in YMCA Exercisers." *Behaviour Research and Therapy,* 48(8):805–9.

Tsafou, K, et al. (2016). "Mindfulness and Satisfaction in Physical Activity: A Cross-Sectional Study in the Dutch Population." *Journal of Health Psychology,* 21(9):1817–27.

Sleiman, MB, et al. (2022). "Sex- and Age-Dependent Genetics of Longevity in a Heterogeneous Mouse Population." *Science,* 377: eabo3191.

Chapter 12

Olson, KL, et al. "Psychological Resilience in Older Adults with Type 2 Diabetes from the Look AHEAD Trial (2023)." *Journal of the American Geriatrics Society,* 71(1): 206–213.

Macía, P, et al. (2020) "Expression of Resilience, Coping, and Quality of Life in People with Cancer." *PLOS ONE,* 15(7): e0236572.

Zhao, X, et al. (2021). "Effects of Social Support, Hope and Resilience on Depressive Symptoms within 18 Months after Diagnosis of Prostate Cancer." *Health and Quality of Life Outcomes,* 19: 15.

Lai, HL, et al. (2020). "Resilience and Coping Styles as Predictors of Health Outcomes in Breast Cancer Patients: A Structural Equation Modelling Analysis." *European Journal of Cancer Care,* 29:e13161.

Ristevska, DG, et al. (2015). "Resilience and Quality of Life in Breast Cancer Patients." *Open Access Macedonian Journal of Medical Sciences,* 3(4):727-31.

Mihic-Gongora, L, et al. (2022). "Psychological Distress and Resilience in Patients with Advanced Cancer During the COVID-19 Pandemic: The Mediating Role of Spirituality." *BMC Palliative Care,* 21: 146.

Talepasand, S, et al. (2013). "Resiliency and Quality of Life in Patients with Cancer: Moderating Role of Duration of Awareness of Cancer." *Iranian Journal of Cancer Prevention,* 6(4), 222–6.

ACKNOWLEDGMENTS

SPECIAL THANKS to my wife Lisa Gao for recommending the title of this book and to Nick Georgandis, Mary Walewski, Patrice Rhoades-Baum, and Victoria and Richard Wolf for their assistance with writing, reviewing, copy editing, formatting the manuscript, cover design, and marketing guidance. Payam Kourosmehr, Joel Shomaker, Jose Kriedler, and David Arase also provided important direction. I would like to thank all of you who have shared your thoughts about *Break Through,* and I wish you health and happiness on your journey.

ABOUT THE AUTHOR

HOSEIN KOUROS-MEHR, MD, PHD is a physician-scientist and cancer drug developer in the biotechnology sector who has spent over two decades studying and developing new medicines for cancer patients. He received his MD and PhD degrees from University of California, San Francisco. He has coauthored over twenty scientific publications and patents related to cell and cancer biology.

Thanks to his background, Hosein recognized the extraordinary ramifications of a recent scientific discovery: the default mode network (DMN), which encodes the human ego and influences our thoughts, emotions, and behaviors. Recognizing the profound impact of this breakthrough on self-understanding (both from clinical and personal experience), he wrote *Break Through: Master Your Default Mode and Thrive* to help readers master the DMN and live happier, more fulfilling lives.

An avid reader and student of science, philosophy, and religion, Hosein draws on a depth of understanding from medical science, neuroscience,

Buddhism, Judeo-Christian teachings, and ancient philosophy. *Break Through* connects the medical and spiritual realms to help readers unlock health and well-being and awaken their higher self, opening the doors to new possibilities and experiences.

Hosein is also the author of two novels, *Extinction 6* and *Project Bodi: Awaken the Power of Insight*, that explore how mindfulness cultivates insights and scientific innovation. He lives in Los Angeles, California, with his wife and children.

Printed in Great Britain
by Amazon

41600460R00148

What The Fire Left Behind

A SPIRITUAL MEMOIR

Malcolm K Rowe

For permission requests, contact:
Malcolm K Rowe

Email: therowes5342@gmail.com

Registered with the U.S. Copyright Office
Registration No. 1-15035501791

Publisher: Self published
Cover: Sure Print & Design.

First Edition

Digital ISBN: 978-1-0699476-0-4
Book ISBN: 978-1-0699476-1-1
Printed in Canada

Disclaimer

This book includes firsthand accounts of life under apartheid, including references to racism, segregation, and violence. These depictions reflect historical realities and are presented for the purpose of truthfully documenting lived experience.

What The Fire Left Behind is a personal narrative and reflection on spiritual growth and life experience.

It is intended for informational and inspirational purposes only.

The author is not a licensed therapist, counselor, or medical professional, and the content of this book should not be considered professional, clinical, or medical advice.

Readers are encouraged to seek the guidance of qualified professionals for any physical, mental, or emotional concerns.

The author and publisher disclaim any liability arising directly or indirectly from the use or application of any of the ideas, suggestions, or techniques described in this book.

Contents

Contextual Foreword

There are places where the law was never meant to protect, only to control.

I served in one of those places.

During South Africa's long winter of apartheid, the uniform I wore carried two weights: the authority of the state, and the quiet ache of conscience. We were trained to maintain order, yet the order itself was built on separation. Every patrol, every arrest, pressed against the edges of what it meant to be human. To serve justice inside an unjust system is to live with a fracture that never fully heals.

Many of the scenes that follow were lived within that fracture.

They are not offered as defence, nor as confession, but as witness - to the complexity of those who stood between violence and the vulnerable, and to the moral confusion that seeps into a person when duty and humanity collide. In those years, I saw both the cruelty of the system and the courage of individuals who defied it in quiet, unseen ways.

When the sunburst of self-governance dawned, it did not erase the past. It merely revealed what the fire had left behind - the embers of guilt, grief, and the fragile hope of renewal. My journey through policing, loss, and spiritual awakening is not the story of a single man's redemption, but of a nation learning to breathe again after decades of smoke.

For readers beyond our borders, know this: apartheid was not only a political structure. It was a moral climate, one that shaped every breath, every order, every silence. To serve within it was to live inside contradiction - and to survive it, one had to search for a deeper truth, concealed within the scar tissue of lived experience.

That search is what this book is about.

It is the record of a soul learning that justice without compassion is hollow, and that even after the flames, something luminous can remain.

The pages ahead are simply my way of sifting through the ash - to find the ember that still burns, quietly, in all of us.

Malcolm K. Rowe

Preface

What The Fire Left Behind

There are lives that unfold quietly - routine, linear, known. And then there are lives like mine: shaped by contrast, stretched across continents, tested by darkness, and tempered by choices that define not just survival, but essence.

Some people are born with a soft landing. I arrived as if dropped from another realm of peace and gentleness into a world that felt, from the very beginning, too loud, too hard, too misaligned. From a young age, I felt like I didn't belong here - not in a poetic sense, but in a deep, cellular way, as if my soul had taken a wrong turn.

I wasn't unhappy in the traditional sense. I had food, shelter, and family. But the emotional terrain was barren. My mother, wounded by her own history, struggled to express love without control. My father, kind in his own way, numbed himself with alcohol and kept his distance. My brother and I existed like satellites around an absent sun - near, but never truly connected. I was the immature younger brother, orbiting my own quiet confusion.

That childhood taught me not just what love is, but what it is not. And in that contrast, I found my first clarity: **I would not become what I was born into.**

At eighteen, I joined the police force. Not for authority, but because something in me needed to protect. It felt like a sacred vow I hadn't realized I'd made. Suddenly, I was thrust into one of the most violent cities in the world during one of its most volatile periods.

This was where the fire truly began.

I saw things no one should see. I held dying men, kicked down doors, faced gunfire, and became the one who walked into chaos when everyone else ran out. And yet, even in that world of blood and exhaustion, something inside me began to awaken.

In the still moments between sirens and screams, I sensed a quiet presence - a knowing, a connection to something deeper than the physical. I felt guided, protected even, as if something unseen walked beside me.

This wasn't religion. I've never been one for dogma. It was an undeniable spiritual awareness that I was more than a body in a bullet-proof vest - I was a soul learning something ancient in a modern hell.

The fire took things from me. It burned away innocence, trust, and sometimes hope. But it also left behind treasures the flames could not consume:

- Strength, not bravado, but the kind forged from facing the worst and choosing not to become it.
- Discernment, the ability to sense truth beneath words.
- Presence, the quiet knowing that being here fully is more powerful than performance.
- Purpose, not grand or heroic, but simply the hope that my life might help another survive theirs.

As you read these pages, know that I'm not writing to impress or preach. I'm writing because I've lived through things most people only read about. From warzones to wild gardens, from murder investigations to conversations with plants, I've learned that truth rarely lives in one extreme or the other.

It lives in the space between.

This book is not a doctrine, nor a catalogue of perfect choices. It is a reflection - a journey through extremes and what they left behind. A story not of a hero, but of a human. Someone who fell down, got up, saw too much, and kept searching for meaning.

Fire does not only destroy.

It clears the ground for renewal - as I would learn years later, in exile, in loss, and in rebuilding.

Reflection - The Ember Within

When have you mistaken destruction for ending, only to discover it was the start of renewal?

What parts of your own story might need to burn away for new life to take root?

A Message To The Reader

The Road Between Extremes

This book is my gift to you. I hope my experiences and insights offer inspiration in times of struggle, perspective in moments of success, and companionship on the road between.

As a young man exposed to the darkest side of humanity while trying to build a "*normal*" life, I had no mentor, no inherited wisdom to guide me. I had intuition - and the choices I made shaped everything that followed.

What you'll read is not mythology polished for effect. It is raw truth: tragedy and triumph, cruelty and compassion, depression and grateful acceptance, and the choices that ultimately defined my path.

Before solitude gave me perspective, I could not see the purpose behind those extremes. Now I understand that even the most unbearable experiences held fragments of meaning, waiting to be uncovered.

This book is not about perfection or certainty. It is not about someone who has all the answers. I am not a Hollywood celebrity, nor a slick self-help guru. Society's hunger for heroes often blinds us to the everyday ones - the World War II veteran in the care home, the middle-aged stranger at the bar with a story of courage, even the man who failed publicly and warns others what not to repeat. Sometimes wisdom comes dressed in ordinary clothes.

In these pages, you'll encounter stories of abuse, bravery, a collaboration with a murder victim's spirit, a friendship with one of Interpol's most wanted, an unexpected moment with Nelson Mandela, and years of wrestling with depression, leadership, laughter, and loss. Each story is offered not for spectacle, but for what it revealed about choice, presence, and the wisdom that lives in the spaces between.

Some details will be difficult to read. I'll spare the unnecessary gruesomeness, but not at the expense of honesty. To truly understand resilience, one must glimpse the weight of what was endured.

From time to time, you'll also find questions waiting for you.

They are not tests or assignments; they are invitations to pause, breathe, and notice what stirs within you as you walk beside my story.

Sometimes fire teaches through words; sometimes through silence.

These questions are ways of listening - to yourself, to what the flames have left behind in you.

Take them gently. Let them rest like embers, warming you quietly. This book carries my story. The reflections belong to both of us.

So, if you are yearning for perspective, searching for purpose, or simply curious about one life lived in extremes –

You are very welcome here, my friend.

A Note on the Spiritual Threads to Come:

Some parts of my story reach past logic into the spiritual. I've learned that life doesn't always speak in straight lines, and sometimes it whispers through moments we can't explain. I'm sharing those moments as they were - not as instructions, but as lived experience. If they challenge your beliefs, that's perfectly fine. I invite you to meet them with curiosity. They're simply part of the path I walked.

This story may sound stranger than fiction, but it is true.

I offer it with unconditional love and the hope that it enriches your own life experience.

So let us begin - not with the answers I hold now, but with the roots of where it all started. To understand what the fire left behind, we must first return to the quiet before the storm.

Chapter I

The Outsider's First Glimpse

My earliest childhood memory was around 3 years old. I felt that I didn't belong. I had no explanation, but I felt it in my body - a homesickness for a place I couldn't remember, a silent wish to go back to a place I had no memory of. This is quite troubling for a child that age with no life experiences to draw that conclusion. Even though I was 3, something deep inside me knew that life ahead would be a struggle. This would be a life filled with danger and adversity - it felt as if my soul was hesitating before fully committing to this lifetime. Even as a child I was open to emotions. I wasn't psychic, but my intuition was naturally strong. I sensed moods shift before words, tension before arguments. I was aware of a dense energy around me, it felt heavy and incompatible.

I have always been a very sociable person in childhood and in later life. Always the jokester, always smiling on the outside, inside, I have maintained an awareness that whatever I experience in this life pales in comparison to where I came from.

My earliest childhood memory was comforting my crying mother after her friend committed suicide. She had shot herself after finding out that her husband had cheated and was divorcing her. I remember her tears, the weight of them, and the strange knowledge that life could end by choice. Looking back now this was probably too much information to share with someone under 5, however with no experience to reference, I was able to effortlessly place myself in that woman's position. I felt her despair and pictured myself in her body I felt all her emotions up to the point of shooting herself. This was uncommon for someone around 4 years of age, but it was my first experience of being open to soul energy.

The next childhood memory was overhearing my mother on the phone telling a friend that one son was born with the brains and the other the looks, not sure if that meant I was dumb, but it certainly lowered the bar of expectations. My brother was very bright, so I guess I had been assigned the "looks category".

I was never an A student, but I was above average and never failed anything at school. My studying routine including my finals were all the night before. My brother in contrast would spend his entire life studying and credit to him he was an A student and excelled in academics.

I found that music lifted my spirits, and I appreciated every genre. I would maintain this love of music throughout my time as a police officer, with a part time business as a Wedding DJ. My first gig was a house party at 13 and by 17 I was spinning at Weddings. Today in my late 50's I retreat to my listening room and mix everything from Hip Hop, Pop and Rock and Dance depending on my mood. Whether uplifting or calming - music is a vehicle for happiness, transformation and healing. Music moves what words cannot touch.

Looking back now, I see that nothing about those early years was random. The outsider in me was not a flaw - it was preparation. A soul noticing the world before the world noticed me.

Love's Absence, Love's Lesson

My father left school at 14 to work in a printing press to support his family after his father died in his 50's. He never went back to school. He never had the guidance to develop a work ethic or improve his social standing. That lost little boy grew into a man and married my mother, who was desperate for her independence after some family turbulence. What followed was a marriage born more from escape than love. We would be a representation of everything she failed to achieve in life.

My mother belittled my father in front of his children. I remember her throwing his clothes out of the window and telling him he didn't own her house. His safe space was the local bar and tennis club – judgement free zones where people laughed at his jokes and accepted him as an individual. He had very little interest in his kids. His wife had told him she was the boss, she made the rules. We were expected to obey her every instruction. We were her property and her life's achievement. We were actually quite poor, but we never showed it.

My childhood was uneventful, neither happy nor unhappy. We were not abused or starved. There was always food on the table, and my mother went to great lengths to portray the family as middle class when in fact we were probably just below that threshold. Beneath the façade, I sensed an emotional emptiness – like a family photo missing warmth. In all my years growing up I never heard the term good job, however there was a great deal of I love you but…

I am very grateful that my parents sent my brother and I to a good government high school. There is no substitute for a good education. It was my portal out of narrowness. This is where I learned about life and formed my opinions through friendships. I credit my education as the reason why both of us grew up to be successful in our own fields of business.

This was my introduction to a life of extremes. A loveless marriage and a seemingly loving family absent love. Sometimes the absence of love speaks louder than its presence. As a child, I didn't just learn from affection - I learned from its opposite. That contrast carved deep grooves in me, shaping my understanding of loyalty, of belonging, and of what it means to give love freely when you've known its scarcity. Looking back, I see how those early lessons weren't just wounds. They were maps, pointing me toward the role I would one day claim: protector, even when protection had not always been mine.

Reflection - Lessons in Contrast

When in your own life has the absence of something taught you more than its presence?

Which silences still echo in you - and what truths might they be asking you to hear?

Forged in Fear

My school life was also a landscape of extremes. While my home environment was emotionally turbulent, I was about to encounter physical abuse sanctioned by the government. A culture of corporal punishment with no guard rails.

I would love to say this perfect storm helped me retreat into my head or cower away in a corner. I did not. This was the only life I knew, and I was going to survive it. Little did I realize that this would be the moment I chose to be a Soul Protector.

I entered school with such naïve anticipation, following in my brother's footsteps. I was already trying to read his schoolbooks and for the first 4 years and knew them by heart. It was a magical place of learning with supportive teachers. I was thriving and at the top of my class!

I was just a 10-year-old sweet, jovial, impressionable child in grade 5, where I had the displeasure of having a nightmare of a teacher. Mrs. J was an embittered woman, painted in layers of makeup as if to hide her own unhappiness. Impatient, volatile, and cruel, she wielded her authority like a weapon. A wrong answer meant screaming rather than explaining, or worse - a heavy ruler slamming down on your open hand. Sometimes she hurled keys. Sometimes she made us hold our fingertips together and struck them with a heavy piece of wood.

The crack of wood against skin still lives in my memory - sharp as a gunshot in a church hall. The smell of chalk and fear hung in the air, a sour mix that settled into my clothes and followed me home

My confidence and attitude towards school changed that year. I dreaded going to school. Fear had replaced curiosity, and I developed a stutter that took me 3 years to break.

At the end of the year, she wrote the following in my memory book. "*Your future lies before you like a path of driven snow. Be careful how you tread on it because every mark will show*". It was meant as an insult, but it became fuel. I decided then that no one would ever break me again. Somewhere in my ten-year-old heart, I vowed to protect others from the helplessness I had known.

And just in case I didn't get the point, the universe, as if to test that vow, gave me more to endure. In high school, Mr. S arrived - a narcissistic teacher with a wooden cricket bat and a taste for domination. He beat students publicly for missing gym clothes or nametags, taking pleasure in their pain. Once, when he asked who had not been beaten that semester, I raised my hand. He summoned me forward and beat me anyway "*so I'd know what it felt like.*"

Each blow reinforced my resolve: I would become strength itself. I would not repeat their cruelty - I would *defy* it. By the time I left school, fear no longer silenced me. It forged me. I was surrounded by unjust laws like corporal punishment and apartheid so I would not follow these laws. I would become the law! Protectors are not born in peace. They are often created in the shadows of fear, carrying within them the choice to break the cycle or to repeat it. I chose to break it.

Years later, I discovered that both Mrs. J and Mr. S became principals. I considered confronting them, but realised they were products of their own pain. I let go. My freedom lay in forgiveness, not vengeance.

Reflection – Fear And The Forge

Recall a moment where fear threatened to break you –

Did you face it or turn away?

What did surviving teach you about who you truly are?

Becoming The Protector

In my teens, my classmates sought my protection. I simply couldn't stand seeing others afraid. Bullies became scared of me and tried to befriend me, so they didn't look weak, but in truth they were just scared kids trying to shift the focus from their own insecurities. I managed to divert fights and become friends with all sides. My powers of persuasion were strong, and I became popular.

I recall a time as a 13-year-old on the playground during recess, a large 18-year-old bully came over and demanded my friend's lunch and then my own. We weren't rich and it was a steak sandwich. What can I say, I was looking forward to that all day and there was no way I was handing it over. I looked at this large boy and told him we were not going to give him our lunch. He tried to take it, and I erupted, grabbing him and managing to turn him onto his back and began laying down some punches. He was clearly stronger than me, but my pride and heart were larger. If I got beaten up, I would go down fighting to defend my honour. I was pulled off him, and we were both sent to the principal's office. The principal heard both sides and gave me a grin and excused me. I heard later that the lunch bandit got 6 lashes. This was my first taste of sweet justice. When I walked back into my classroom, the whole class erupted in applause, and I spent the rest of my school days known as *Rocky*. In fact, when I met my wife, I was introduced to her as *Rocky* by an ex-classmate. Today my wife has other names for me – depending on her mood.

In my final year of school, I planned to join the police. I joined as a junior police reservist at 17 - to be certain this was the career I wanted. I spent every moment after school helping at the local police station with any task they would give me. I helped feed prisoners in the cells and at times they would take me out in the patrol vehicle to attend to real crimes. I learned that justice wasn't only about laws - it was about humanity.

My final exams came and went. I passed easily despite studying the entire year's work the night before. At 18, I jumped on a train to Police College to start my career in policing. My spirit braced itself to serve, protect, and perhaps to heal what had been broken in me - but that would have to wait.

I was entering an institution that was responsible for enforcing apartheid and desperate to maintain the status quo. The training would be top notch but rooted in the philosophy of breaking young men before remoulding them.

Reflection - The Call to Protect

Where in your life have you felt the pull to defend, to heal, to stand between harm and the vulnerable?

Is protection always strength - or can it sometimes be love in disguise?

Chapter II

Trained In Fire

Growing up under apartheid, I had witnessed racial discrimination, but nothing prepared me for the level of racial hatred that the Afrikaners had for English speaking people. The public service and military were run almost exclusively by the Afrikaners, and all our instructions, tuition and exams were solely in Afrikaans. They refused to speak English and reminded us that our English forefathers put their forefathers in concentration camps during the Boer War which I found to be true. This was something that was omitted in our history lessons and 100 years later those memories were still fresh, and we were guilty by association.

We were all placed in a block of 1300 boys and the English recruits were separated and evenly dispersed across all platoons. The instructor proudly announced that it was, so we don't get too friendly and speak English.

What followed was next level emotional abuse breaking our spirit and indoctrination of old school political ideology. Selling a message of hate and fear was not a hard sell. The country was nearing the end of the Apartheid regime. There was a power struggle amongst three black political parties and unprecedented levels of violence and bombings of soft innocent targets with weapons and explosives obtained through communist led countries.

One of the doctrines forced into us was the fear of cowardice. The greatest honour was to die in a heroic way in the service of your country. That mantra would echo throughout my career - both driving and haunting me.

First Supper, First Flames

The Police station was a mirror of the country's segregation, with separate entrances for white and black people. The charge office counter had two sides to one large table. Whites lined up on the right and blacks lined up on the left-hand side. There was no barrier in between and people instinctively knew to stand in the appropriate spot.

We were told that white cops served white residents and black cops served black residents. Interestingly enough, Indian (Southeast Asian) and Bi-racial cops could serve both. There was a police training facility for each race of police officer.

I had already experienced this inequality during my year as a junior reservist, but I couldn't help wondering when this stupidity would all fall apart. Then came the first supper (in contrast to the last supper). All of us gathered in the filthy parade room that was often used to process suspects or hold drunk homeless people while they sobered up. The table was wiped and my Sergeant said, *"okay boys empty your pockets"*. All the cops (of all races) emptied their pockets and threw in a few bucks. Then I received my first official order "*Foxy*" (A term for a newbie) "Go down to Theo's café and get us a couple of loafs of hot bread, two packets of chips (fries) and a 2L of coke and make sure it's cold - Are you back yet"?

I arrived back with the spoils and what followed was the opposite of the racial theatrics that took place in front of the public. Hands of every colour hastily ripped pieces of bread and chips and the room was filled with mm, mmm sounds. They passed the bottle of coke around. Nobody dared to wipe the lid before drinking. This was clearly a brotherhood ritual, and I was amazed.

In that smelly parade room, I was witnessing far more than hungry men devouring food. And then I realized something unexpected – Survival creates its own kind of fellowship - not holy, not polished, just real. For a few minutes we weren't uniforms or ranks. We were just men trying to keep our humanity intact while everything outside those walls was coming undone.

That night taught me something powerful: even inside a corrupt system, humanity could still break through. The brotherhood of the badge stretched beyond the lines politicians drew. Black cops were being targeted as agents of the State and killed quite frequently. We drove each cop home at the end of their shift at great danger to ourselves and they appreciated that. From time to time, we honored our fallen fellow black officers as they were murdered on the trains, ambushed as they reached home or left for work. This was an unprecedented time for all. There are too many stories to share.

Reflection - Beneath The Uniform

What masks have you worn to survive a divided world?

When have you glimpsed unity beneath separation?

From Apartheid To Democracy

When I joined the police, South Africa was on the brink of civil war. Violence wasn't a headline - it was the air itself. Brutal home invasions, car hijackings, political assassinations, and bombings of soft targets filled the air we breathed. For a time, the country held the highest murder rate in the world, a title some wore perversely as pride.

The African National Congress (ANC) was still banned, operating underground through sabotage and urban terrorism. The townships were burning, not just from poverty but from political killings. The ANC and the Inkatha Freedom Party (IFP) were locked in a deadly rivalry, and ordinary residents were caught in between. Even black officers in the force weren't trusted. Citizens never knew which political allegiance a uniform might secretly carry.

Democracy should have been the calm after the storm, but in those years, it was the opposite: the storm before the calm.

The faces behind the headlines were complex. Oliver Tambo led the ANC in exile. Govan Mbeki - father of future president Thabo Mbeki - helmed its military wing. The South African Communist Party lurked in the background, influencing policy and strategy. These men were aging and knew they could not carry the movement into power themselves.

And so, they chose Nelson Mandela.

At that time, most South Africans had heard his name but never seen his face - his image was banned from publication. To many, he was less a man than a myth. Yet he was the figure they elevated as their leader and thank God they did.

Mandela's story itself was one of extremes. A young lawyer drawn into violent resistance, convicted of sabotage, and sentenced to life in prison. For 27 years he lived behind bars, his body confined but his mind sharpening. In solitude, he studied philosophy, poetry, and politics. He emerged not hardened into bitterness but softened into clarity - a man who chose reconciliation over revenge. From prisoner to president, his very life became a lesson: greatness is not always chosen, sometimes it chooses you.

As South Africa shed its chains, I felt my own begin to loosen. The country and I were evolving together - both trying to reconcile light and shadow, anger and hope. The political fires outside mirrored the personal ones within me. That parallel was no accident - it was another lesson written into the fire of my life.

In the smouldering remains of our pasts, we each faced the same question: *What will you do with the freedom you have earned?*

Whispers Through The Flames

Looking back at these early chapters, I see how the themes of my life began long before I had words for them. The outsider's awareness, the silent lessons of family, the early encounters with fear, the instinct to protect - all of it was a kind of apprenticeship. Life was preparing me for the crucibles to come. The wisdom I carry now is this: what feels like weakness in one season often becomes strength in another. The fire that threatens to destroy you can also be the fire that shapes you.

The flames that consumed my world were never just physical. They symbolized the burning away of illusions, the stripping down to what truly matters. In the smoke, I saw both destruction and rebirth. The lesson was never that fire only takes. It also clears the ground for what must grow next.

Reflections - The Ground Cleared By Fire

What in your life has burned away that, in hindsight, needed to go?

What new growth has quietly taken root in the ashes?

Some seasons don't announce themselves - they just arrive and ask who you're willing to become.

Chapter III

From Campfire To Bonfire

Some fires warm you; others transform you. This chapter begins the slow burn - the moment the boy I had been stepped aside, and the protector I would become stepped forward.

It did not take long for me to feel the heat of the hellfire I had chosen for a career. The night of my "*first supper*," a commotion near the cells pulled me in. I watched a prisoner get slapped - my first time seeing that level of violence face-to-face. For context: it was a white cop striking a young black prisoner. That contradiction - brutality followed by a fatherly gesture - would be a lesson I'd come to see again and again.

My immediate reaction was simple: that's wrong. But then I learned the slapped man had just raped a fellow inmate. I remember a smaller boy, head bowed, tears streaking his face, being led into an adjacent cell separated from the perpetrator. In a fatherly gesture, the same officer who struck the perpetrator put his arm around the young victim and asked if he was all right. The victim refused to press charges. Life at the station moved on as if nothing had happened. What the hell had I signed up for? The darkness I'd been sheltered from as a child had moved into daylight. My childish worries evaporated. This was a world where pain was currency and innocence burned fast.

People ask me at barbecues, "*You were in the police - you must have a ton of stories.*" I smile, and they have no idea what they're inviting. It's impossible to truly understand unless you've lived it. The world needs protectors, and sometimes you must become the thing criminals fear.

After the initiation duties - guarding the station overnight (a shift nobody wanted) - I moved onto the frontlines – driving patrol vehicles and attending calls. The rush was addictive. I was nervous, but I never showed it; bravado was armour. I learned the job from my colleagues. The sense of brotherhood was powerful. Not many jobs require you to literally place your life in the hands of another. We protected one another. The indoctrination that dying heroically was the highest form of courage echoed loudly, but the reality was cruder: we protected each other's families because none of us wanted to be the one who had to tell a partner's family that they'd failed. It was a sacred pact.

Every shift stripped away another layer of innocence. But in the embers of each call-out, I felt something unexpected rising - not hardness, but clarity. The fire wasn't just consuming me; it was shaping me.

Walking Among The Dead

Some jobs change what you see. Others change what you can never unsee.

My first contact with a dead body came at a train collision involving a vagrant. They handed me black bin bags, and my partner and I walked the tracks in a tunnel, picking up pieces. The air in the tunnel was thick with iron and smoke - that strange metallic scent of blood and diesel coated my throat.

Every step echoed off the walls, too loud, too human. It was the kind of silence that screamed.

Later, a bus struck a tractor-trailer, and I scraped fragments of a driver from the twisted metal where his body had been imprinted, like a grotesque relief. At that time, we often didn't wear gloves; I scrubbed my hands until they hurt.

You never get used to it. Death went from headline to everyday reality. Shootings, stabbings, suicides, crashes - the morgue overflowed. We'd sometimes bring bodies back to the station for lack of space. Crime scenes were triaged by forensic need and severity. Our after-work gatherings were barbecues and beers, our way of surviving. Beneath that laughter sat horror too heavy to name. We were still young, but our conversations were threaded with scenes most people could never imagine.

One call still lives inside me. A serial killer had raped a woman and left her on train tracks to erase evidence. The train cut her in half like a cruel medical experiment. These images never fade; they etch themselves into your subconscious and reemerge in the quiet moments – denying solitude and peace. Each time I thought I'd seen the worst, life reminded me that I hadn't.

There were so many bodies I couldn't possibly count, but the ones that reach inside your soul are the ones that move you emotionally - dead children, ordinary people burnt or mutilated. Those scenes make you question everything in the quiet hours.

I remember a woman necklaced because neighbours accused her of witchcraft. She'd watered her vegetable patch, and it began to flourish. Her neighbours did not take the same care and theirs wilted. To us this is simple reality but to them it was signs of hexing and witchcraft laced with a healthy dose of jealousy and the rumours began. They doused her with petrol, put a tire around her waist, and watched her burn. Ordinary people watched. With no witnesses willing to speak up, I knew the case would likely be unsolved. I imagined her final moments and said a quiet prayer for her soul.

Inhumanity and suffering are deeply troubling to witness. Compartmentalisation and detachment are only temporary, until the weight of the trauma becomes too heavy and we lose the strength to keep it buried. Mental health support didn't exist; to need help meant weakness. The institution's solution was silence. But silence is not healing - it is slow corrosion masked by bravado.

Hearing the screams of family, holding someone as they bled out, comforting a child while lying about what was coming. No amount of therapy erases certain images. My wife knows to turn the TV's volume down at the sound of screams, because it can take me back - instantly - to the darkness best concealed in the deepest depths of my subconscious mind. It permeates your soul. You breathe, you release, and you divert your thoughts elsewhere.

One suicide remains vivid: an investment banker who shot himself in bed while his family watched TV in their lounge. He was still alive when I arrived on the scene - his wife and child screaming uncontrollably. I held his head as he died, telling his terrified son everything would be okay, knowing it was a lie. Another time, a man begged me not to let him die after a car crash. I held him until his pulse stopped. Those moments rewire something fundamental.

Then there was the night of the apartment disturbance: a man covered in blood trying to climb out a window, and inside a woman in her nineties slumped against a door, stabbed more than a hundred times with a blunt butter knife, a ligature around her neck. I had never seen so many stab wounds. We covered her half-naked body with a blanket and called an ambulance; she died on route. The suspect tried to feign mental illness; he even removed his hospital cast later to force a return visit. I warned the next shift to guard him. The next day I heard he'd jumped from a window and was never rearrested. Many cops carry a single case that haunts them because it never closed - that was mine. Nothing haunts the soul more than a lack of closure and the absence of justice.

The Weight Of Loyalty

Then there are quieter reminders of life and loyalty: a middle-aged woman collapsing from a heart attack with her two faithful dogs at her side, licking her face as if asking her to wake up - confused and afraid. Their cries were half hope, half heartbreak. I remember kneeling there, feeling their desperation like a pulse. It wasn't just grief; it was love refusing to understand death.

This would not be the only time I experienced the heart wrenching devotion of animals. I would attend the funeral of two close colleagues in the K9 unit. Both tricked into an ambush and executed in their vehicles. Eddie's K9, who witnessed it all, would be whining and sniffing his coffin at the funeral as if he were begging it to be opened to reunite with his owner. Even now, years later, that sound - the soft, trembling whine of loyalty - can undo me. The innocence of children and animals is the purest contrast to evil. When they suffer, something in the universe shatters.

Animals are loyal in a way people forget how to be. I'm besotted with my dogs. They are literally daddy's big sausages - tender hearts in fur coats who shadow me everywhere. They carry the same duality I do: a capacity for protection and a capacity for tenderness. They are my therapy - lifting my spirits in times of darkness and a daily reminder that love can be both fierce and uncomplicated. I have trained protection dogs as a hobby and chosen to own rottweilers because they embody traits I look for in a best friend, love, loyalty and a fierce protector that has your back. Ironically, they protect their protector.

Training protection dogs taught me something that no academy ever could: strength without love is just aggression. True guardianship - of people, of values, of peace - comes from empathy. My dogs don't just guard my home; they keep the best parts of me alive.

Every protector pays a hidden cost. To carry the grief of others, to stand where death has visited, leaves scars that uniforms cannot conceal. I learned to smile, to joke, to keep moving - but inside, the echoes of those moments stuck. Protectors often look unbreakable, but that's an illusion. We are simply skilled at hiding the cracks. Silence becomes our armor. But it's also our burden.

Even now, when I watch my dogs sleep - peaceful, unguarded - I find a strange comfort. They remind me that loyalty is sacred, that love without words can still heal the deepest wounds.

Reflection - Echoes Of The Fallen

Which losses still whisper in your quiet hours?

What did they leave behind that still lives within you?

Dancing With Mortality

As the years rolled by, I wanted out of the darkness, but adrenaline is its own addiction. Each shift felt like an invitation to die or to prove I couldn't. I sometimes ditched my bulletproof vest, claiming it restricted movement. The truth: I didn't care if I survived. Yet somehow, I always did. Despite my reckless bravery, I kept surviving and the meaningless commendations kept coming. Bullets missed. Fights resolved with me still breathing. I was either very good, very lucky or being protected by something unseen.

A colleague once told me he'd felt an invisible hand pull him backward just as a bullet tore through the air where he'd been standing. He turned to thank his partner, only to find him still kneeling and firing. He was too embarrassed to tell anyone. Stories like that linger. Maybe this unexplainable event was the universe nudging me to expand my limited understanding. Later in my career I would encounter something stranger - spiritual communications that helped solve a murder.

When Death Came Calling

There were many times I faced danger; There are so many instances where I narrowly escaped death, but the memories that stick are the incidents where I literally fought for my life.

One night, while feeding prisoners, I was attacked by fourteen inmates. They pulled my service pistol from its holster. In a flash I stripped the magazine free and guarded it with my life. Fourteen against one are not good odds. I curled into a ball and protected that magazine like it was all I had to keep breathing. Miraculously, one prisoner hid the gun down a toilet while the others searched, and within minutes my colleagues rescued me.

On other nights I fought off attack from an attempted murder suspect with a broken bottle and later a robbery suspect with a large homemade knife he had used to stab his victim. The chase would end with a lengthy fight in the middle of a highway in the dead of night and a good Samaritan shielding us with his car as I placed him under arrest. Ironically, I faced a greater danger from being struck by a car than disarming a man who tried to stab me.

The most memorable was a double-murder-in-progress call. Two women had been stabbed - one in her apartment and the other bleeding in the stairwell. We realized they were mother and daughter and that the boyfriend, high on drugs, had gone berserk, stabbed them both and stolen their newborn child. I left my partner with the injured mother, bleeding profusely from the neck, chased the suspect alone, arrested him at gunpoint, and freed the child. A mob gathered; his mates wanted to pull him free. In the back of the van, he grabbed for my weapon.

We crashed into each other, fighting in cramped metal. One of his friends locked the van and left me alone with a desperate man trying to kill me. That fight lasted a few minutes that stretched into eternity. I thought about the kid on the playground who once fought for his sandwich and thanked whatever had made me strong. Backup arrived. Later, at his trial, he admitted how drugs and anger had consumed him. I sat with him in court and, strangely, asked the prosecutor for leniency; My anger had dissolved into something quieter: understanding.

A few years later, I lost my best friend and longtime partner Andre - fiercely brave, steady - killed execution-style after chasing robbers. His killer laughed in court, but his wife and 7-month-old daughter didn't see the funny side of it. Colleagues would die in shoot outs or by their own hand, and you learn the cost of the role.

Pointing Fingers

I've always been the joker - the one to break the tension with a dad-joke and a grin. It's how I survived a job that could otherwise hollow you out. But even jokers have their narrow escapes, and some stories, as ridiculous as they sound in the retelling, were close calls that could easily have ended differently.

This was one of those days.

We were in the office when an urgent call came in: an armed robbery in progress. My station commissioner and I left immediately. We knew the area, its shortcuts and its blind alleys like the back of our hands. While driving we spotted one of the suspects running down a ravine into a maze of shacks. I gave chase on foot.

The ravine swallowed radio signals and cell reception. My partner circled round the other side and said he'd lie in wait in case the suspect tried to double back. I pushed through the twists and turns, but he was fast, and he disappeared into the maze of shanties. Minutes went by, then on instinct I looped to a likely escape route and crouched near the roadside waiting patiently like a lion stalking a gazelle.

When he appeared, he looked exhausted. Our eyes locked for a second. Everything slowed. He began to reach into his belt – I was unarmed, and I had to think on my feet. My choices condensed into a single, sharp question: do I bluff my way through this? It wasn't bravery so much as calculation mixed with a hefty dose of foolishness. I reached behind my back as if for my firearm, screamed a command, and let the threat in my voice do the heavy lifting.

"Get on the floor or I'll blow your f---ing head off," I bellowed.

BS, by the classical definition, was doing its job. The suspect dropped to the dirt. I moved in, cuffed him, and found a large knife. When I revealed there was no gun - only my finger tucked like a pretend pistol - I gave the fingertip a gentle blow - the air between us shifted from fear to disbelief. He looked at me, then at my hands, then let out the strangest half-laugh.

I was lucky. My quick thinking saved me from being stabbed. The line between heroism and catastrophe is thin. That night reinforced two truths: trust your instincts, and never mistake lucky outcomes for smart planning. Today I'm grateful my bluff worked. Tomorrow I still recommend being properly armed, trained, and cautious.

The Thin Line

Looking back, what strikes me most is not the bravado, but the fragility of it all. One finger tucked behind my back was the only thing standing between me and a knife buried in my ribs. One bluff, one moment of eye contact, one decision to act as though I was armed - and the story tipped in my favor.

The truth is, we all bluff sometimes. In arguments, in boardrooms, in moments where we feel outmatched. Sometimes it works. Sometimes it doesn't. The lesson isn't that bluffing is clever. The lesson is that survival often hangs by the thinnest of threads - and that humility must follow close behind.

This day taught me three things:

- **Instinct** is a compass, but it's not a guarantee. Trust it, but back it with preparation.
- **Luck** is not strategy. Be grateful, not arrogant.
- **Courage** is not the absence of fear but the space between fear and action.

I walked away with cuffs on a suspect and a story that still makes me laugh nervously at the absurdity of it. But underneath the laughter lies the real takeaway: life gives us narrow escapes not to inflate our ego, but to remind us of the sacredness of caution, gratitude, and the thin line we walk between disaster and deliverance.

Every narrow escape leaves behind a question: *was I just lucky, or was I being shown the thin line between who I was and who I might yet become?*

The Silent Saviour

This is a story I never put into an official report, and one that none of my colleagues even know took place. It sits in the quiet archive of small secrets we first responders carry - reminders that not every act of heroism is celebrated. Some are messy, forgotten, or deliberately left unsaid.

A municipal - worker strike had turned the city's streets volatile. Demonstrations in our region were rarely peaceful; they had become pressure cookers where anger could ignite into fire, looting, or violence without warning. My station commissioner and I were called out together - two older cops still carrying the old-school energy to teach the younger ones how to hold the line.

The chanting grew louder as a mob of more than a hundred surged down the main road. We parked our vehicle across the tar to block their path. My partner walked forward, rifle raised, hoping intimidation alone would disperse the crowd. In an instant, everything changed. A man lunged, grabbed hold of the weapon, and before my partner could react, the rifle was torn from his hands.

A fully automatic rifle in the hands of an angry mob is a very short bridge to catastrophe. My heart sank. For a brief second, I pictured the worst - dozens gunned down, blood in the dust, my partner killed before my eyes. A thousand outcomes filled my head, none of them good.

I didn't hesitate. Some might call what I did reckless; others might call it decisive. I ran straight at the man, shotgun leveled at his head, screaming orders with a ferocity that left no doubt I would act. He froze. Then, almost reluctantly, he dropped the rifle.

We secured the weapon, but the danger didn't vanish with it. Tension still rippled through the crowd like electricity searching for ground. Switching into broken Zulu, I shouted: "*Be calm! Don't do anything you will regret. No one needs to die today.*"

Something shifted. One of the men at the front recognized me. He had seen me years before - maybe in a school, maybe at one of the township programs where I'd volunteered my time. He raised a hand, muttered something to those around him, and slowly the crowd began to move on. Later that day, the same mob would clash with police riot units in another part of the city. Cars would burn. Shops would be destroyed. But not here. Not on our street.

When the dust settled, my partner looked at me, eyes wide, and mouthed a quiet "*thank you.*" We never spoke of it again. In police culture, revealing his mistake would have been seen as weakness, and weakness is rarely forgiven. We both carried it as an unspoken pact, tucked away like so many other untold stories.

What stayed with me was not the danger, nor even the theft of the rifle. It was the realization that small choices made years earlier - speaking kindly to a child, showing up in a township hall, treating people with dignity - had created an invisible ledger of goodwill. And in that moment of crisis, that goodwill saved us both.

Lessons From The Crowd

What saved us that day wasn't the shotgun in my hands. It wasn't the threat in my voice. It was the unseen weight of choices made years before - moments of showing up, listening, and treating people with dignity.

That's the part of policing, and of life, that doesn't make the reports: the quiet investments that sit in the background until the day you need them. A kind word spoken to a child, a talk at a school, a moment where you choose respect instead of arrogance - they all go into an invisible ledger. One day, that ledger may be the difference between escalation and peace.

The other truth is harder: leadership sometimes demands that you act before you think. There isn't always time to calculate. You move, you decide, and you hope the training - and your intent - is enough to tip the scales. That weight is yours to carry, whether anyone else ever knows about it or not.

And finally: force doesn't always win. Sometimes the strongest shield you can raise is your humanity - your ability to remind people, even in the heat of anger, that they still have a choice. When the crowd had passed, I was reminded of this: peace is never won in a single confrontation. It is built long before; in the ordinary ways we treat one another.

Reflection - The Ledger Of Grace

What quiet investments have you made in the lives around you?

How might they return to you in a moment you least expect?

Chapter IV

Heartfelt Protection

Wife Protector

Some stories feel too small to tell - private moments we imagine belong only to the quiet vault of a marriage. But sometimes those moments reveal something essential about who we are, and they earn their place in the larger story of what it means to protect.

My wife and I had been out partying. It was late, about one in the morning - the streets were empty, the air heavy with that peculiar stillness that only cities at rest can hold. As we were crossing a quiet street my instincts lit up. Four youths emerged, arranging themselves in a pincer formation the way predators circle prey. It was textbook: the recruiter - the one who steps forward - flanked by lookouts ready to close in. I felt the geometry in my ribs before my mind even named it.

The night air shifted - that sudden, electric quiet signaling imminent danger. The hum of the streetlights gave way to a different sense of urgency. I could hear their shoes scuffing the pavement, slow, deliberate, closing the distance. The smell of damp concrete and stale beer hung between us, a reminder that this wasn't a movie - it was real, and trouble was seconds away.

I turned to my wife and said quietly, "*Stay behind me. Don't run.*" That wasn't bravado - it was deliberate. Running invites a chase; staying close, deliberate, calm, keeps the energy grounded and less likely to spiral.

The main suspect stepped forward, his body language practiced, the kind of swagger that aims to distract while his friends flank. Four against two is never good odds, and in that split-second calculation, I knew the only way out was to interrupt the rhythm - to break the choreography before it set.

I struck first. Not a wild swing, but a precise blow to the jaw and neck designed to interrupt blood flow, shock the nervous system, and drop him cleanly. It was fast, clinical. His eyes rolled back and he collapsed, unconscious before he hit the ground.

For one breathless moment, the world froze - as if someone had pressed pause on a television show. The remaining three stared, then laughed nervously, trying and failing to lift their motionless friend. In the end, they abandoned him and scattered into the night.

We walked briskly to the car, pulse thundering, breath shallow but steady, not running, not showing fear.

The cool night breeze brushed against my face, the heat still pulsing in my hands. Somewhere a car horn broke the silence - a single, impatient note that felt almost human, as if the city itself had finally exhaled. Later, sitting with the aftermath, I felt a strange mix of relief and disquiet. The strike had worked, and part of me - the old cop ego - wished my colleagues had seen the precision of it. My wife certainly had. But when the adrenaline drained, the reflection set in. I hadn't just won a fight. I had crossed a threshold: using violence, even calculated, to protect the one I love.

The truth is this: not all violence is wrong. Sometimes it is necessary. But violence always leaves its mark - not just on the one who falls, but on the one who delivers it. The role of protector is never clean. To protect someone, you love is both instinct and burden. It is the willingness to stand between them and harm, knowing that the cost is yours to carry.

Reflection - The Protector's Weight

Not all violence is wrong, but all violence leaves a mark.

Protection is love wearing armour.

Heart And Hand

Protecting those you love is rarely graceful. It isn't the stuff of choreographed movies, and it isn't about showing off strength. It is about a heart that refuses to stay silent when danger circles close. Sometimes the hand must follow that heart - swift, decisive, unwilling to bargain with fear.

But the lesson isn't in the strike. It is in what happens after: the quiet walk to the car, the slow breath that returns, the silent prayer of gratitude that you made it through. Protection is not only about force; it is about presence. It is about teaching those we love how to face life's challenges with awareness, humility and reverence, and teaching ourselves how to sit with the weight of choices we did not ask for but could not avoid.

True protection is an act of love, even when it wears the mask of conflict.

Reflection - Love in Motion

Who do you stand before when danger circles close?

And who stands before you when you cannot?

Between Fear And Courage

Looking back, these stories form a single thread woven through my life. Sometimes I bluffed with nothing but my finger and a shout. Sometimes I ran headlong into danger and prayed the crowd would recognize my intent. Sometimes I struck with precision to shield the one I loved most.

Different settings, different risks - but the same calling. Each moment asked me the same question: *will you step back, or will you step in?*

Being a protector isn't about never feeling fear. It is about what you do with that fear - whether you let it paralyze or sharpen you. But every act leaves an imprint: every decision leaves a trace.

But here is what I've learned: protection is not just about surviving the day. It is about realizing that the hand may strike, the voice may command, but it is the heart that decides.

The role of protector has been mine. Yours may be different - Anchor, Mirror, Vessel, Guide - but the thread is the same: life will ask you, again and again, to choose between stepping back or stepping in.

And the answer you give will shape not only your story, but your soul.

Before Nisha's story of fragility and loss, there was Kwazi - a brother forged in fire. His story carried a different weight: not of endings, but of survival, defiance, and the unspoken bond that grows when protectors stand shoulder to shoulder.

Kwazi

Kwazi joined us as a new recruit and quickly became part of the inner circle. He carried an odd mix of worlds: his mother worked as a domestic in the then white suburbs, a wealthy liberal family had paid his tuition, and he'd grown up straddling two very different lives. He hadn't been raised in the townships, and he didn't fit neatly into expected cultural boxes - belonging everywhere and nowhere at once. He was curious, ambitious, and grateful for opportunities he hadn't been born to. With no money for university, he joined the police.

I liked him immediately. He was sharp, driven and brave. Language and cultural differences sometimes separated us from others, but with Kwazi you felt the easy chemistry of adopted brothers. We loved sport, music, and the same stupid jokes. We became partners in crime - literally and figuratively.

One day I'd chromed a CZ75 9mm with custom grips. Kwazi coveted it. So, we went down together and bought him his own "*baby*." Back then young officers were encouraged not to take service pistols home, so having your own was a small, private declaration of belonging.

I remember a night shift when Kwazi was late - not his pattern. He finally strode in - uniform stained with blood. I ran to him. "*Don't worry,*" he said. "*It's not mine*." He told us how, earlier on a train home from visiting a friend, a gang had tried to rob him of his firearm and kill him. He'd drawn his pistol and fired at point-blank range. One man was hit in the neck, another leapt from the moving train. It sounded cinematic – but it was raw survival.

Kwazi said he planned to open an attempted-murder case to cover himself. I was furious. I would not let this stand – it had become personal. In my absence, Kwazi had managed to defend himself on the train – this was my time to stand side by side with him and do my part to bring these killers to justice and give him the peace he deserved. I mapped every hospital for miles, divided the calls between us, and left names and numbers with emergency staff - a long, almost hopeless drag through the system. But we kept at it.

Hours later an urgent-care nurse called: a man with a gunshot wound to the neck had been admitted. We raced to the hospital. In the waiting room sat a couple of men with blood on their shirts. There was a patient bandaged around the neck, waiting for surgery. Kwazi stepped forward, greeted him in blunt, unrepeatable language, and made sure he was booked and guarded. That night, the patient's bed would become a holding cell after surgery. The wound had led us directly to our man. Even now, I sometimes wonder if I acted out of courage or fear disguised as purpose."

We did the police work that followed: statements, custody, evidence. It felt like raw justice. For Kwazi it was survival; for me it was proof that the pact we'd made as protectors - to look out for one another - actually meant something.

What Kwazi Taught Me

Kwazi's story sits at the intersection of belonging and bravery. He wasn't from the place his colleagues expected him to be from, and that difference made him a target - yet it also made him fearless in ways others weren't. Two lessons stayed with me:

- *Belonging isn't about origin - it's about loyalty.* Kwazi's background could have isolated him. Instead, he chose to join, to learn, to be part of something larger. That choice made him family.
- *Courage sometimes arrives in ordinary packages.* He was not a mythical hero; he was a young man who answered violence with decisive action. The hero is often the person who simply refuses to let evil pass unchallenged.

Hold that: protectors are crafted, not born. Kwazi didn't need to be polished by pedigree; he was forged by circumstance, and in that forging he became one of us.

Carrying Nisha

One memory that still weighs on me is the senseless death of Nisha, a fellow officer and close colleague. We trained together during the SWAT course, and I remember the day we were tasked with traversing a ravine over a body of water using only a rope. Nisha couldn't swim. I saw the fear in her eyes, so I swam back across, carried her on my back, and made sure she completed the task. Her father was a police superintendent, and I knew she could never face the disappointment of failing. When we reached the other side, she hugged me in a way that said more than words: thank you, my friend. In that moment, I was her strength, her protector.

Later, Nisha ended her own life to escape the turmoil that weighed on her. Her soul was never meant for this kind of work. Losing her reminded me that bravery doesn't always save us - sometimes it just hides our pain.

Sometimes even protectors cannot protect the ones they hold most dearly. I carried Nisha across a river once, but I could not carry her across the darker waters of her own pain.

Reflection - The Weight We Cannot Lift

Nisha's story reminded me that strength has limits, and that even those who seem resilient can break silently. To be a protector is to know both triumph and heartbreak - and to carry both with equal weight.

The Silence Of Healing

Healing does not always arrive like a dawn breaking the night. More often, it comes disguised as stillness - so quiet we almost miss it. It begins in the ashes, long after the flames have passed, when the smoke has lifted and only silence remains. At first that silence feels unbearable, like standing in the hollowed-out shell of all that was lost. Yet if you stay with it, if you resist the urge to rush past it, something begins to stir.

A breath that no longer catches in your chest. A night of sleep unmarked by shadows. A laugh that feels unforced, entirely your own. These are the first green shoots pushing through scorched ground. These moments are sacred because they mark the return of life.

The silence after fire is not emptiness - it is the soil of renewal. It is the pause where the soul regathers itself, where strength roots itself unseen before it blooms again. Do not mistake the quiet for absence. Healing lives there, waiting patiently to be noticed.

The Fire That Teaches

There is a sacred rhythm in destruction and rebirth - the soul's quiet curriculum written in flame.

At first, all you see is loss. The smoke, the silence, the hollow ache where something once lived. But if you stand still long enough, you will hear it - the whisper beneath the crackle, the invitation to rise again, lighter, clearer, unafraid.

Perhaps survival is not a reward, but a calling - to live awake, to walk softer upon the earth, to love without the armour that once felt necessary.

The fire never came to punish. It came to refine - to melt illusion, to reveal what cannot burn.

Every ember carries a message: nothing true is ever lost.

What remains after the flames are not ruins, but foundations - the soul's architecture of strength, compassion, and grace.

When I look back on my life, I no longer ask why the fire came.

I ask instead: what light did it leave behind?

Reflection – What Truly Remains

What has your own fire revealed that could not have been seen in the calm?
What light has it left glowing quietly within you?

Chapter V

A Garden In The Fire

We made extraordinary arrests. At times I felt like a hero; more often I felt like a man responding to crisis. Silence became my quiet teacher. In it, I learned that the protector's journey isn't only about standing guard - it's about learning when to rest the sword and simply breathe.

And then - amid the chaos, life offered me a gift – my soulmate. At twenty-five I met the love of my life. She steadied me and brought me back from the edge on more than one occasion. Professionally brilliant, she's also a guardian at heart. We share a love of gardening and built a home that became our refuge – a place where the chaos would quieten.

We bought a small plot and built a house, turned it into a garden, a safe space. That all changed the night our house was broken into while we were dining with friends. Four guns, my uniform, and some wedding photos - gone. My sanctuary had been violated, and I felt I had failed my role as protector.

It took a year to piece the crime together through informers and long, patient work. We identified suspects but lacked ironclad evidence. One gun ended up taped inside a speaker sold anonymously at auction; someone out there inherited a crappy old speaker with a .38 tucked inside. My shotgun was sold at a hostel; my favorite pistol was dismantled and thrown down a well. I got a small closure - they wouldn't return the stolen items - but our illusion of safety was destroyed forever. Innocence and nativity were replaced with insecurity and vulnerability. South Africa was a place where criminals often had no use for human life, so every drive had windows up and a weapon within reach, and our sleep was always light, a pistol under the pillow.

Even in the ruins of what we built, I sensed a strange mercy. Endings have a way of clearing the path for beginnings we cannot yet imagine.

Soul Protector

There are moments when life pushes you past logic into a deeper kind of knowing.

I remember Olga, an elderly woman in her late 80's, who used to make me tea whenever I checked on her. When she was found strangled, beaten and left for dead, I responded to the call alone. My intuition drew me to someone innocently walking near a railway track. His heartbeat betrayed him before his words did. This was someone who had been running. When his story fell apart, he confessed and led me to the scene where I found Olga still alive. That day, I served as her *soul protector.*

On a day I should have been heading to court, an older man and his son burst into the station, frantic. They'd seen the suspect who'd tried to murder their mother a year prior. We drove around searching for him - then I spotted him sitting casually at a bus stop. I calmly walked up and sat down next to him - greeted him in Zulu to confirm identity, and then put the barrel of my 9mm to his temple. The precision of the arrest and his expression of horrific confusion felt like justice breathing. The victim later told what had happened: her ex-gardener had tied her up, beaten her with a hammer, broken her skull and every bone in her hands and feet as he demanded the key to her safe.

Then lying helpless near death, he shot her in the head. The bullet hit her ear, missing her skull. She miraculously recovered, learning to walk and speak again. That was a satisfying day: giving her the closure she needed.

Lessons In Restraint

Some calls pull at a different part of your chest - not the adrenaline, but the place that holds outrage and sorrow. Those calls test everything you think you stand for. They tempt you to become the thing you hunt. I've had a lot of difficult calls, but two cases stand out because they forced me to choose restraint over vengeance - to hold the line between protector and judge.

Anger is a fire of its own. Left untended, it devours everything in its path - reason, compassion, even our own health. But fire, when contained, can become a force for light and warmth. I learned that anger could be both my enemy and my teacher. It showed me where injustice lived. It revealed what I could not ignore. And in learning to harness it, I discovered that true strength lies not in suppressing anger, but in shaping it into resolve. The fire of anger asks us: *will you burn with it, or will you burn it into fuel for justice?*

Reflection - The Fire Of Anger

When anger rises like flame, how do you hold it?
Do you let it consume—or light the dark with it?

Innocence Lost

I remember the call like a punch to the gut: a thirteen-year-old girl, walking home from school, pulled off the road in broad daylight and raped in the bushes. It was the kind of opportunistic, senseless evil that rearranges the world for the victim and everyone who loves her. When I arrived, the scene was clinical and terrible at once - a frightened girl, the evidence to preserve, the beginnings of a life that would now always carry this wound.

She could not name her attacker, but she remembered one small detail: another man nearby called him by his first name. That shard of memory - so small, so human - became the single lead we had. In an affluent, quiet, treed neighbourhood like that, my first instinct was to go door to door. I knocked on hundreds of doors. I asked about gardeners, domestic workers, handymen, contractors - anyone who might answer to that name. It's tedious work; it's heart work. It's detective work - the endless hope that you'll find the one person who fits.

Intuition drew me to a golf course some distance away. Their payroll didn't show what I needed - no obvious cook or grounds man with that name - but when I thought of how people hide in plain sight, I asked about caddies. Those part-time workers were often off the books. One name seemed to fit. I returned that night to surprise him. He was not home. I informed his family that he was a person of interest in a rape case of a young girl. After I had left, his family and the victim's family connected. He was rounded up by the tribal court - where elders convene and vigilante justice is metered out. He was badly injured when I was called to come and collect him, and he confessed to the charges.

It's complex. The rage is righteous and immediate. You watch a child carry the moment into adulthood and you ache for something decisive. But what I learned again and again is that the long arc of justice isn't ours to replace with our fists. My job was to secure him, present him to the court system, and let the law - imperfect as it is - take its course. The protector's job is not to destroy - it's to preserve. Even when every cell in your body screams otherwise. That was a restraint I had to practice, day after exhausting day.

A Mother's Face

Another case: a young offender who was brazenly stealing and bringing goods home. His mother refused to be complicit; she wanted nothing to do with his crimes. In an act of shocking brutality, he bit off a large part of her cheek. The wound was grotesque in a way that lodged itself in your throat; I will never forget the sight: a gaping hole in her cheek, bone and jaw exposed. It was the closest thing to the horror I'd seen in films. I noticed the cruel irony – flesh devoured by her own flesh and blood.

When we arrested him, something primal flared in me - not just anger, it was unbridled vengeance - a deep desire to make him feel the same pain he had inflicted. I could have done something out of earshot, something that would have felt like justice in the moment. Instead, I held myself to the rule I was taught as a young cop: secure the suspect, get medical help for the victim, and deliver the case to the courts. Our role is not to sentence; our role is to present. The judiciary - even with its flaws - must be the arbiter.

In both cases, restraint was fierce discipline. It required: turning fury into evidence, anger into investigation, revenge into testimony. When the impulse to break the rules is strongest, that is usually the moment you must be most careful to follow them.

Reflection - Holding The Line

When emotions cloud the mind, find the clarity to act authentically?

The line between protector and punisher is razor thin. But that line is everything.

Resisting Temptation

The temptation to become vengeance is natural; resisting it is moral work. Restraint isn't passivity - it's mastery. To hold back your hand when your heart burns for justice takes more courage than any act of violence.

Anger can destroy, or it can illuminate. Compassion doesn't excuse cruelty - it transforms it. Each time I resisted vengeance, I honoured not only the victim but also my own soul's integrity. In a profession built on confrontation, that's the real measure of strength.

Flames Of Deception

Evil doesn't always wear the mask of a monster. Sometimes it comes dressed as an ex-detective, a grieving partner, or someone who knows exactly how to use your trust against you. I learned that lesson the night I was called to a burning car in a quiet residential area.

By the time I arrived, the vehicle was fully engulfed, a furnace of twisted steel and fire. The air tasted of burning rubber and gasoline - bitter, chemical, alive. The heat pressed against my face, humming like an engine that refused to die. Beneath it all, the faint pop of cooling metal sounded almost like applause. Inside, strapped into the driver's seat, was the body of a man already gone, reduced to ash and bone. His seatbelt was still intact. The gas tank cap was open. I'd seen dozens of suicides in my career - I knew their rhythms, the grim variety of methods - but this didn't add up. Nobody douses their own car, buckles their seatbelt, and calmly sets themselves on fire. It reeked of staging, not despair.

When the flames died down, the air was filled with an unfamiliar odour – the scent of everything familiar turned strange. I peered into the wreck. In the back seat was a small handgun, charred but still intact. Had he shot himself after setting the fire? The theory collapsed the moment I pictured it. It was absurd. The scene radiated not just heat, but the restless, unsettled energy of a lie.

Then he arrived. A face I knew - not well, but enough. A former detective, the kind of man you'd once trust to have your back on a case. He introduced himself as the victim's best friend, collapsing into noisy grief. He clutched a chain-link fence, rattling it while wailing "*Why? Why?*" with the performance of a man who wanted every eye on him. Too emotional, too loud, too theatrical. I wasn't buying it.

While his colleagues - his former colleagues - hovered around, I scanned the perimeter. Down the slope of a nearby embankment, I spotted a plastic fuel canister. Carefully, I retrieved it, preserving it as evidence. "*Preserve this can, there may be prints on it,*" I told the lead investigator. But before the scene could be properly locked down, the grieving "*friend*" strolled over, picked it up in plain sight, and casually announced, "*Oh just so you know I touched this, so my prints are going to be on it".* His voice cracked just enough to sound convincing. No experienced ex-investigator makes a rookie mistake like that. In that instant, I knew: that I was standing in the presence of a murderer. He had intentionally destroyed a vital piece of evidence, and he knew exactly what he was doing to derail the case.

The mask slipped, just for a second. I saw the calculation beneath the tears. He was too comfortable, too knowing. And then came the wife. Her performance was different - guarded, quieter, more restrained - but still something off. She cried, but the tears didn't match the display. I watched them embrace, two actors in the same play, and felt the cold certainty of betrayal hanging in the smoke.

The autopsy confirmed what my instincts already told me. The victim hadn't died by fire. He had been shot, and the weapon found was unregistered. Odd, considering he already had a legal firearm at home. But an ex-detective would have access to "*spare*" guns - confiscated, never logged, kept for moments just like this.

I pressed my concerns with the lead investigator weeks later. He agreed: nobody siphons gas, douses a car, straps themselves in, and then shoots themselves in the head. It was a murder dressed up as suicide, clumsy but covered by familiarity and timing. Still, without forensics, without surveillance, without the tools we now take for granted - cell tower dumps, DNA databases, security cameras - we were stuck.

And so, they got away with it.

It is one of the few cases that still sits on my shoulders. Not because of the gore or the shock, but because of the betrayal. A wife, who should have been a sanctuary, turned conspirator. A former detective, who once wore the same badge I carried, turned predator. Betrayal is its own kind of evil, worse than violence from a stranger. It is intimate, personal, corrosive.

I carry that case not because I failed to work it - I did everything I could with the tools available - but because it taught me a brutal truth: not every story has closure. Justice is not a guarantee. Sometimes, evil gets away with murder.

I had to learn to live with that. To trust that reckoning exists beyond my reach. To keep faith with my intuition, which had screamed the truth to me long before the evidence could. And to carry on doing the work, even knowing that some cases will remain ashes in the wind.

Reflection - Betrayal's Shadow

Some wounds heal, but betrayal lingers.

It burns slower, deeper - because it's personal.

The Weight Of Unfinished Stories

Some cases close in the courtroom. Others close only in your gut. This was one of the latter. Standing in the heat of that burned-out car, I realized that intuition is often more honest than appearances. It won't always be enough to convict, but it will always tell you where to look, who to question, and when to stay wary.

Betrayal cuts deeper than violence. A stranger's cruelty wounds the body, but a friend's treachery wounds the soul. That's what I felt at that scene - the deep fracture that comes when trust itself is weaponized. And maybe that's why the case lingers: because it wasn't just about a man murdered, it was about the bonds of loyalty burned alongside him.

Not every story ends with justice. Some end with silence, with unfinished files, with killers who slip through the cracks. The temptation is to let bitterness take root, to let that shadow grow. But the harder path - the one that has kept me steady - is this: accept that closure is a luxury, not a certainty. Justice is not always ours to deliver.

What remains in our hands is discipline, honesty, and the memory of the dead. I couldn't give that man his justice, but I could give him my truth: I knew what had been done, even if the courts never said it. And sometimes, naming the betrayal is its own form of witness.

Reflection - The Protector's Prayer

Let me act with courage, but not cruelty.
Let me see truth, but not lose compassion.
Let me protect, but never harden.
And when the fire comes again, let me remember -
it can destroy, or it can cleanse.

Chapter VI

Flames Of Betrayal

When I first joined the police, I recall a statement posted on the noticeboard as an example for new recruits to admire. Beside it was a letter from the Attorney General to the Station Commissioner, congratulating a Constable Jean Marc for what he claimed was the best written police statement he had ever read in his career.

Jean Marc was only about three years our senior. I had the privilege of partnering with him on numerous shifts, and he became a mentor to me. It was from Jean Marc that I learned the art of writing a police statement - clear, detailed, professional.

He was high potential. A short, dark-featured, good-looking man's man, with effortless charisma. Women loved him, and his motorcycle didn't hurt his cause. It was said that pretty girls loved bad boys, but Jean Marc wasn't really a bad boy - not in those days. He was kind, fun, and magnetic. We partied together, and our friendship carried through those early years.

Then came the news: Jean Marc had gotten a barmaid pregnant. They barely knew each other, but he was determined to do "*the right thing*." He told me he didn't want his child to grow up the way he had. So he married her. We threw him a bachelor's party worthy of the occasion, and I stood with him at his wedding.

He rose through the ranks. Promoted to Sergeant, then to the detective branch. From time to time, he'd sign out cases at the station, and we'd reminisce about the old days. His little boy was now a toddler, and Jean Marc seemed to embrace fatherhood with surprising tenderness. I remember being struck by how affectionate he was, how naturally he seemed to take to being a dad.

And then, darkness descended.

The Unthinkable

The accusation arrived like a punch to the chest: he had allegedly abused his partner's two young children when they were left in his care. I was stunned. Surely not Jean Marc. I wanted to see the evidence. He was suspended and charged. My wife and I bumped into him in a mall not long after. He was apologetic, insistent it was all a misunderstanding, certain the truth would come out in court. My world closed in around me that day, restricting my breathing. The air felt heavier, thick with something unsaid. My pulse was loud in my ears - the sound of a truth I wasn't ready to hear.

But the truth that did come out was darker than I could have imagined. Jean Marc was convicted of sexual abuse - not only of those children, but of his own son. Repeatedly. He remained on bail awaiting sentencing, and I was left speechless. How had I missed this? How could the man I had admired, learned from, partied with - my friend - be a predator?

Days later came another call. An adult had exposed himself to children outside a nearby school. My colleagues responded, gathered a witness, and went looking for the suspect. They found him sitting at a bus stop. It was Jean Marc.

He was arrested and begged not to be detained at his old precinct. He didn't want to face the humiliation of being processed where he was once respected. They agreed and left him locked in the back of a police van. When they returned, he had managed to hang himself with his shoelaces - an almost impossible feat in such a confined space, and yet, there he was.

The Shattered Mirror

I struggled to process it. I had once worked with the very first Child Abuse Unit in South Africa - the precursor to what later became Child Protection Units across the country. We were young, eager, and determined to expose hidden crimes. I still recall running surveillance on known offenders, photographing them, gathering evidence. I remember the father who burned his newborn's skin with cigarettes, and how deeply it affected me. I knew then I could never have the restraint to serve in that unit long term. My rage toward those crimes was too great.

And now here it was, not in the shadows of society, but standing before me in the face of a man I knew. A friend. A mentor.

The betrayal was staggering. Different from the betrayal of a wife and lover conspiring to murder her husband - that was cold, calculated, and intimate in its own way. But this - this was personal. I couldn't dismiss it as greed or lust or a crime of passion. I was forced to face the horrifying truth that even people I trusted, people I admired, could be living a lie so dark it poisoned everything around them.

I couldn't bring myself to hate Jean Marc. What I felt was sorrow. Sorrow that he carried a sickness that had no cure, sorrow that he had hidden it behind his charm and intelligence, sorrow for the children whose lives were scarred by it. And sorrow for the part of me that had to confront this lesson: evil doesn't always wear the face of the stranger. Sometimes it wears the face of a friend.

The legacy Jean Marc once carried was erased in an instant. The statement that had once been celebrated and pinned proudly on the notice board was quietly removed, as if to deny it had ever existed. His name was no longer spoken with admiration, but in hushed tones over late-night drinks - not as an example to follow, but as a cautionary tale of how quickly trust, respect, and promise can be shattered.

The Betrayal That Cuts Deepest

This betrayal was different. Flames of Deception showed me murder born of greed and hidden desire - evil wearing the mask of passion. But Jean Marc's story was soul-level treachery. It wasn't about strangers or lovers. It was about friendship. Trust. Brotherhood.

The lesson it left me with was sobering. Sometimes the deepest betrayals come not from enemies, but from those we call friends. Sometimes evil wears the mask of laughter shared, of lessons taught, of nights spent side by side. And when the mask falls, we are left not only with anger at their crimes, but with a wound inside ourselves - the wound of questioning our own judgment.

I had to accept that no amount of intuition can pierce every mask. Sometimes the predator hides in plain sight, shielded by the love and loyalty we give them. And when that happens, the only way forward is not to drown in anger, but to acknowledge the sickness, protect the innocent, and let go of the illusion of who we thought they were.

Jean Marc's betrayal reminded me of this: trust is sacred, and when broken, it doesn't just shatter the bond - it reshapes the one who trusted.

Some betrayals destroy illusions. Others refine intuition.

Either way - they change the way you see the world forever.

Reflection - The Fire of Trust

Has anyone ever betrayed your trust?

Have you forgiven them, or allowed the betrayal to live rent-free in your heart?

What did that betrayal teach you about discernment, about your own light?

The Cop, The Witch and the Broomstick

I recall lighter stories that still bring a smile to my face - moments of foolishness that, even then, held filaments of wisdom that would return to solve a murder many years later.

Mrs. O was straight out of central casting for one of Macbeth's witches. Barely five feet tall, an unredeemable alcoholic in her seventies, she was combative, foul-mouthed, and disheveled. She lived alone in a small house that resembled a hovel straight out of Hansel and Gretel. To fund her drinking, she rented out rooms to vagrants and fought constantly with her neighbours. At the station, we'd draw straws to see who'd handle her complaints - they always involved rambling, incoherent explanations and an invitation to sit on her flea-infested couch.

One day she was at it again. Her neighbours called to report her screaming abuse in the street. We reluctantly secured her in the police van and brought her to the station. My partner Michael - who remains a close friend to this day - was on duty. Mike was an excellent cop with a mischievous streak. When bored, he'd sing the Gummy Bears theme song just to irritate us.

It was early Sunday morning when I arrived with my "present" for him - someone to keep him company. Feeling sorry for her, we let her sober up in the charge office instead of the cells.

It didn't take long before conflict erupted. Mike glanced at the greasy nest on her head and said, "I love what you've done with your hair." That single comment lit the fuse. What followed was a masterclass in profanity - and before long, Mrs. O had hurled not only abuse but DNA at Michael before bolting from the station.

Michael, enraged, grabbed a broom and chased after her, shouting, "Come back, you filthy witch!" Down the road he ran after this wizened old woman, screaming uncontrollably - until he froze. Staring in horror was a group of conservative Dutch Reformed parishioners emerging from their Sunday service, witnessing what appeared to be a young cop wielding a broom and chasing an elderly lady. Context and optics matter, I guess - but fortunately, this was before cell phones. Otherwise, that moment would have gone viral.

Sadly, a couple of years later, Mrs. O was found murdered - the suspect one of the vagrants she'd let sleep on her porch. There was no motive; she had nothing to steal. Perhaps her belligerence was the catalyst.

Dangerous Liaisons

More than a decade later, I was working at a different precinct, a hundred kilometres away, when I attended a troubling crime scene.

Mrs. M was in her sixties, living alone on a hillside we called the buffer zone. During apartheid, zoning laws placed Southeast Asian communities between white residential areas and black townships. Though the laws were repealed, the landscape remained eerily unchanged. The township had sprawled into her area, bringing with it elements of crime.

Like Mrs. O, Mrs. M was an alcoholic - troublesome, well-known to local police. Her only family was an autistic son in his thirties, who wandered aimlessly through the township. She was unemployed and rented out rooms to survive.

The moment I entered her house, my breath caught. The place was filthy, overturned - the walls painted with blood. Someone had fought for their life. Then I saw it: Mrs. M reduced to a half-naked pile of body parts, hacked apart with a machete. It was not just murder - it was enraged butchery.

After preserving the scene, I canvassed the area. No one would talk. On her dusty table, I noticed one clear rectangle where something had recently stood. The only missing item: a small black-and-white television.

Sitting alone in that chaos, I was overcome with the persistent thought of Mrs. O - the old witch Michael had chased with a broomstick. This time, the memory wasn't humorous. It was a whisper of intuition. The similarity wasn't in the victim or even the method, but in the circumstance of death. I trusted that feeling and began asking about tenants. One name stood out - "Michael."

Something stirred in me. Was the link to Mrs. O's case simply that she too had been killed by a tenant - or was my former partner's name a sign, a message from spirit, pointing me toward the murderer's identity?

I tracked the tenant, but he had vanished. With no witnesses, no record, and no motive, I could only wait for his fingerprints to one day surface if he reoffended. I felt defeated. In a world of headline-worthy tragedies, the brutal death of an impoverished woman drew little attention.

Yet, as I've come to learn, the universe has its own timing. Revelations arrive when your intuition whispers - if you're willing to listen.

The Universe Lends a Hand

*O*ver a year later, I was at home when the call came.

"Inspector, we've arrested someone who says he has information."

The man was a low-level burglar. In exchange for freedom, he'd give up details on a murderer. My jaw tightened when he said the name: Michael Majola. Apparently, he had hacked a woman to death with a machete - and yes, she had been his former landlady. My intuition had been dead on.

He confessed it wasn't Majola's first murder. Years earlier, he and his gang had invaded a home, tortured an old man and suffocated him to death with a plastic bag. I asked where to find him. "He's working as a gardener nearby," the informant said.

The next day, we arrested him - an ordinary-looking man, calm and thin, innocently sweeping leaves in a driveway. How could such frailty house such violence? When I showed him the crime scene photos, the mask fell. He knew the game was over.

I asked, “What did you do with her TV?”

Without hesitation, he replied, “I took it to my mother’s house.”

“Where’s that?”

“In the Transkei.”

Transkei was seven hours away. We had no time to lose before he had a change of heart. I assembled a team and drove through the night.

During the journey, he was quiet. To keep him cooperative, we gave him cigarettes and a burger - small kindnesses to sustain fragile truth.

In the rural village, I met his family before bringing him inside. They were simple, decent people. When I showed them the photos and told them what he’d done, they broke down in tears. They embraced their son, weeping in disbelief. In the corner of the room sat a small black-and-white television. His mother handed it over as if it were cursed - tainted by the horror it represented.

The Stillness After the Siren

After a nonstop thirty-two-hour investigation, I arrived home, exhausted but strangely calm. The suspect’s honesty had softened my anger. I was forced to face an unsettling truth - that even the most ordinary looking souls can carry extraordinary darkness.

At my gate, I paused to gather myself. The night was still - a tranquility so complete it felt alive. And in that stillness, I sensed a presence beside me, as if the universe itself whispered, “You did good.”

Peace, I realized, doesn’t always come after justice. Sometimes it arrives *in spite of it*. The badge taught me procedure; the streets taught me truth. But it was the silence afterward that taught me who I was becoming.

The stillness didn't erase the pain I'd seen, but it showed me that beneath every human cry lies a silence large enough to hold it. Later, I would call that silence God - or grace - or simply the breath I'd been ignoring all my life.

And maybe that's the lesson: that the universe doesn't speak in thunder, but in whispers; not in the clamor of pursuit, but in the hush that follows - where truth, and mercy, finally meet.

Reflection - After the Stillness

Looking back, I've come to see that none of it was random. It's strange how the people we pity most often reveal the truth about ourselves - that the broken are rarely beyond repair; sometimes, they're the ones holding the map back to wholeness.

I used to believe that police work was all about evidence - the things you can measure and prove. But there are moments when logic runs out, and all that's left is the whisper of spirit. That's when intuition steps forward, asking you to trust what the mind can't explain. I've learned that truth doesn't always arrive through the front door; sometimes it drifts in quietly, carried by something unseen, waiting for you to notice.

Over time, compassion became both my weakness and my strength. I thought it would empty me, but instead it filled me - each act of mercy seemed to replenish what the world had drained away. I came to understand that feeling deeply isn't a liability in this work; it's proof that you're still alive. Every small kindness circles back, and even in failure, there's a kind of grace that refuses to vanish.

I also learned that redemption doesn't always come through justice - sometimes it comes through presence. Simply staying with the wounded, the guilty, the grieving, without turning away. Not everything can be fixed, but everything deserves to be witnessed. Justice may balance the scales, but presence heals the soul - it's the quiet courage to stand in another's darkness until the light shifts.

And through it all, I stopped seeing the universe as indifferent. It was never silent; it was speaking in coincidences, in timing, in the stillness after the siren. Maybe grace isn't earned at all - maybe it's just recognized when we finally grow still enough to feel it. Peace doesn't arrive as a prize for what we've done; it comes as a soft confirmation that the work - and the authenticity behind it truly mattered.

So now I listen differently. To the pauses between sirens. To the breath between questions. To the silence that follows violence and somehow holds it all. Because beneath the noise, I've come to believe there's a single enduring truth: that every life touches another, that even the absurd has its purpose, and that love, when it finds us again, is never new - it's simply the next verse in the song the universe has been singing all along.

Chapter VII

Breath Returned

There are miracles too. A four-year-old Bongi - the son of a domestic worker - fell into a swimming pool and was pulled out by his granny after fifteen minutes. I held the lifeless child, inverted him to clear water, began CPR, and he started to breathe. He made a full recovery with no brain damage. A year later I saved my own eighteen-month-old son from drowning in a friend's pool - a collision of emotions, disbelief and triumph. Witnessing your child suspended between worlds - that image never leaves you.

Even today, water carries two meanings for me: life, and the terrifying nearness of loss. I learned that day that fatherhood sharpens fear into something almost sacred - a fierce awareness of how quickly a world can break, and how miraculous it is when it doesn't.

By then, I'd learned that survival wasn't always explained by training or luck. Sometimes there's a current moving through life that defies explanation, something bigger than breath itself.

Embers of Change

South Africa stood at the edge of history - filled with hope for rebirth and haunted by fear of collapse. As the first democratic election approached, the air was charged with uncertainty. The ANC had been unbanned, Nelson Mandela had been released from prison, and for the first time the possibility of real change stood before us.

Would this mean civil war? Would the fragile constitution endure? Could reconciliation be more than words? I was cautiously optimistic, but my skepticism ran deep. I had seen the weapons caches, the violence that scarred our streets, and the Soviet and Cuban influence on the resistance. My head whispered caution; my heart longed for a miracle.

And then, by chance, I met the man himself.

One evening, dining with my wife, Mandela appeared in the restaurant after a speaking engagement. He moved calmly among the tables, shaking hands with patrons, cooks, and waiters alike. He was flanked not by enemies, but by bodyguards who once would have hunted him.

The myth became the man before my eyes. He was older, ordinary, and yet extraordinary all at once. He carried peace the way some people carry perfume - you felt it before you named it. His charisma was quiet, not forced - the kind that settled something deep inside you. In that moment, I felt hope take root.

In that brief encounter, something quiet shifted inside me. Not because Mandela was famous, but because he embodied a kind of peace I had never known - the kind forged through suffering, not in spite of it. I remember thinking: If a man who survived so much could carry this much gentleness, then maybe there was hope for the rest of us too.

Mandela went on to win the election and guide South Africa back from the brink. He was called Madiba, father of the nation. But leaders of that caliber are rare. As the years passed, the honeymoon faded. Funds were scarce, dreams went unmet, crime soared, and unemployment reached staggering heights. The miracle became fragile.

I served eleven years under Mandela and Thabo Mbeki. I witnessed the shift from military-style policing to a new, democratic service. At first there was camaraderie - the sense of being part of history in the making. But soon, ambition and tribalism eroded it. "*Everyone has your back*" became "*everyone for themself.*"

That miracle of the "*first supper*" turned into a "*last supper.*" Police lunches divided into cliques. Veteran officers left for the private sector, draining the force of experience. Smaller precincts struggled with staff and vehicle shortages. Response times lagged. Private security and medical services became the lifeline of ordinary citizens.

The light of a fledgling democracy began to flicker, This was an opportunity lost.

A nation can survive many storms. A family cannot survive the slow erosion of hope. And so, a question formed quietly inside me - not out of fear, but out of love: What future am I handing to my child?

Reflection - In The Glow

What embers still glow in the ashes of your past?
Which of them call you now, asking to be breathed into flame again?

When the Dead Spoke

In 2002 I investigated one of the strangest, most meaningful cases of my career - a case that reached beyond the visible world.

Greg was a town planner and an active member of neighbourhood watch. After a break-in at his home, he followed a trail of stolen goods into the nature reserve with a neighbour and elected to wait in the dark to catch the thieves. The neighbour left: Greg stayed. Hours later Greg was ambushed and shot multiple times.

We processed a scene that offered little: some property, a TV with potential prints, no eyewitnesses. I did something some police would call unwise - I told Greg's wife Jenny I'd find the killers. It felt like the right thing to say.

We worked informers and offered rewards for information to hundreds of people. Two names surfaced: one was a known hitman I'd arrested before; the other was a local man, Sibongiseni M, whose name tugged at my memory. We had only whispers. My wife, sensing my unease that night, pushed me to call Verna - a psychic I'd known through hypnotherapy training. I was skeptical, but I called.

What she told me stunned me: Greg was speaking through her, she said. Three suspects - two men and a fourteen-year-old boy. She said Greg had fought back and cut the shooter's eyebrow, leaving a gash. She mentioned a white van. I wrote everything down.

At the midnight briefing I repeated her words. A few laughed. We went anyway. After hours of searching and canvassing, we found ourselves at Phumlani's house (Phumlani was the brother of a man I'd arrested years before) - and there, parked outside, was the white van. We made entry into several houses until, in the early hours, we pulled a blanket off a sleeping figure: Sibongiseni. A bag next to him held a CZ 75 9mm pistol. Under the streetlight his left eyebrow bore an infected gash. I asked him, "*How did you get that*?" He said, with a chilling casualness, "*I got it fighting with the boss when I killed him.*" He admitted there had been three of them; one was fourteen and had been used to carry the stolen goods.

Forensics tied the pistol to the killing. We had a confession. I kept my promise to Jenny and sat at the front of Greg's funeral with a complicated ache of satisfaction and loss.

But the courts are messy. At trial Sibongiseni withdrew his confession. His lawyers argued self-defense - that Greg had attacked him, and he'd shot in fear. The judge acquitted him of murder. He was, however, convicted on a weapons charge and sentenced to fifteen years, largely because of his criminal history. He served eleven years and was released. Years after I emigrated to Canada, a mate visiting me told a story about a home invasion in my old neighbourhood, where a husband was shot in bed and the wife forced to load stolen goods. When I looked the case up later, the shooter was Sibongiseni. The case that had haunted me had resurfaced - 11 years later and thousands of miles away.

The Unseen Thread

There's one more twist. Over a decade later, Verna contacted me out of the blue after a reading for a stranger. She'd connected with the spirit of a young man killed in a restaurant shooting - the man turned out to be Greg's nephew. Greg came through too, and he wanted to thank me.

Here's something I never put into an official file: I did not record Verna's involvement in any statement or the criminal case file. I knew that introducing psychic testimony would have tainted the proceedings and undermined the investigation. To the system, Verna never existed. To me - and to Greg's family - her message shaped the pursuit of justice.

When the lab confirmed the ballistics, I felt vindicated and unsettled. I had always trusted evidence. Yet the improbable details from an unlikely source had led us to a man with blood on his hands. The world, apparently, permits mysteries and spirit holds truths beyond our earthly comprehension.

I sat down and wept. I cried for Greg and for the strange sense that life and death are threaded together in ways I don't fully understand. It would take years to trace how all the pieces connected - the promise to a widow, a dogged informer, a psychic on a phone, the lab results, and a friend telling me a story across an ocean. In time I came to believe that Greg nudged events from the other side - sharpening my attention, pushing for closure.

One day I'll have that beer with Greg if they serve beer in the afterlife. It had better be cold.

I have placed a detailed version of this case in the Appendix.

Verna

But there is someone else I know I will sit down with on the other side. I had planned to contact Verna to tell her that I was writing this book and that her story would be included. I wanted to send her an advance copy to honour her and to thank her for being the silent spiritual teacher who opened my heart and mind to the possibility of life after death.

Sadly, when I went online, I discovered that Verna had passed away. And so, I want to draw attention to what truly allowed me to call her that night.

When I first met Verna, she was a highly respected hypnotherapist - at the time, I believe she was the chairperson of the South African Association of Hypnotherapists. I learned a great deal from her about the subject, but something far deeper stirred inside me from the moment we met. I was overcome by a sense of love – a very unfamiliar and magnetic feeling. My soul opened to her, and I was consumed by a state of peace and love that I could not explain. I know now that my soul was being enriched by the sheer energy of unconditional love, something I had never experienced before.

She began speaking about past lives, and the police officer in me immediately thought, "*Oh no - here we go. This person is a bit out there.*" Yet I listened with an open, yet skeptical, mind. Then she turned to me and said, "Malcolm - your higher self is standing right behind you."

I thought to myself, "*What nonsense*," and replied politely, "*Oh, that's nice.*" She then looked directly through me and said calmly, "*You know it is there, because you felt it. It feels like a shiver, as though someone has walked over your grave. I saw it touch you - you felt it.*"

I was stunned. I had indeed felt a huge shiver but had never shown it. That was something I could not explain.

Later, she told me that my father, who had passed away, wanted to know why I had not put batteries in his clock. Years before, after a burglary, the suspects had taken a relatively inexpensive peach marble clock my father had given me for my twenty-first birthday - a year before he fell down the stairs and broke his neck. That clock was obviously important to him, and it was the only thing I had left of his memory. For context, I often forgot to put batteries in it, so it never told the correct time. Apparently, this was my father's way of coming through with information only I would know.

I also met a lovely young lady that Verna proudly introduced as Sharon, her miracle child. I felt a similar friendly energy, a familiarity, as if we had crossed paths in a previous life. But I said nothing for fear of being ridiculed. Still, I believe these souls knew mine.

Looking back on this spiritual catalyst and absolute angel who crossed my path, I know it was no accident. When I ask spirit for answers, I am overcome with the feeling that I was blessed to have met one of heaven's special angels. She lived life fully and practiced what she preached. I cannot recall her exact age, but she was older, and her husband knew exactly what would delight her on her birthday: a bucket-list experience in a fighter jet. Most people at that age might choose a quiet night of bingo, but not Verna - a trip in a military fighter jet was far more her style.

When my wife pressed me to call Verna that night, I was curious to hear what she might say. But the thought of asking her whether I was going to die that night held me back. In the end, I gave in to the possibility and called her - and thank God I did. It was another gift, another verifiable incident that I will take to my grave. Over drinks with friends, I often share this experience to open others to the secret wonders that await us on the other side.

I only wish I had kept in regular contact with Verna and told her what an inspiration it was to have known her. If there is someone in your life who is growing older, let them know. Remind them of the memories they have created and the legacy they leave behind in the hearts of those they have touched. Let them carry that knowledge with them when they go.

If there is one truth I now carry without hesitation, it is this: nothing we love is ever lost - only transformed, waiting for us in a place where the fire no longer burns.

Reflection - The Teacher Beyond the Uniform

Most of my wisdom has been gained through adversity - the lessons I learned from Verna were learned with grace and joyfulness. Her memory will always occupy a special place in my heart.

She was a special angel who taught me that the unseen is as real as evidence, and that sometimes the truest justice begins when the heart finally believes in something greater than proof.

But there is one final lesson drawn from our collaboration: *Love unspoken becomes regret. Gratitude expressed becomes legacy.*

JC: The Devil's Couple

I could write an entire book about him, but in this volume, he serves as a lesson in extremes - the magnetism of danger, and the cost of being fascinated by it.

They called him JC. He arrived in our world like a movie-star apparition: French charm, a private jet, a Ferrari he expected others to admire, and stories that smelled like the scripts he'd hint at writing. JC said he co-created reality police TV; he talked about weapons companies in France and diamond mines in far-off places. He told the kind of tall tales that make a skeptical man listen twice: half show, half confession. He loved to be surrounded by admirers, but he had a private loneliness that he wore like an expensive watch - visible, valuable, and hollow.

He courted danger for sport. He'd fly down to visit, take us out on jet skis, wine us in the best hotels, and open conversations with impossible questions about where the line sits between a cop and a killer. When a man like JC says that the difference is intent, you listen - not because he's wise, but because he invites you into the dark. There was a thrill to knowing someone who lived on the edge - and a recoil beneath the thrill I felt as clearly as my heartbeat.

He had a wife - a pale, quiet woman – a doctor from Germany - who accompanied him to dinners like a shadow. She rarely spoke, and that silence was part of the act: perfect contrast to his spectacle. He had the trappings of wealth and the posture of a self-made man. I was not impressed by the glitter; I was wary of the other things he never said.

JC asked favours. Would I buy a pistol for him in my name? Would I consider a loan to make an investment? He pushed, then schemed, then laughed it away. I declined the risky offers with a flatness he didn't expect. I was, after all, a cop who knew the weight of choices. I also saw the way his talk of glory masked a man who had learned to perform power rather than be governed by it.

When the truth later came out, it was worse than any of his stories. JC was not merely a fabulist; he and his partner were part of a dark reality. Accusations mounted - fraud, conning businessmen, and a violent trajectory that ended in murder and a life on the run. The glamorous images were quickly replaced by headlines I wish I had never read. The woman whose delicate hands once poured wine at our table was later known in court files as part of the "*Devil's Couple*." Their glamour was a façade stitched from other people's losses.

I remember sitting on my own porch with him, sharing long, philosophical conversations that now read like auditions. He delighted in being believed. He relished proof he could control the narrative. But there were moments he showed something softer - a man who said he had no true friends because money made people turn. Perhaps he felt isolated by his own manipulation. Perhaps that was the kernel of truth in his performance.

When he fled, when his stories turned from bright to brutal, I exhaled with gratitude that I had kept my distance from the things that mattered: the gun, the loan, and the conveniences that would have entangled me. That restraint kept my life on the path I chose - to protect the innocent, not to be seduced by a dangerous idea of being untouchable.

Years later, I saw photos of his arrest: a man once sleek and defiant, now diminished - older, thinner, a face chastened by consequence. He had become the caricature his bravado always promised to make him. The Ferrari was gone. The jet was gone. What remained was a silence that said: everything taken eventually has a price.

The lesson sits with me the way all extremes do: power without accountability decays into harm. I'm glad I met him on my terms - curious, sure, but not complicit. In the ledger of my life, his entry is a warning, not a trophy.

There is a strange magnetism in darkness. JC embodied everything I was not, yet for a time our lives intersected. Looking back, I realize it wasn't admiration that bound me to him. It was a mirror - a glimpse of what I might have become had I chosen differently. Protectors are always walking that thin line: between power and corruption, between service and self-interest. In seeing him clearly, I saw myself more clearly too. Fascination ended where wisdom began.

I have placed a detailed account of this encounter in the Appendix.

Reflection – The Broken Mirror

Who in your life has shown you a version of yourself you didn't want to become?

What did that mirror teach you about power, choice, and restraint?

Farewell to the Fire

After three long years of waiting for our Canadian immigration application to come through, the confirmation finally arrived. We gleefully ripped open the letter and read it together - we were about to become Canadians.

We began dismantling our life piece by piece. We sold the house ourselves. Then the cars, furniture and the small things - the ones you don't realize hold so much memory until you are forced to let them go. The house we had built with love turned into a showroom of memories on auction. Every sale felt like betrayal. We left only our beds so we would not have to sleep on the bare floor. The house felt ghostly. It was ours, but it no longer belonged to us. We were squatters in our own home, wandering from room to room like strangers.

It broke our hearts to part with material things we had cherished. We received so little money for them it felt almost insulting – cherished memories, bartered away for a handful of worthless coins. Yet even as our hands trembled with grief, our hearts beat with a cautious hope. We were terrified but determined, telling ourselves repeatedly that this upheaval was for our son, for his future, for a life without the shadow of violence.

The Last Three Signs

But confirmation, I have learned, rarely comes just once. It comes in threes.

The First Sign: One morning, while burning garden refuse in the back yard - I saw a man walking up along the side of my fence. Immediately, something in my gut tightened. He was not there to ask for sugar or directions. He was hunting.

He beckoned me toward the fence. I had lived in South Africa long enough to know this was a trap. Either he was luring me away from the house, or someone else was already circling around the other side.

I shouted in Zulu, my voice rough with adrenaline, "Ufunani"? (What do you want)

"Ngifuna umsebenzi," he replied. (I want a job)

I told him there was no work. He kept calling, his hand curling in a gesture for me to come closer. Then, without warning, he began to climb the fence in my direction.

I had seconds. I was unarmed. My three-year-old son was inside, watching television with the front door wide open. All I could think of was to focus on keeping him safe and getting my weapon.

I sprinted to the house, slammed the door, locked it, and screamed for my boy to lie down and not move. Then I raced upstairs for my pistol.

I went back outside in time to see the man jump back over the fence and run. I fired a single warning shot, and he disappeared in the bushes. I called the police and gave a description.

Thirty minutes later, sirens howled on the other side of the road. The K9 unit were chasing a suspect in the bushes after another attempted break-in. It was the same man.

That was the first sign.

The Second Sign: Days later, my wife had her own experience that galvanized her decision. On her last day at work, sitting at a red light, she watched the car in front of her hijacked at gunpoint. Just like that. Broad daylight. Life and death measured in inches.

We spoke late into the night after that. We knew, in our bones, we were making the right choice. But people always say - things happen in threes. And so, it did.

The Third Sign: A few nights later, we awoke in a panic - a creaking sound of twisting aluminum echoed downstairs as our garage door was forced open. The alarm sounded – entry had been gained. My service pistol had already been returned. I was unarmed. Even the kitchen knives had been sold, a wink and a smile would be inadequate tools to defend my family. We pressed the panic button for the private security armed response. The suspects fled into the night.

It was like an exhale of fate. That was the moment we decided: enough. The last two nights in our home country we spent in a small bed-and-breakfast near the police station, our life in three suitcases- stacked at the door, our son asleep between us.

Sometimes survival means staying. Sometimes survival means leaving everything you love.

A Final Farewell

Then, at last, the flight. I sat at the window, staring down as the country of my birth shrank beneath the wings of the plane. Hills and highways, rivers and rooftops - a tapestry of danger - a patchwork of beauty and brutality, of home and hurt. You could never tell from up there how much blood had seeped into that soil. In my mind, I saw the headline the local paper had written about me before my departure: *"Highway Superhero Leaves for Distant Shores."*

I smiled at the irony. I was no superhero. Just a man who had seen enough fire to know when it was time to walk away from it.

And in that moment, I knew the truth. I was not just leaving one country for another. I was stepping across an invisible threshold - from one lifetime into another. Carrying the fire of my old life with me, yes, but also saying goodbye to it forever. Leaving meant surrendering the role of protector I had worn like armor. It meant learning to live without a gun under my pillow. It meant trusting that peace was not weakness.

As parents, we carry both the weight of what we leave behind and the quiet, stubborn hope of what lies ahead. And though we walked away from the fire, from the heat of a country we once called home, we carried its embers with us - not as a burden, but as a reminder: we did not leave because we stopped loving it. We left because we loved our son more.

Reflection – The Extra Heavy Baggage Pass

What have you had to walk away from - not because you stopped loving it, but because staying would have cost too much of your soul?

Chapter VIII

Crossing the Threshold

Leaving your homeland doesn't happen at the airport - it happens in the heart. It is the quiet burial of an old life, and the trembling birth of another. When I stepped onto that plane, I couldn't see the road ahead, but something inside me knew I was crossing far more than a border.

We left South Africa with three suitcases, our life savings, and a fragile dream. The money, once converted into Canadian dollars, looked pitifully small. We rented a modest semi-detached house and bought a second-hand minivan that swallowed much of what little we had.

I thought I understood hardship - I had faced gunmen, corruption, and death. But nothing prepared me for the slow erosion of dignity that comes when you cannot provide. There is a special kind of despair that comes not from danger, but from irrelevance - from watching your skills, your identity, your worth evaporate in a land where nobody knows your name. New beginnings, as I learned, can feel oddly like endings.

Canada was safe, yes, but strange. I found myself fumbling through the smallest tasks. At the gas station, I proudly pumped fuel into my car for the first time in my life. In South Africa, labour had been cheap - one never touched the pump, and to remain inside your vehicle was also a survival tactic against hijackings. Now, standing in the crisp Canadian air, I felt oddly powerful.

The card reader asked me if I wanted a discounted car wash. "*Yes,*" I thought, grinning at this little luxury. But after circling the station twice, I could not find the wash. I walked back inside, sheepishly clutching the receipt. "*I bought a car wash,*" I explained, "*but I can't find it.*" The attendant shrugged: "*Oh, we don't have one here.*" I looked for the hidden camera. Surely, this was a joke. It wasn't. Welcome to Canada.

There were many such moments: the overpriced, half-done car washes where I demanded a cloth to dry the droplets; the confusion over local slang; the pride that kept us from applying for assistance, even as our bank balance thinned to desperation.

My wife, once a senior biologist in South Africa, took an entry-level administrative job. She accepted work her boss dumped on her gratefully - better to be burdened than unemployed. I, on the other hand, began applying for anything: cashier, dog walker, industrial cleaner. Who would hire an immigrant with SWAT and Counter-Terrorism training to walk their dog?

It was humbling - and profoundly humiliating.

I walked into job "*interviews*" that turned out to be scams: door-to-door alarm sales disguised as "*security management*" roles; strike-breaking work advertised as "*investigations.*" My lowest point came when I applied for a bouncer job. Dressed in a suit and tie, résumé in hand, I sat across from a manager with cocaine dust on his nostrils. He looked me up and down and sneered: "*So, are you a tough guy? Can you growl?*"

I stared at him. "*Like a dog?*"

"*Yes. I'm being serious – Growl for me.*"

I shook my head. "*No. I don't bark.*"

The interview ended there. But the humiliation lingered. My mother-in-law had driven me. I climbed into her car, swallowing the lump in my throat, holding back tears I refused to let fall. I had fought men with knives and guns - and here I was, defeated by a question.

Four months in, the money was gone. Rent was borrowed from my in-laws. And I, who had once been a protector of the innocent, a man of courage and authority, felt reduced to nothing.

I spiraled into depression. Not the chemical kind, but the kind forged by hopelessness. I was humble – when people called me a hero, I knew it was true, but I always dismissed it, never truly appreciating the difficult and dangerous circumstances that allowed me to perform heroic deeds. How could all that eroded in a few months? I had spiralled into a darkness, robbing me of all self worth - there was only one means of escape. I forced myself to go through the motions - an hour applying for jobs I didn't believe I'd get - before collapsing back into bed, disappearing beneath the blankets. Sleep became my refuge, my anesthesia, the only place where existence didn't ache. It was peace, or something close to dying without the finality.

One day I surrendered to the darkness and despair. I wrote letters to my wife and son. I made a CD of songs that would play after I was gone. "*Wherever You Will Go*" by The Calling. "*One Last Breath*" by Creed. I planned my death with the same calm precision I once planned operations. As I write these words, I am reminded of those lyrics that played in my head like a tragic prophecy.

But despair is a liar. And love has a louder voice.

I broke down and confessed my plans to my wife. We wept together, not just for what we'd lost, but for what we still had. I remembered that young boy I had once held, comforting him after his father's suicide. I could not put my son in that same darkness.

Days later, I received a call. A hotel offered me a security job. Not glamorous, not prestigious - but it was hope. I took it, humbled, grateful, still broken, but alive.

Every morning, I endured three-hour commutes in dress shoes through the snow: walk, train, subway, walk again. My feet froze, my spirit cracked, but I endured. Eventually, I bought a small car. The journey shortened, but the lesson didn't: survival isn't just about courage under fire. It's about courage under failure.

And then, unexpectedly, something stirred inside me - for the first time since landing in Canada, I felt the fire of my purpose return.

Celebrity Protector

The hotel job was not just a job. It was a doorway - one that reintroduced me to the role I was born into: protector.

Celebrities passed through daily. I had seen fame from afar, but here it was up close: the smiles, the egos, the fragility behind the glamour. Some were genuinely kind, greeting staff with warmth. Others, consumed by their reflection, treated people as props when the cameras weren't rolling.

I kept my professional silence. No autographs. No photos. No stories. Just watchfulness. Just service.

One pop icon teased me about my hairstyle and complimented me on my accent. Another smiled across the lobby in a way that momentarily patched my wounded ego. Then there were the difficult ones: the singer who demanded attention like oxygen, the starlet who escaped her security detail for the thrill of being recognized in public. Fame, I realized, could be a prison with velvet ropes.

But the encounter that cut the deepest was with a band I adored. I had every one of their records, their guitar riffs etched into my soul. When they arrived, I was starstruck. They were down-to-earth, friendly - but the lead guitarist, my idol, was absent.

He arrived later, clutching a bottle of wine he finished before the elevator doors even opened. The next night I escorted the band after their concert, and they broke into an impromptu a cappella of one of their biggest hits. Just me, them, and the song - a private performance I will never forget. But again, no lead.

Later, he came staggering in later, fragile, lost in addiction, hiding pain behind the bravado of fame. He was not the hero I had imagined. He was just a man fighting the same familiar demons. In the restaurant, ripped jeans, slurred words, cigarette dangling. I asked him politely not to smoke indoors, and he stubbed it out in a flowerpot. A sad gesture, almost symbolic - beauty smothered by ashes. Fans swarmed, cameras poised. Without thinking, I stepped in, shielding him from humiliation. I wrapped my arm around him, his frail body leaning into mine, and guided him quietly to his room. That night, I was his protector. Not with guns or SWAT tactics - but with compassion.

It was then I realized: protection is not about status. It's about soul. It's about being the steady presence when someone else is unraveling. Even stripped of my weapons, my badge, and my uniform, I was still what I had always been: a protector.

He has since passed on. They say he found sobriety before the end. I hope so. Maybe one day, in whatever comes after this life, I will finally ask him for his autograph.

For me, that night was enough.

Reflection – Redefining Protection

True protection is not measured by the uniform you wear,
but by the moments you choose compassion over judgment.

Political Protector

After the hotel job, I spent 6 years as a Director of Facilities at Canada's second largest convention centre - absorbing every scrap of knowledge and gaining valuable Canadian experience and regaining my credibility. But the universe conspired again - this time pulling me into the orbit of politics.

At first, it was small: helping to plan security for a political convention. I wasn't there to impress, only to apply the instincts and discipline forged through years of service. I mapped vulnerabilities, neutralized risks, and ensured there were no ambushes, no ugly surprises.

It was noticed.

A kind man in his sixties, DG, approached me afterward. He was gracious, observant, and I had no idea of the influence he held. He thanked me warmly, and we shared a genuine connection. What I didn't realize was that he had already begun drawing me into a role far larger than I could have imagined.

A few months later, my phone rang. DG's voice was warm but serious: "*I've been trying to retire. The Prime Minister won't let me until I find a successor. I believe that person is you.*"

I was stunned. *Me? Head of security for the Prime Minister of Canada?* I had gone from a man rejected for jobs as a dog-walker, to being asked to protect the leader of a nation. The irony was dizzying. My mind flashed back to the cocaine-snorting nightclub manager who once demanded I "*growl like a dog.*" Now here I was, entrusted with the safety of the highest office in the land.

The owner of the convention centre told me to go and pursue my dream and if I decided to return, my job would be waiting for me.

The role was intoxicating. Meetings with law enforcement. Venue sweeps. Flying ahead of the PM to assess risks. Watching as luggage, buses, and even planes were methodically searched before every move. And always, the quiet pressure of keeping the leader of a nation one step ahead of danger. Every moment a reminder that vigilance is both an art and a burden.

I would be there as he entered venues, catching his eye and smile which said – *we got this* - not for recognition, but for the silent nod protectors share with those they serve. I wasn't there to be seen. I was there to be invisible, steady, and unyielding.

And yet, beneath the pride, doubt stirred. DG warned me: "*During my time with a former Prime Minister, I missed most of my child's life.*" His words lodged in me like a seed of unease. I had already sacrificed much for duty. Was I willing to sacrifice my family too?

Sleepless nights followed. My sense of duty wrestled with my sense of purpose. One morning, exhausted and clear-eyed, I made my choice. I picked up the phone and told DG I couldn't continue. It broke my heart to step away, but my soul whispered that this was not my path.

I still remember my last detail: standing close to the PM as he walked onstage. An RCMP officer whispered to his superior, "*Who's that guy*?" The reply came in a hushed tone: "*That's the Prime Minister's new head of security.*" For a brief moment, respect radiated from those words - and I smiled quietly.

I walked away with no medals, no photographs, no fame. Just the memory of being trusted at the highest level, and the clarity that even the grandest stage is meaningless if it costs your family.

That truth became my compass.

Reflection - When Presence Trumps Ego

Is success worth more than your presence?
The world may remember what you built,
but your family will remember whether you were there to hold them.

Government Protector

Walking away from a role protecting the nation's leader felt like pulling a plug on part of myself. The invitation had been intoxicating - a sign, perhaps, that I still mattered - and yet the quiet truth I carried in my chest was louder: whatever glory the job might bring, it would cost me the thing I'd learned to cherish most - my family.

I returned to my job to the delight of the owner and shortly after that decision, the universe nudged me again. My first boss - the one who had been my guardian angel when I needed work most - called to say there was a civil service post advertised. It was a long commute, and I wondered whether the juice was worth the squeeze. I said no. Then he called again. Strange how persistence sounds like destiny. I applied. Out of hundreds, I was chosen.

The contrast of private sector and civil service was an extreme. It would become a doorway, giving me stability, a pension, and the space to rebuild. The department had problems: unions snarled like brambles and entitlement had hollowed out morale. It needed someone who would lead by presence more than by proclamation.

I set about doing the practical things that actually lift people: show up, listen, be accountable, notice the quiet performers, and call out the disruptors with fairness. I learned the power of a well-timed compliment and the quiet authority of someone whose word equals action. Slowly, cynicism softened. People began to trust that this office wasn't just another place to hide poor behaviour.

From Shadows to Substance

There are victories we celebrate out loud, and there are others that never make the history books - the ones that live only in our own conscience. My time protecting political power reminded me that sometimes the highest stages aren't meant for us, even when they're within reach. It also revealed something deeper: leadership is not about standing closest to authority, but about standing true to your values. That lesson would echo louder in the years to come, shaping how I chose to lead and how I chose to live.

Lessons in Leadership

When a consultant's 360 survey landed on my desk, the numbers stunned me. The average score across management was under fifty percent. My score was in the nineties. The consultant eagerly wanted to know my secret. I was flattered and humbled but at the time I struggled to articulate - I was simply being the product of my life's experiences. Now I have a clearer language for it.

Leadership Is:

- **Not restricted to managers**. Leadership begins with how you carry yourself, every day, whether or not you hold a title. It is about leading by example, showing others the way - through your own actions.
- **Actively listening.** True leaders quiet their own judgments, biases, and filters to truly hear what is being said - and sometimes, what is left unsaid.
- **Turning every interaction into an opportunity.** Even the smallest exchange can be shaped by empathy, accountability, transparency, and authenticity.
- **Earning trust daily.** Credibility is everything, and it is built in the quiet consistency of your actions, not in grand speeches or promises.
- **Lifting others.** Your success is not measured by titles or possessions, but by the people you have lifted, the courage you have shown, the culture you have shaped, and the values you have lived.
- **Mentorship that outlives you.** Every word, every choice, every act of guidance leaves an imprint. The leaders you mentor today will carry pieces of your wisdom into tomorrow.

- **Openness and presence.** Leadership is knowing your people - their strengths, their weaknesses, and their humanity - and making space for them to grow.
- **Celebrating and correcting.** Taking the time to acknowledge a job well done matters as much as having the courage to give constructive feedback. And when needed, to look in the mirror and give yourself the same.
- **Humility as strength.** Leadership is not about being flawless. It is about owning mistakes, learning from them, and modeling that vulnerability is not weakness - it is growth.
- **Consistency under pressure.** Anyone can look composed when things are easy. Real leadership shows itself when chaos arrives, when others look to you for calm and steadiness.
- **Courage in decision-making.** Leaders are often called to make difficult, unpopular choices. The measure of a leader is whether those choices align with their values and protect the greater good.
- **Protecting the vulnerable.** Leadership is not about power. It is about using whatever strength you have, to shield those who cannot shield themselves. Sometimes leadership is simply standing in the gap.
- **Vision and hope.** Leaders don't just manage the present - they point toward a better future, even when the path is unclear. They help others believe it is worth walking toward.

A memory sticks. A junior colleague emailed me one frantic morning asking for a complex deliverable by noon. I was juggling eighteen-hour days and felt the world pressing in. I fired back an email – Help me understand, this request has a 48-hour lead time, and you are asking me to deliver it in one hour? After reading it, apparently she burst into tears. She'd looked up to me; my curt reply felt like betrayal. I called her, explained my day, heard her fear, and apologised. We laughed later, and she still works with me now - stronger and more confident. Leadership isn't earned in the roar; it's sustained in the quiet fixes.

That job lasted years and gave me something I'd almost forgotten: the capacity to breathe. I was no longer constantly bracing for chaos. Instead, I had the bandwidth to mentor, to take risks that were not life-or-death, and to plant seeds in younger people who would one day lead. That, more than any medal or commendation, felt like redemption.

The Mirror of Leadership

I once thought leadership was reserved for titles, uniforms, and command structures. Experience taught me otherwise.

True leadership begins quietly - in the daily choice to listen before speaking, to act with integrity even when no one is watching, to lift someone else when you yourself are weary. It is tested most when our patience runs out, when the easy answer is anger, and when others look to us with unspoken expectation.

In those moments, leadership becomes less about the role we hold and more about the reflection in the mirror.

Fools Rush In

There's a well-known television series called What Would You Do? In it, unsuspecting members of the public are faced with staged moral dilemmas while hidden cameras roll. The question is always the same: will they step in, or will they walk away?

For me, there's never been much of a question. The answer is always clear. I've never been able to shake the "Protector" instinct in me. It's part of who I am.

Years ago, my wife called me from her nail salon just before closing. Two suspicious-looking men had walked in as they were cashing up, and something about them didn't sit right with her. Without thinking, I jumped in the car and drove straight there. I walked in, stood right beside them, and waited for them to make a move.

Looking back, it was a thoroughly stupid thing to do. I didn't call the police - because, in my mind, I was the person people called. My mere presence seemed to be enough. They asked for a flyer and walked out.

To this day, I shake my head at what could have happened. But the truth is, I simply cannot avoid being who I am. That guardian impulse has a mind of its own.

A few years later, that same instinct nearly got me killed - this time, trying to save a child in distress.

We were on a family getaway at Deerhurst in Muskoka, sitting comfortably in our deck chairs by the lake. Even while relaxing, my eyes were scanning the water. Old habits die hard - especially after years living in South Africa, where peace can so quickly turn to danger.

Then I saw him: a young boy, alone on a paddle board, too far out into the lake. He was waving frantically, silently calling for help. No one else seemed to notice. From where he was, no one would hear his cries. He had minutes, maybe less, before he fell off the board and drowned.

I shot up from my chair, threw off my shirt - revealing a well-concealed dad bod and a one-pack that I had cultivated in recent years - and sprinted toward the water – but not with the agility of the fit, SWAT trained earlier version of myself.

"Go get help!" I shouted to my son, pointing toward the bystanders. "There's a kid drowning! Find a lifeguard!"

My commands were met with blank stares. No movement. No action. Just silence. In that moment, I knew: I was his only hope. He was not going to get the heroic Kevin Costner from *The Guardian* – his saviour would carry a pot belly with a heart just as large – running on instinct and adrenaline.

I dove into the water and began swimming with everything I had. Stroke after stroke, pushing hard - he was clearly further away than I had anticipated. I was only halfway there when I was hit with a sobering reality.

I was out of shape. I was exhausted. And I was drunk!

In my haste to be the rescuer, I had forgotten a minor detail: I had already consumed three-quarters of a bottle of rum and coke.

Bravery and common sense, as I learned that day, don't always swim together. But the heart wants what the heart wants.

With my lungs burning and muscles aching, I made a quick assessment. I had just enough energy left to tread water calmly. Panic wouldn't help anyone - not me, and certainly not the boy.

After a few agonizing minutes, an inflatable rescue boat arrived. Ironically, they reached me first. As they pulled me into the boat, I looked at them, completely spent, and muttered one of my classic one-liners:

"It seemed like a good idea at the time."

We quickly reached the boy, who, though clearly shaken, was wearing a life jacket - a small detail I had failed to notice from shore. I helped him into the boat and asked if he was okay. He looked at me like I had arrived from another planet. He had no idea who I was, nor that I had just risked my life - inebriated and underprepared - to save the life of a stranger.

When we arrived at the shoreline, he ran straight to his parents. Not a word was said to me. No thank you. No nod of appreciation. Nothing.

I remember thinking, *What a cheek.* If someone had done that for my child, I would have hugged them and bought them a drink - or at least offered a handshake. But there were no words of gratitude that day.

I collapsed back into my folding chair, panting like a dehydrated dog, and looked at my wife.

"Pour me a double, honey."

My family knew what had just happened. They saw the whole thing. I sat there, drained and dazed, finishing the rest of that bottle, shaking my head in disbelief at the events - at myself, and my foolish recklessness.

Sometimes, we cannot change the core of who we are. That guardian instinct - it's not something I can turn off, even if it puts me at risk, or makes me look like a moron.

But next time - yes, there will be a next time - I'll pause. I'll make sure I am fully capable before diving in headfirst.

Still, I know this: even when I am 80 years old, I will be the idiot who stands up, steps in, and tries to make a difference. Because, for better or worse, that is who I am.

Your soul's unique identity is not searchable online; it is defined by our daily actions; one choice, one scar, and one act of courage at a time. Courage isn't the absence of fear – in the moment, it's simply the decision that something else matters more. In this case, it was the life of a stranger's son.

Reflection – Taking the Plunge

There are parts of us that never retire.
The world still needs its protectors -
even if their bodies are slower,
their courage still runs fast.

Chapter IX

Faith in the Fire

Wrestling with God and Evil

There comes a point in every journey when stories of survival are not enough. When the questions turn inward, demanding answers that no courtroom or battlefield can provide. I had faced criminals, loss, and death - but the hardest adversary was the silence of God.

The mind recalls echoes the soul has buried in silence. During my years in the police, I bore witness to scenes too horrific to fully capture in words. Evil in its rawest form - parents abusing babies, a mentor revealed as a pedophile who ended his life in the back of a police van, an elderly man whose eyelids were cut off and who was forced to watch the rape of his wife. These images seared themselves into me, each one forcing me to confront the same unyielding question:

What kind of God allows this?

Religious leaders often lean on well-worn phrases: *It's God's plan. Have faith. All will be revealed in time*. Spiritual teachers may frame it differently, *saying souls enter into agreements to play the roles of victim and perpetrator, so that higher lessons can be learned*. To me, both explanations felt like intellectual shortcuts. They diminished the suffering of innocents, wrapping human agony in ribbons of doctrine.

I remember one of my first calls: a head-on collision between a Porsche and another car. Both occupants died instantly. They were newlyweds, the bride still in her gown as if frozen in a cruel parody of a fairy tale. How do you reconcile that with "*God's plan*"?

I believe this: people have *free will*. Evil acts are choices, not destiny. Accidents are products of negligence, bad timing, or sheer misfortune. And yet the outcomes - the pain, the loss - are real. It is not the events themselves that define us, but what we do in the aftermath. How we hold the pain, how we carry the weight, how we transmute suffering into resilience.

I cannot pretend to love the murderer, the abuser, the destroyer of innocence. My faith does not stretch that far. What I do hope is that such souls, before they are allowed to enter the peace of eternity, must endure a reckoning - a life review where they feel the devastation they caused. Perhaps then justice and mercy intertwine.

As a boy, I would often demand answers of God. *Why are we here? What is our purpose? What do you want me to do?* And the silence was deafening. Priests told me not to be a "*Doubting Thomas*." I taught Sunday school, played my part, but inside I was restless.

It felt as though God had placed me into a taxi with no destination, no map, and no driver. Just blind faith that the ride would get me where I needed to go. I couldn't accept that. So, I did what I was trained to do: I opened an investigation. The case of my life.

Some truths arrive not in textbooks or sermons, but in whispers carried by experience. I did not discover the meaning of life in a church pew or under the words of philosophers. I found it in the cracks between despair and resilience, in the echoes of my own spirit asking: *Why am I here?*

But not all guidance comes in words. Some truths arrive as a feeling that refuses to leave.

Healing Intuition

I have two lovely Rottweilers. The male, Mr. Shenzi, is a 160-pound specimen of power and loyalty. He is loving in his own way; a dutiful protector and cuddle-bunny rolled into one. But then there is Bella.

Some animals are more than companions; they are sacred gifts from God. Bella is mine. I always wanted a daughter, and spirit delivered her in the form of a bundle of black-and-tan fur with a small white mark on her chest - heaven's way of making sure I noticed her. We share a soul connection. She follows me everywhere, my shadow with four legs. If I leave the house, she sits for hours at the front door, waiting. No human being is capable of showing that level of love and devotion.

Bella became the catalyst for one of the greatest shifts in my life: moving to a three-acre property, reigniting my love for nature and the environment, and creating the sanctuary that now sustains me. She is the epitome of extremes - a bundle of pure love who will transform into a fierce protector if I give the command. She knows how to tap the door when she wants to go out, the cupboard when she wants her ball, and her food bowl when she's hungry. Every day she brings joy to my family, and every day she reminds me of what unconditional devotion looks like.

So, imagine my despair when Bella began to waste away before my eyes. Her muscles faded, her weight dropped, she struggled to walk, and she couldn't keep food down. The vet was perplexed and eventually diagnosed her with an autoimmune disorder - her body was attacking itself. High doses of steroids followed, but Bella's condition worsened. She was desperately holding on to life, her spirit still fierce, but her body betraying her.

Then came the cancer drugs, designed to suppress the immune reaction. They dulled the symptoms but left me with a dog who was only a shadow of herself. Thousands of dollars spent, countless tests, and still no clarity. Her diagnosis - "*protein-losing enteropathy*" - felt like a death sentence. The vet warned she might last a year, but the medication, costing $1,300 a month, would destroy her organs in the process.

I couldn't accept that. Not for Bella. Not for my daughter in fur.

So, in the silence of my sanctuary, I asked God for help. I sat quietly, still, asking my higher self to guide me. And what came to me wasn't words, but a *knowing.* A deep, insistent sense that this was not only her immune system at all - it was her pancreas. When I told the vet, he dismissed me outright. I left that office determined never to return.

If no one would save Bella, then I would.

With my wife beside me, we began to investigate the case like detectives - this time not for the courts, but for the beating heart of our family. We stripped her diet down to essentials. Out went the animal protein that seemed to spark her body's revolt. In came pea protein, easy to digest and unlikely to trigger rejection. We added coconut oil, metabolized differently from other fats, sparing the pancreas. We kept carbs limited. I began administering B12 injections to combat anemia and introduced small, carefully measured doses of probiotics.

It was not a miracle that happened overnight. But in the weeks that followed, Bella's health was restored. Her weight and strength returned. Her sparkle returned. She was no longer a fading shadow - she was herself again.

My intuition had been right all along: her body could not process animal protein or traditional fats. When those were removed, her body healed. Today she takes only a tiny residual dose of steroids, costing pennies a month, and she thrives.

I may never have been smart enough to pass medical school. But I learned something more important: when you listen deeply - to spirit, to intuition, to the silent wisdom within - answers arrive. I realized I no longer needed a badge to be a protector. In saving Bella, I protected the one who had so often protected me. Her heartbeat is proof that love listens louder than logic.

Every day I look at her, my Princess Bella, and I give thanks. She is alive. She is well. And she illuminates my heart in ways no human could ever measure.

Reflection – Your Inner Voice

Sometimes God answers through instinct.

The whisper you doubt may be the miracle you asked for.

Protecting the Protector

Bella's story is not just about veterinary science. It is about listening - really listening - when the world dismisses you. It is about the way love sharpens intuition and how the bond between souls can reveal truths that logic alone cannot.

Intuition is not guessing; it is wisdom whispered from a deeper place. Trust it, especially when everything rational has failed.

Love gives us courage to do what we might otherwise doubt ourselves capable of. Without Bella, I may have ignored that inner voice.

Protectors need protecting, too. The ones who guard us, whether human or animal, deserve our fiercest devotion when they are at their weakest.

Healing is not always found in textbooks or tests; sometimes it is found in presence, patience, and the courage to follow what feels true.

In Bella's healing, I was reminded of my own: that devotion and trust, when acted upon, can bring us back from the brink. Sometimes the greatest case you ever solve is the one that saves the heartbeat beside your own.

There's a strange irony in life: often the very lessons we think we are here to teach turn back on us. Bella reminded me that protecting the vulnerable is a sacred duty - but soon I would be forced to look at my own vulnerability in the mirror. What happens when the protector himself becomes frail? When the one who has always carried others suddenly has to carry the weight of his own broken body? The universe, in its relentless way of balancing extremes, was about to show me that strength is not always measured in muscle or in how many lives you can shield, but in how many times you can choose to rise again when everything inside you wants to stay down.

Strength Defined

For years, I struggled with my back. About seven years ago, it finally gave way, and I collapsed in excruciating pain. This wasn't the usual pinch from twisting too far or sleeping wrong. This was different - nerve pain that set my body on fire, a relentless agony that stole my breath and left me unable to stand.

Surgery or paralysis were the options - an extensive back reconstruction with an 80% chance of success. Unfortunately, I fell into the other 20%.

I could walk again, yes, but with permanent limitations. What I once took for granted was gone.

I used to be strong - not just average strong, but the kind that turned heads. Six-foot-two, 280 pounds. I remember one night at work when a massive roll of industrial carpet was left blocking an entrance an hour before an event. Normally, a forklift would move it, but the staff had gone home. Six custodians tried to lift it - but it didn't budge. The carpet had to move, so I told them to line up three on each side, load it onto my back, and I carried it thirty meters, step by grinding step.

Another director walked by, shook his head, and muttered, "F-ck, that's impressive."

I hold onto that memory now - not out of vanity, but as a reminder of the strength I once wore like a second skin.

But life has a cruel way of balancing the scales. The man who once carried a carpet on his shoulders now bends slowly, carefully, painfully, just to put on socks. Wiping myself involves a daily ritual of awkward, cruel contortion. The spasms hit before I'm even out of bed, and for a while I just lie there, often tearing up. Then the inner voice kicks in: Get up. Move. One foot in front of the other. That's how I begin each day.

Some call it misfortune - and yes, it is. The pain drains me, and I mask it with humor. But this isn't just bad luck; it's a choice life has handed me. Every morning, I stand at the same crossroads: Do I get up, or do I give up?

For me now, strength isn't the power to knock someone out cold or to carry impossible weight. It's the stubbornness to rise each day, to refuse victimhood, to give what I can, and to resist collapsing into self-pity.

And just in case I missed the spiritual memo, life threw another punch.

Last year, long COVID hit hard - swelling in the brain and optic nerve, uncontrolled inflammation, bleeding behind the retinal nerve. Then, suddenly, permanent blindness in my right eye. One day I was watching television; the next, half the screen went dark forever.

Adjusting was brutal. Depth perception vanished in a world suddenly two-dimensional. Driving became a calculated effort; low light a hazard; headlights, blinding. I tripped over furniture, grocery store displays - even my poor dogs. It was clumsy, humiliating, and infuriating. Yet each time the doctors ruled out another fear - no tumor, no multiple sclerosis, no giant cell arteritis - I felt relief. Every "no" was a gift, even if the blindness was irreversible.

And again, clarity found me. Yes, I lost half my sight - but I still have the other half. I can still write, work, garden, marvel at flowers, hear music, play with Bella and Shenzi, laugh with my family. I am not fully blind, and for that, I give thanks.

Strangely, I think I see more clearly now than ever before. Strength, I've learned, isn't measured in how much weight a man can carry or how many enemies he can face down. Strength is found in the grit to face your limits, the gratitude to find blessings where others see only loss, and the courage to keep moving forward when standing still would be easier.

What I lost in muscle and sight, I gained in understanding - that strength was never about what I could lift, but what I could carry within.

Redefining Strength

Strength is not what I once thought it was. It isn't the roar of muscle or the applause of the impressed. Those are moments, not definitions.

True strength lives in quieter places. It's waking up broken and still choosing to rise. It's laughing through pain, so your coworkers see light instead of despair. It's accepting loss without surrendering identity.

And sometimes, it's realizing that while your sight has dimmed, your vision of life has sharpened.

Reflection – When Darkness Calls

Perhaps God never promised to spare us the fire.
He promised to stand in it with us -
until we learn to see light even through the smoke.

The Garden In The Dark

After the diagnosis, I began walking in the garden at night.

I wanted to learn the contours of darkness - to see what my eyes could not. The air carried the scent of lilac and pine, and each calculated step on uneven ground, became an act of trust.

At first, I felt only frustration. The world I had commanded for decades was suddenly fragile; even a curb or root felt like a threat. Then one evening, I stopped fighting the shadows and simply stood still. The wind moved through the leaves, and something inside me whispered, "You are not losing sight - you are learning to see differently."

In that moment the garden came alive, not with images but with presence: treads of sound woven through stillness, air trembling with birdsong, leaves rustling through the poplars like thousands of tiny hands applauding. Everything was part of one vast heartbeat. I realized my work had never been about controlling the world, but participating in it - listening until the quiet spoke back.

The blindness hadn't come to punish me. It had come to slow me down enough to witness what vision alone could never reveal.

To understand where you're going, life sometimes asks you to look back at where you came from. Our ancestors leave more than names; they leave questions. Some linger like whispers, others like wounds. To understand myself, I had to walk back into a story written long before mine began.

Chapter X

Lesson from the Family Tree

I had always been curious about my forefathers, so at one point I began an investigation into the past - digging through censuses, records, and fragments of memory to unearth the family story. Part of me wanted to know whether there were skeletons rattling in the tree, or whether any noble legacies had been passed down the line.

On the positive side, I found no slave owners in my lineage. That gave me some relief. But on the flipside - well, let's just say no Nobel Prize winners either.

My great-great-grandfather appeared on a census in Hertfordshire in the 1800s. He married a farmer's daughter - not uncommon in those days when most families lived off the land. When she died of illness, he married her sister and remained on the farm, raising a few children of his own. One of those sons later married and fathered two boys.

Those two sons - my great-grandfather and his brother - decided to emigrate to South Africa together and start a business. The venture failed. With the Anglo-Boer War looming, both men fled back to the UK to avoid serving. And in that act of self-preservation, my great-grandfather abandoned his wife and seven children.

Years later, he surfaced again in another South African census in a neighboring town, having returned after the war. There was no evidence he ever reunited with his wife, nor that he remarried. He simply reappeared - a man who had severed the thread of his own family line.

My grandfather, whom I never met, was the only one of those children to finish high school. Against the odds, he became an architect, and apparently even designed a famous bridge. He married his secretary, fathered my aunt and my father - and then died young, in his fifties. That left my father with no choice but to quit school and work in a printing press to support the family.

I paused on this story for a long time. What struck me was the consequence of my great-grandfather's choices. His act of cowardice - fleeing responsibility, abandoning his wife and children - had sentenced his lineage to poverty. His failure in business and family duty didn't just scar his own life. It shaped the lives of every descendant that followed.

And yet, here I was. Here my brother was. My brother built a highly successful business. I chose a life of service and bravery. Somewhere along the line, the cycle had begun to shift.

It made me wonder. Were we reincarnated souls of our forefathers, come back to repair the damage they had caused? Or were we living proof that we are not doomed to repeat their failures - that we can carry the baggage, examine it, and then lay it down?

Maybe the answer is both. Maybe cycles break when one generation refuses to bow to them.

One day, perhaps, I will meet the grandfather I never knew, and the others who came before. And if I do, I hope they will see me clearly: the man who did not run, who did not abandon, who kept his commitments and his marriage of more than three decades intact. If legacy is measured in anything, let it be in the courage to choose differently.

The Weight of Inheritance

Family trees are not just branches of names and dates. They are chains of choices - some brave, some selfish, some unfinished. We inherit more than DNA; we inherit patterns, wounds, and debts unpaid. Sometimes we repeat them. Sometimes we break them.

It is tempting to believe we are bound by the actions of our ancestors, but the truth is far more liberating: we are not their sins. We are not their cowardice. We are not their failures. What we inherit is not destiny, but opportunity. The opportunity to see what was broken, and to choose differently.

Reflection – Broken Branches and Clean Slates

Strength is not about surviving pain and loss. Sometimes it is this: looking at the lineage that shaped you and deciding, the chain ends here.
That is how cycles close and new legacies are created.

Thanksgiving

Some of you reading this may think, my goodness, what a catalogue of misfortune. Believe me - if there had been more carefree times that taught me lessons, I would have surely shouted them from the rooftops. But as I look back, I don't see a string of misfortunes - I see opportunities for personal growth. This isn't about being thankful for "*the good*" or "*the bad*." It's about learning to be grateful. Period.

When you live in a state of want, your soul twists itself into knots. You become restless, jealous, resentful. That is not who your soul is - so don't give that energy power. Gratitude is the opposite. Gratitude is fuel for the soul. It expands you. That's why you get a warm, lifted feeling when you practice it, and a tense, uneasy feeling in your stomach when you don't.

We make a mistake thinking Thanksgiving is just once a year - an awkward dinner where everyone prays the relatives don't talk politics. Thanksgiving should be five minutes carved out of every single day. You don't need a turkey or a tablecloth. You can do it silently while driving to work, or lying in the bath, or even while watching your dog snore on the floor. Gratitude isn't a ritual. It's a rhythm.

Here are some of the things I am grateful for:

- **I am grateful to be alive.** I cheated death too many times to count. It took me too long to appreciate the life force I had been given, but I see it now.
- **I am grateful for my health** - not perfect, but still mine. For the one good eye that allows me to see beauty. For the body that still lets me work, garden, drive, and play.
- **I am grateful for the Creator** - the source that comforts and guides me daily.
- **I am grateful for adversity** - those extreme moments that forced me to decide who I am and who I want to be.
- **I am grateful for stillness and solitude**, for the way they open a channel to wisdom I can't reach through the noise.
- **I am grateful for my family**. Thirty-two years of marriage and still walking side by side through storms.
- **I am grateful for my dogs** - my angels, my shadows, my companions.
- **I am grateful for my bosses**, past and present, who believed in me even when I didn't believe in myself.

- **I am grateful for my career** - for the chance to protect, to serve, and to grow into a different kind of protector later in life.
- **I am grateful for my sharpness of mind** - for the choice to endure pain rather than dull myself with narcotics. My body may falter, but my mind is still sharp and free.
- **I am grateful even for the pain**, because it forces me to rise each day and choose life again.
- **I am grateful for my ability to speak from the heart** - raw, unfiltered, with truth, credibility and emotions that often bring grown men to tears.
- **I am grateful for humour** - my secret bridge to survival. It kept me human when the world tried to make me hard.
- **I am grateful for music** - the soundtrack to my life, the comfort when words failed me.
- **I am grateful for my garden** - my Eden, carved out of vision, sweat, and soil. Each corner whispers peace back into me and grounds me to nature's energy – a place where my body will return when my soul ascends.
- **I am grateful for safety** - to live in a place without war, without venomous snakes at my feet or intruders at my door.
- **I am grateful for my car** - my Mercedes AMG, sleek and powerful. I treat it like an old man behind the wheel, but every time I see it, I remember the days I walked in snow without a cent to my name. It is more than metal. It is proof of what was overcome.

When my wife asks what I want for Christmas or my birthday, my answer is the same: "*Nothing.*" At first, it sounds boring. But in truth, it says everything. It says I am content. I love my gadgets, my music room, my car, my house - but I don't need more. That kind of contentment is worth more than anything you can buy.

And yet, I think of the monks in Tibet, who live with nothing. No cars, no widescreen TVs, no gardens. Just stillness. At first glance, it feels over the top. But who am I to judge? If they can be grateful with nothing, perhaps that is the purest lesson of all. My life is not more meaningful than theirs, nor theirs than mine. Meaning comes from living it fully, with gratitude and humility, no matter the trappings.

So here is my challenge to you: make your own gratitude list. Write it down. Keep it somewhere safe. Add to it. Revisit it when life feels heavy. And be honest: is your list filled with things, or with truths? There's nothing wrong with being thankful for a car or a house - provided you know what it really represents.

For me, gratitude is not just a practice. It is a vibration. One of the highest a soul can reach, right alongside unconditional love. So let me leave you with this truth: happiness is not stumbled upon. It is built - through hard work, through wise decisions, through gratitude and acceptance. Write your list, read it back to yourself, and see what kind of soul you are building.

Because in the end, it's not what we have, but how we give thanks for it, that writes the story of our lives.

Reflection Exercise: Your Gratitude Ledger

Find a quiet moment - maybe in the car before work, in the garden, or just sitting on the edge of your bed. Take a notebook, a piece of scrap paper, or even the back of an envelope. The tool doesn't matter. The honesty does.

1. **Write "*I am grateful for…*" at the top of the page.**
   Don't overthink it. Let whatever rises come out. Maybe it's a person, maybe it's a moment, maybe it's something simple like a morning coffee.

2. **Push past the surface.**
   Once the obvious things are written, ask yourself: *Why does this matter to me? What does it represent?*
   For example, instead of just writing "*my car,*" maybe it's "*my car - because it reminds me how far I've come from walking in the snow with nothing.*"
3. **Balance the list.**
   Make sure it isn't only material. What about the people who shaped you, even in hardship? What about your inner qualities - humour, resilience, faith?
4. **Sit with it.**
   Read it back to yourself slowly. Notice the shift in your body as you do. Gratitude isn't only an idea - it's a vibration, and you'll feel it when you're aligned with it.
5. **Keep it alive.**
   Put the list somewhere you'll return to - a drawer, a journal, even taped to your wall. Add to it whenever life gives you another reminder of how much you already hold.

This simple practice doesn't erase pain or struggle. It reframes them. And maybe the simplest truth of all is this: gratitude is not the reward of a good life. Gratitude is the good life. Gratitude doesn't deny reality; it changes the way you carry it. And that can be the difference between a restless soul and a peaceful one.

Common Ground

If there's one thing my years of policing taught me, it's that people are never as simple as their labels. Discard the uniform, the faith, the accent, and you'll usually find someone with the same fears, the same hopes, the same love for their kids. This little experiment in conversation proved that to me again.

I grew up steeped in church ritual. I asked Father Ivor the big questions and his answers were perfunctory - the same puzzled look, the same "*have faith*" shrug. Later, rumours of inappropriate behaviour surfaced, and he was moved to another parish. It was a lesson that institutions can hide rot under nice pews.

From the start I'd been curious about where scripture itself came from. I wasn't trying to be clever - I was trying to make sense. The Bible, like all holy books, sits in history. It was compiled by people, influenced by politics and power, trimmed and translated across centuries. That bothered me less than the way people treated it as a club to beat anyone who dared to question.

So, when a devout contractor tried to convert me, I braced for argument. He came at me with verses, certainty dripping from every paragraph. I could have matched him with counter-arguments, but I chose a different approach. I set religion aside and steered the conversation toward practical things: kids on the streets, the collapsing schools, the violence that tore communities apart. I asked about his fears for his own children. Slowly, the hard edge of his certainty softened.

What surprised me most wasn't that we disagreed less than I expected - it was how quickly the noise fell away when we stopped trying to prove who was right. Two men from different races, backgrounds and religious beliefs could effortlessly find a middle path of decent common sense. We talked less about doctrine and more about our human experiences. We found shared outrage at what was being lost and shared ideas about what might help. The conversation turned from conversion to companionship.

That's when I understood the simple trick: remove the weapon of certainty and you'll find the person. Religion - like politics, becomes dangerous when it stops people from talking. Strip it down and what's left is usually the same basic humanity: fear, pride, regret, love for family, a wish to belong.

So, I practiced it more. I stopped trying to win debates and started looking for overlap. When people are paranoid that their identity is under attack, they defend it fiercely. But when you meet them where they're vulnerable - their kids, their work, their home - the defenses drop. You can disagree about metaphysics and still agree on how to get a rubbish bin emptied or a child into an afternoon program. Those small agreements matter. They are the scaffolding on which trust is built.

If the world is burning with division, the solution won't start at the podiums. It will start on porches, in small talks with tradesmen, at school gates and hospital waiting rooms where two people discover they want the same thing: safety for their children and a chance to sleep at night.

What this means, and what to do with it

This isn't a sermon about faith being wrong or right. It's a practical manual for staying human. You don't have to strip away your beliefs - keep them proud and whole - but don't let them be the first thing you place between yourself and another person.

When you meet someone whose beliefs jar you, try this: ask them one honest question that matters to them, not to your argument. Listen. Resist the urge to produce the clever retort. Find one area - education, safety, dignity, work - where you can nod and say, "*Yes, that matters*." That nod is more powerful than a lecture. It's a tiny bridge. Cross it.

We are told to fear our differences. I've learned to do the opposite: look for the small common thing and nurture it. That is where real change starts - not from the pulpit or the press release, but from the quiet, human work of recognizing someone else's pain and responding with a measure of decency.

If your faith leads you to kinder acts, then keep the faith. If your doubt leads you to harder questions, ask them with compassion. Either way, the test is simple: does what you believe make you more humane, or less? If it makes you more humane, you're on the right road. If it makes you less so, then maybe your highest duty is to simply "*change your mind*" and love the person in front of you.

Society

As a boy obsessed with superheroes, I used to ask myself what power I'd choose. Would I fly? Possess superhuman strength? Teleport through walls? For a while, I was convinced I wanted the mind - a super-brain. Imagine being able to answer any question, solve any problem instantly. That was my fantasy: Super-Brain. Especially for someone who only got the looks in the family.

Funny thing is, years later the world gave us something close to that dream. The internet arrived. Anyone, regardless of their intellectual capacity, could type a question into a box and pull an answer out of the ether in seconds. No more hours in libraries, buried in dusty books. Then phones put that power in our pockets. And now AI is building a path toward having that kind of super-brain at our fingertips - maybe one day directly inside our own heads.

But here's the twist: all that knowledge hasn't made us any wiser. If anything, it's made us lazy. We've become nations at war with each other, while our youth disappear into screens, numbed by games, mindless videos, and the empty pursuit of likes and followers. The tools of infinite learning are right there, yet too often they're used to consume noise instead of nurture growth.

Take something as simple as fixing a car. I remember when mechanics actually fixed things. They'd strip down a part, recondition it, and put it back together, good as new. Today, the part just gets swapped out. It's too much trouble, too costly, too inconvenient to think. Somewhere along the way, we lost the collective hunger to understand how things work. But real solutions come from understanding. So does invention.

I think of my brother at nineteen. No background in mechanics, no YouTube tutorials, no instant answers at the tap of a screen. He got hold of an engine diagram, pulled a car apart piece by piece, and rebuilt the entire engine. By hand. By thought. By sheer will.

Or myself at thirteen. All I wanted was to be a DJ, but I had no money for speakers. I remembered a lesson from school - necessity is the mother of invention - and I put it to the test. My mother drove me to A1 Radio, where I asked for a copy of a loudspeaker diagram. I saved every cent for cones, woofers, tweeters, wires, capacitors, and connectors. I borrowed a soldering iron. Piece by piece, I built my own system inside the shell of an old speaker box, complete with a bass reflex hole for resonance. And it worked. Not because I was a genius, but because I was hungry to learn, curious enough to try, and stubborn enough to see it through.

Now I ask myself: how far could today's youth go if they diverted their attention of social media and poured that same energy into invention, creation, or starting businesses that put food on other tables?

Technology has accelerated. Humanity hasn't. We can split atoms, transplant hearts, and send cameras to Mars, yet we still fall to division, violence, and the same tribal conflicts that scarred our ancestors. Progress without wisdom is no progress at all. But history teaches us that the rhythms of life are cycles. Adversity has a way of jolting us awake, of forcing unity where comfort breeds apathy. Maybe we've swung too far into distraction, and maybe the pendulum needs to swing back before our brilliance - both individual and collective - is revealed again.

Reflection - What Society Teaches Us

The tools we have today are extraordinary, but they are only tools. They amplify whatever state we're in. If we are lazy, they will fuel our laziness. If we are hungry to grow, they can accelerate that growth faster than any generation before us. The real superpower isn't technology. It's curiosity. It's the courage to learn, to build, to try when no one hands you the answers.

Society will always be a mirror - showing us both our decay and our potential. The challenge is to decide what reflection we're going to leave behind. Will we be the generation that drowned in distraction, or the one that turned noise into wisdom?

Chapter XI

A New Sanctuary of Extremes

Bella was the catalyst for moving to a three-acre property where she could run free, and where we could take a blank canvas and turn it into something beautiful. It had been 18 years since my last garden, and I was itching to transform this land into a place of peace. What began as weeds and patches of wild turned into a living, breathing sanctuary. It took thousands of plants and trees, meticulous study to restore indigenous vegetation, and careful planning to attract birds, rabbits, raptors, and all of God's creatures. The result was a biodiverse paradise - rolling lawns, rockeries, quiet reflection spaces, and even fairy gardens.

It is a garden of extremes. Bird-rich woodland edges seamlessly into manicured beds bursting with color and pollinators. Nature and nurture co-exist here, as if to remind me that life's beauty is found not in choosing one or the other, but in holding both together. But the cruel Canadian winters provide *another set of extremes* to marvel as the garden transforms from sticks to luscious beauty - buzzing with life in the Spring.

Our first week was a shock. We killed seven snakes. It was instinctive - after all, I was used to black mambas, puff adders, and spitting cobras. In South Africa, snakes were death sentences, not creatures to co-exist with. But this was Canada, and soon I learned they were harmless garter snakes, allies in keeping the mice, frogs, and chipmunks in check. Snakes are now welcome in my sanctuary. They still make me jump out of my skin, but instead of reaching for a weapon, I guide them gently out of reach of my Rottweilers, who don't have the benefit of Google to know the difference.

This garden has become my true refuge. Yes, it is the result of hard work, but it is more than that - it is my communion space with Spirit. Here, time can pause. I can sit and marvel at the stillness and the colors, the multitude of birds (sending out their tweets), and feel a reassuring sense of peace and wellbeing enveloping my soul.

And just because the trees and flowers cannot speak does not mean they do not communicate. Without sounding like I should be committed, I sense energy from them. Healthy trees emanate calm; diseased ones emit a faint unease. I don't hug them, but I'll admit, I sometimes speak words of encouragement. My spruces even have names: Spruce Willis, Spruce Wayne, Spruce Lee, Spruce Almighty, Spruce Springsteen, Spruce Hornsby, and, of course, Robert the Spruce. Please don't judge.

In many ways, I am their custodian. I defend them against invasive species. I can't reverse climate change, but I can honor this land - land once walked by Indigenous peoples - and leave it better than when I found it. Perhaps that will be part of my legacy: proof that passion and hard work can transform not just soil, but spirit.

You don't need three acres to find this peace. Gardening in any form teaches patience, responsibility, and humility. It pulls the mind away from the noise of life and grounds you in the sacred. Nelson Mandela often spoke of the peace he found in tending gardens during his incarceration. For me, too, gardening is more than a hobby - it is therapy, sanctuary, and prayer all at once.

When the Walls Tremble

For a time, I believed sanctuary was something you could build with your hands. A garden, a refuge, a fortress of trees and stone. And in many ways, it is. The work, the soil, the sweat - all of it creates a space that feels safe.

But no matter how carefully you design it, life has a way of sending storms that shake the very walls. Sometimes the intruder is outside the fence. Other times, it walks through the front door carrying your own last name.

That was the lesson I had to face next: the realization that the toughest battles are not always with criminals or strangers, but in the fragile space we call family.

The Test Within

Thus far, I have poured out the stories of my life hoping they carry some wisdom for you. But this one is harder. It is ongoing, unresolved, and raw. I share it not to expose, but to be honest - because life is not just about victories. Sometimes, it is about learning to stand in the storm with no umbrella or barefoot in the snow.

People once told me what a good father I would make. And when my son was born, I believed them. I still remember him as a little boy in a Spider-Man suit, shooting imaginary webs while I held him aloft. We shared a close bond, especially when my wife traveled for work. He was my shadow, my joy, and the little reflection of myself I never thought I'd have.

But at 22, his life changed in an instant. A car ran a red light, struck him, and left him with brain damage that altered everything. His memory and emotions were fractured. He became someone I barely recognized - filled with anger, depression, and addiction. Violence, property damage, and outbursts strained our marriage and turned our sanctuary into a living nightmare.

My fatherly instinct was to discipline, to call out behavior. But I learned quickly that anger met with anger only destroyed us further. I had to learn silence, restraint, and strategies I never imagined I would need in my own home. Neighbors sometimes hear shouting. My mute button gets a workout during virtual meetings. Every day requires adaptation and patience that tests the core of who I am.

We focus now on guiding him toward small goals, crumbs of purpose in a life marked by struggle. And I reflect daily: *Why him? Why us?* But I also know this is his path to walk, and ours to support. We are, strangely, well-prepared - two parents with the financial means and the resilience to carry him when he cannot carry himself.

It feels like a cycle repeating. Earlier in my life, sanctuary was destroyed by criminals and chaos. Now, the invasion has come from within my own family. Perhaps this is the true test - not whether I can build a garden or a fortress, but whether I can build sanctuary inside myself. A safe place that no outburst can destroy, no addiction can shake, no pain can uproot.

One day, this external garden will belong to someone else. But the inner sanctuary I build now will live on in my soul. My lesson from the family tree still echoes: break the cycle, do not abandon, even when it hurts. And perhaps the deepest test of all is this: can I still choose love, even when love is the hardest choice left?

Sanctuary Redefined

There's a bizarre irony in the word sanctuary. We think of it as a place outside of us - a garden, a church, a home, a retreat. And yet, sooner or later, life will send storms that breach the walls. A snake in the grass, a betrayal from a friend, or even the struggle of your own child can dismantle what you thought was safe.

What I see now is that sanctuary is not about walls or fences, not even three acres of Eden. True sanctuary is the one you construct within your own soul. It is the discipline to stay standing when everything around you trembles. It is the choice to keep tending the garden of love, even when the weeds of anger or grief grow thick.

We cannot always control the outer landscape, but we can decide what seeds we plant inside. That is where the real sanctuary lives - the one no one can take from you.

Legacy

I havc always felt compelled to help people. That's the essence behind this book - to give someone a way to make sense of life's challenges, to find meaning in it all, to walk away with a renewed perspective.

I thought about my son, about grandchildren I shall never hold, and I found myself staring at a pile of commendations when laid out, spanned 2 rooms. Pieces of paper with brave-sounding words. I remembered the bronze war medal my grandmother gave me - a stranger's medal, a signed letter from King George tucked away in a box - and how I'd passed it on to a collector when we emigrated. Someone else displayed it now. That felt like a metaphor for everything I was worried legacy might be.

I asked this question in quiet moment of reflection, and the answer was instantaneous.

"Your bloodline is not your legacy".

That was a revelation. My mother believed legacy was her children. For a long time, I'd been tempted to think the same. But the more I sat with it, the clearer it became. Legacy isn't a birth certificate; it's the trace you leave in the lives of others and in the world you touch. It can be an album you recorded, a book you wrote, or an office culture changed for the better - a thing people point to and say, "*They did that*!" Or it can be quieter: the way you steadied someone at a crucial minute, a thoughtful email of encouragement, the lessons of patience, empathy, humility and courage you taught someone when you thought nobody was watching. And it can be as simple as sparking an interest in a child as you teach them how to write or do mathematics.

Sometimes it's the tiny validations that envelop your heart with far greater warmth than any commendation can. Years later, a young director told me I'd been an inspiration. A consultant said she had learned so much from me when I wasn't teaching. Those comments moved me. They're the kind of legacy that won't fit into a display case but will sit in someone's head and heart and change how they live in gratitude that I am creating my own legacy.

This book has been heavy at times. I didn't hide the flames or the things that almost burned me. I walked you safely through them because I wanted you to see the kinds of choices I was given to make - and the way those choices built or broke things. Now I want you to turn the same bright, sometimes uncomfortable light on your own life. *What legacy are you building?* Have you been distracted by daily noise so long that you missed the lessons adversity was trying to hand you? Are there patterns repeating in your family, at work, in the way you love or avoid loving? Be honest.

Recently I was offered an industry award for a large project I had led. I instinctively shrugged it off. Material trophies of recognition are not as powerful as a genuine quiet word from your superior that says "*Thank you. I acknowledge what you did*". But I've learned that recognition has value too. It signals to other people what's worth copying. If your integrity or compassion gets noticed, maybe someone watching will choose the same. If the world remembers you for helping another human, it's not vanity; it's planting the idea that this behaviour matters.

I wrestle with anonymity. Part of me wants the book to be a quiet offering; part of me knows the market demands a name. If this book helps people, if it pushes even one person toward meaning and purpose, then it's done what I set out to do - whether I hide behind initials or sign my full name.

So what do I do with this clarity? I keep protecting, but from a distance where my family's peace matters first. I mentor. I plan to volunteer. I keep showing up for people who need a steady hand. The work of a protector doesn't always need an automatic weapon - often it needs time, consistency, and the courage to be useful without fanfare. That is the quiet legacy that fills up a life and, quietly, keeps reshaping the world.

There is a sweeter truth too: broken family patterns can be changed. My great-grandfather ran, abandoned his responsibilities, and set a course of hardship for many. But the story doesn't have to stop there. We can choose differently. Mrs. J - the ogre who scarred my early spirit - somehow later became a mentor to my sister-in-law when she entered her teaching career. People change. History rewrites itself when we decide to act differently.

If you want to leave something that matters, start small. Teach something. Show up when it counts. Be the credible person who keeps their word - those little deposits compound into something real. Ask yourself, honestly: when my name is said in a room, what do I want people to remember? If your answer is "*I was famous on social media, or they never had anything good to say*", change your habits now. If your answer is "*they were brave; they were kind; they made a life better*," then keep modelling that mindset - you are on the right track.

There's warmth in quiet giving. There's electricity when chosen actions move someone from stuck to stepping forward. Pay it forward not for applause, but because the act itself feeds your soul in a way nothing else will.

What the fire leaves behind is not only scars, but stories. Some will be told by us, some will be carried in whispers by those who loved us. Legacy is not about statues or headlines. It is about the choices we made in private, the kindness we showed when no one was watching, the dignity we gave even to those who didn't deserve it. My legacy is not the cases I closed or the arrests I made, but the lives I touched, the souls I protected, and the seeds of resilience I left in others. That is what endures when the flames have passed.

So here's my dare to you: pause. Sit with your life for a little while. Ask the hard question. If you don't like the answer, it may be time for a change. Mentorship, consistency, and courage aren't glamorous, but they last. If this book nudges one person to pick up that habit - to choose presence over performance – that ripple effect will help build my legacy too.

Go forth, do the small things, and unleash the power of you. If for no other reason – do it for me – I need the good karma!

Legacy Starter – A Quiet Challenge

Legacy isn't something you wait until the end to build. It's a living thing, shaped daily by what you choose to do, ignore, or walk away from. If you want to start now, here are a few simple prompts to guide you:

- **Name one person you've quietly shaped.**
  Think of someone who learned something from you - a child, a coworker, a friend. Write their name down. That influence is already part of your legacy.
- **Choose one act of protection or kindness you can do this week.**
  It doesn't need to be dramatic. A phone call. A piece of honest feedback. A simple presence when someone feels alone. Do it without announcing it to the world.
- **Ask the hard funeral question.**
  If someone stood up tomorrow to speak about you, what story would they tell? What story would you want them to tell? Write both down. Then notice the gap between them.
- **Plant something lasting.**
  This can be literal - a tree, a garden bed - or symbolic: a project, a note of encouragement, a tradition in your family. Leave behind something that continues without you.

- **Choose one pattern to break.**
  Look honestly at your family, your workplace, or your habits. Is there a cycle that keeps repeating? Anger, silence, avoidance, dishonesty? Decide where it ends, and let it end with you.

Your legacy doesn't have to be grand. It just has to be yours. Each choice is a brick in the story people will one day tell about you. Start laying them down with care.

The Quiet Echo

Legacy is not something we write only at the end of our lives. It is written now; in the choices we make every day. Most of it won't be carved into stone or printed in a newspaper. It will be carried quietly in the hearts of those who walked beside us.

Sometimes legacy is the child you raise. Sometimes it is the stranger you protected, the kindness no one saw, the courage that cost you more than anyone will ever know. It doesn't matter how small, the act feels at the time - one word, one gesture, one smile, one refusal to turn away - all of it leaves an imprint.

Reflection – A Call to Act

Pause - Look at your own life, not as a list of achievements or failures, but as a trail of echoes.

Ask yourself: What will remain when I am gone? What story will others tell when they speak my name?

The answer isn't waiting in the future. It is being written in this moment - in how you live, how you love, how you choose to show up for the world.

Sacred Levitations

As far back as I can remember, I have been obsessed with one question: *what happens when we die?* A qualification in hypnotherapy expanded my understanding of the capability of the human mind and I was fascinated by one's ability to recall almost every childhood detail while under hypnosis. Regression therapy revealed the possibility of memories from a past life. Was this fantasy or something deeper?

My investigation led me to books by pioneers like Drs. Ian Stevenson, Brian Weiss, Raymond Moody and Michael Newton. Past-life regression, near-death experiences, reincarnation - these weren't just curiosities anymore; they felt like clues on a trail I was determined to follow. Greg's case accelerated that hunger. Was this spirit's way of telling me I was on the right track?

An Uplifting Dream

For a few years prior, I had experienced a recurring dream - exciting and unbelievable but never fearful.

The dream was always the same. I'm in a room, surrounded by friendly faces - not frightening, not judgmental - people who seem to be waiting for me or focused on me. I would tell them, "*Watch this*," and hold my breath, and slowly I would begin to rise up, slowly at first, then steadier. I'd look beneath my feet and see the bed getting smaller and the room receding. The sensation was one of lightness, like being unburdened of gravity and worry. At the point where the levitation felt effortless, I would start to rise faster and wake up with a jolt - not panic, but surprise. The more I experienced this dream, I would gain further control over my ascension; but when I began to rise too quickly, I lost that control and would snap back, delighting at the cool experience that nobody else could do.

Over time the dreams became very infrequent. Many of you may agree that dreams are usually remembered directly after you wake and fade - especially when they are nightmares. But this dream would be fully recoverable, and I recalled every detail well into the following day. A part of me missed that feeling of flying and I never gave it a second thought. I would have the dream again once a month or so and secretly look forward to them, because I never seemed to remember any other dreams.

One day it hit me. The frequency of those vivid dreams stopped when I started to use a CPAP machine. Was this related? I tracked my sleep, and the pattern was hard to ignore: the dream remained identical, and it correlated with the apnea episodes. Was this dream a result of my brain being starved of oxygen, or was this a repeated near-death experience?

Was my soul enjoying a spirit vacation and flirting with the joy of returning to its origin? Either way, I knew it was physically harmful and unavoidable. I was bothered that I had no conscious control when I was asleep. However, I was consciously holding my breath to produce this phenomenon - this wasn't a sensation of being suffocated or starved of breath; it was holding my breath in anticipation of the wonderful experience of levitation. The only encouragement was that my apnea episodes had gone from 32 per hour to 2 per night.

I will not pretend I can explain it. All I can say is what I felt: the dream-space was friendly, bright and calm. There were no angels surrounding me; in fact, the spirit witnesses were eerily unidentifiable and all I got was a feeling of support.

Defying Gravity – Not Logic

There are two practical lessons here. First: if you have symptoms of sleep apnea - snoring, waking gasps, chronic fatigue - get it checked. The spiritual stuff is fascinating, but your physical health is paramount. Second: don't fear the metaphysical - I did not see heaven or hell or scary beings waiting for me, nor did I witness any vibrant colours or symphonic sounds - not to say they do not exist - I was left with a sense of excitement and peace.

What stays with me most is humility. I've spent decades as an investigator - trained to measure, test, and prove. Yet the best evidence I have for anything beyond this life is not a lab result; it's a persistent, intimate *knowing* that has shown up again and again in very human ways: a voice on a phone, a dream that returns, the sense of someone's gratitude across the years. If these levitations were a preview, then they were gentle and kind. If they were a trick of a tired brain, they were nonetheless profoundly instructive. Either way, they stopped me from shrinking my curiosity to fit my skepticism.

Sneak peeks or brain fantasies

If you wake choking, gasping or feeling like you've been yanked back from somewhere warm and strange, don't romanticise it - get a sleep study and act on it! Sleep apnea is real and dangerous. Treat the body and keep the mind curious. If you have had a similar dream, it may not be a coincidence. Track your apnea episodes and document them – they may reveal patterns.

The investigator in me dissected the dreams to see if anything I had experienced was my mind drawing on the near-death cases I had read about, but the surroundings did not mirror what I had read. This was a personal experience. I never met a guide, and I was never told to return and finish my soul's purpose. I was always left with the feeling of, "*Look what you can do - you are much more than your body.*"

If this was a doorway to another plane of existence, then I am thankful for the sneak peeks - but if it was something physiological then I am thankful I keep my CPAP on every night. But sometimes, before sleep, I am drawn back to that magnificent feeling of flight, and I whisper to the quiet:

If there's more to see, show me again - just not tonight.

Chapter XI

Altered States of Consciousness

To understand solitude, awareness, and the higher states many gurus strive for, we first need to understand states of consciousness - and the truth is, we all pass through them every day.

Some people argue about whether we can sense these states as energies around the body, or whether they can only be measured in the brain. I have never seen an aura, and I cannot judge anyone who has claimed to. But I can tell you this: I absolutely feel shifts in energy - in people, in spaces, and even in plants. I've tested myself, walking with eyes closed, paying attention to what I felt. More often than not, that uneasy sensation corresponded with a plant in distress - drought, fungal infection, or infestation. Conversely, I feel peace around healthy trees or certain quiet places in my garden. I've learned to trust that intuition - it's not mysticism; it's connection.

Everyday Mysticism

Many people believe that altered states are only attainable through prayer, meditation, or self-hypnosis. But that's not the whole picture. In fact, we all experience them naturally. From the sharp alertness of a meeting, to the drift of a daydream, to the depths of sleep - we are constantly shifting between states. Scientists have measured these patterns of thought as frequencies in the brain.

Beta State (12–35 Hz):

This is alertness and concentration. It's the everyday state where the conscious brain takes in data, analyzes, and makes decisions.

Alpha State (8–12 Hz):

This is relaxed awareness. Think of driving a manual car in traffic - you're not consciously changing gears, it happens intuitively, while your mind is focused elsewhere. This is also the daydream state - half aware of the meeting in front of you while your thoughts wander to what's for dinner.

Theta State (4–8 Hz):

This is where things get interesting. Hypnotists know it well: the state of deep relaxation where the conscious mind quiets, and the subconscious opens. Elders reached it by gazing into firelight or swinging a pendulum. For me, it's that fleeting moment before waking or just before sleep, when someone speaks and you hear them, but you simply don't care to respond. In Theta, suggestions bypass the conscious mind. The body can heal. Pain can be ignored. There are cases of patients undergoing dental surgery with no anesthetic, guided only by suggestion.

Delta State (0.5–4 Hz):

This is deep sleep, or REM sleep. The conscious mind is entirely offline, while the subconscious busily weaves memories and dreams.

Have you noticed a pattern? Your vibration and intuition increase when you relax and your brain waves decrease. Mystics have long maintained that quietening the mind is the portal to achieving spiritual awareness – well before science measured brain waves. Of all these states, Theta is where the door cracks open. Here is the secret: prayer, deep meditation, or hypnosis are reliable doors into this state. But I have found I can sometimes reach Theta by simply being. It sounds strange, but it aligns with what yogis and mystics have described for centuries: a state of union with the universe, radiating energy rather than grasping at it.

Simple does not mean easy. When I have managed to rest in Theta, I have held deep conversations within myself, receiving insights and answers that felt far beyond my life experience. Sometimes it's a clear thought, other times just a feeling. But it is always significant and comforting.

Reaching Theta

So how do you reach this state? You begin with awareness, acceptance, trust, truth, love, and a genuine desire to commune with spirit. You also need calm, patience, and a body completely relaxed. With practice, the doorway opens more quickly. But there is a caveat: you cannot fool yourself. You cannot enter Theta asking for wisdom, then return unchanged, clinging to old habits and selfish motives. The soul knows.

If guided meditation works for you, use it. If prayer is your way into that communion, embrace it. If visualization unlocks it, then let that be your path. The method matters far less than the intention. What matters is the honesty of what you ask - and the willingness to listen - in that silence.

Theta is the state where magic happens. What you ask in those moments of solitude matters most. It is here, in this quiet space, that we glimpse both who we are and what we might become.

And this is where the power of imagination begins to take shape. In Theta, the mind is fertile ground - open to suggestion, rich with possibility.

What we hold in focus here, whether it is peace, healing, or a vision of the life we want to live, can ripple outward into the physical world. This is where visualization is born, and where manifestation begins.

The Power of Visualization

Visualization is not a fantasy. It's not wishful thinking or passive daydreaming. It's a vehicle for creation - a sacred tool through which we co-author our reality. It isn't just theory. It's a practice. A way of gently rehearsing the life you want until your soul begins to believe it's already yours.

I've included guided meditations and simple exercises in the Appendix to help you ease into this space. This isn't something reserved for the few who meditate in silence or manifest under the full moon. This is for anyone - for you - if you are focused on a goal and willing to meet yourself honestly along the way.

The truth is many of us are already visualizing without even knowing it. Whenever you imagine a desired outcome and mentally run through strategies, risks, or future scenarios, you are visualizing. But often it's from a place of worry or fear, not empowered creation. That's the difference. One is survival. The other is alignment.

In the previous chapter, I spoke of the Theta State that quiet, dreamy space between sleep and waking where the mind is soft and open, and the soul is listening. It's in this frequency that visualization becomes especially powerful. Why? Because you're closer to your true self - not the version of you who reacts to traffic or emails, but the one who remembers what you came here for.

I once read someone say, "*Raise your vibration.*" At the time, I had no idea what that meant. But now I know: Begin by knowing yourself. Then, like yourself. And finally, gently shift or release what no longer serves you.

Think only your highest thoughts. Quieten the noise. Be truthful. Fill your heart with love, acceptance, and gratitude. Eliminate the static of fear, jealousy, or resentment - those are just white noise blocking the signal.

Then, when you're ready, sit still. Breathe. And bring your focus to the outcome you desire - not with desperation, but with devotion. Picture it vividly. Add color, sound, texture, emotion. Feel it as if it's happening right now. See yourself smiling, living it, holding it. And above all, feel the gratitude as if it were already yours. Repeat as often as you like. This isn't Beetlejuice - there's no need to chant and spin. Just return to the vision like it's already part of your life. Trust - let go – rinse and repeat.

A Cautionary Tale – Lessons From The Genie

As Rumpelstiltskin once said, "All magic comes at a price". The universe responds, but not always how we expect. Sometimes, we are granted what we asked for, but it comes with unexpected consequences. I learned this the hard way.

There's an old story about a man who found a magic lamp. When the genie appeared, the man asked to be the richest person in the world. Poof! He got his wish - but he was now in a wheelchair, alone, and unhappy. When he protested, the genie reminded him, "*You should've been more specific.*"

I know someone who visualized her horrible boss disappearing. She imagined the woman gone from her life - and sure enough, within a few weeks, her wish was granted. She was let go. Her boss remained. But in time, spirit revealed the greater plan. She found a new job, a fresh start. Eventually, her former boss was fired for underperformance. But only after she had learned the lessons she needed.

So yes - visualization is powerful. But always remember to pair it with purity of intention. Petty wants or ego-driven desires may be granted, but they often come with a wicked sense of irony buried in the fine print. Be careful what you wish for.

I've reflected deeply on this in my own life. I used to speak wistfully about working from home - and then, after a failed back operation, I was forced to. The physical pain and loss of vision in one eye became the cost of my unfiltered desire. My son, who never appreciated his blessings, now lives with brain damage and faces heavy decisions daily. So, I share this with sincerity: There is a deeper truth to all of this. Only one path truly holds - the path of righteousness, of sincerity, of love.

But let's return to brighter things.

Let's say you want a new job, but you don't yet know what it looks like. Does that matter? Not really. What matters is how you want to feel. Visualize yourself smiling at your desk, surrounded by people who uplift you. Picture a fair, kind boss, and the steady rhythm of a balanced, fulfilling workday. Focus not on the title or salary, but the feeling of purpose and peace. If it's money you seek, ask - but be mindful. More money at the cost of your soul is a high price to pay.

Use your emotional energy wisely. Charge your visions with love, not fear. With joy, not desperation. That's the sweet spot where the universe meets us halfway.

And if you've ever prayed - "*Please God, give me this job, I'll start going to church!*" - only to be turned down, don't fall into despair. It's not that your prayers weren't heard. It's that something better - or more aligned - is on the way. Faith is not measured by results. It's measured by trust.

Free will is your compass. Intuition is your guide. Spirit - whatever name you give it - is the wind that fills your sails when you're headed in the right direction.

When The Universe Says - Yes

I once wanted a new DJ mixer. It was expensive and frivolous. But I set it as my laptop wallpaper - a small act of belief. I sold a few old things, saved what I could. Then came a budget crunch, and I had to hand over my savings. I was back at zero. But shortly afterward, my wife received a bonus, and I got the mixer. It arrived - beautiful, sleek - a reward for patience. And let's be clear: I'm talking about both the mixer and my wife - Beautiful not sleek – Okay let me stop while I'm ahead.

Later, I tried to manifest new speakers. These weren't just any speakers - they were $7,000. I added them to my wallpaper, envisioned them in my listening room, imagined their sound. And then - a storm hit Toronto. Our basement flooded. Months of repair followed. But through that upheaval, insurance paid out just enough to bridge the gap. I combined the funds and bought the speakers. They now sit in my listening room – *my precious* (that sounded like Smeagol) - a testament to the mysterious ways the universe answers.

Yes, they're material things. But the joy they brought was rooted in appreciation, not greed. I asked not for the object, but the feeling they'd give me - and that, I believe, is why the universe said, "*Yeah sure – be patient I'm sending you a storm*".

Manifesting People, Not Things

I've used this same practice to manifest people - specifically, bosses who have changed my life.

Each time a VP left, I stayed calm. I didn't beg for status or salary. I visualized one thing: a kind, empathetic, fair person. And each time, spirit delivered. My last boss - once my peer - became a soul connection. During my most difficult times, I never abandoned my integrity. Even while losing vision, I stayed on to finish a project because I had made her a promise. And promises mean something to me.

When it came time for a new VP, I once again asked only for kindness. I released all fear and said, "*Spirit, I leave this to you.*" And once again, I was blessed. My current boss is calm, fair, grounded. He listens, values my contributions, respects my limits. I joke that I'm manifesting him staying until I retire - because breaking in a new one would be far too much work.

But seriously - I do not take these blessings lightly. Each day, I wake up in gratitude for the people, the peace, and the quiet wisdom that has come through communion with something greater than myself. Whether you call it Spirit, the Universe, or God - it listens. And it responds.

Now, a word on words.

The Weight of Words

You've heard the rhyme: "*Sticks and stones may break my bones, but words will never harm me.*" I disagree completely.

Words can heal. Words can destroy! Under hypnosis, words can influence thoughts, calm pain, and even rewire our beliefs. A cruel comment in childhood can become a lifelong prison. I've seen beautiful girls develop eating disorders after being called fat. I've met brilliant people who still carry the sting of being told they weren't enough. And I know the effect on one's self-esteem when one hears their mother refer to them as the one who didn't get the brains!

But used with love, words are powerful tools of creation. They're keys. Spells. Catalysts.

Speak from your heart. Speak with kindness. Use your voice to uplift, not condemn. And when you speak your desires into the universe, do it with clarity, humility, and truth. The soul hears. Spirit hears. And when you send out loving thoughts for others, you are planting those seeds for yourself too.

We are all connected at a soul level. When you wish good for another, you vibrate with that same goodness.

The Closing Breath

This book describes my journey from darkness to light. Along the way, I’ve left breadcrumbs of wisdom that I only came to understand in hindsight. If you're reading this, you're on your own path, and I honor that.

So, take a breath. The book becomes lighter now.

Everything you’ve read, everything that’s stirred within you - it was meant to. Adversity is a teacher. Darkness is a mirror. Through every loss or struggle, there’s a hidden gift. Did you see it? Do you see more than I did?

Now is the time for you to ask the tough questions. Reflect. Revisit old habits. Investigate the recurring patterns. What’s your soul trying to show you?

I’ve cracked the case of my life, but it’s still unfolding – let’s say the prosecution has not rested, if you will. My hope is that my journey helps you uncover some of your own truths, mysteries, and miracles - no matter your age, your faith, or your past.

And above all - I hope it helps you rediscover the radiant purity of your soul, one loving choice at a time.

Bless you, my friend.

Chapter XII

The Meaning of Life

A Protector's Perspective

For centuries, philosophers have debated the meaning of life.

I hadn't read them. Instead, I asked myself.

One day, in a moment of clarity, the answer appeared like a verdict delivered in court:

"*Spiritual growth through physical experience.*"

The simplicity of it stunned me. Was it God's voice? My subconscious? Either way, the phrase lingered, pulsing with truth.

But if that's the overarching meaning, what does it look like in practice? Do we all learn the same lessons, or do we each walk unique pathways shaped by our soul roles?

Patterns began to surface. My life had been one of extremes - light and dark, loss and renewal, despair and resilience. It wasn't random. It was as if I'd been given sharp contrasts to make my choices unmistakable: protector or predator, servant or tyrant, faithful or faithless.

Over time, I came to see that each of us embodies certain soul roles - recurring archetypes that guide our growth:

- **Protector** - Guardian of people and energy; brave, empathetic, a warrior for truth and justice.
- **Vessel** - Channel of wisdom or higher consciousness, awakening connection to something greater.
- **Mirror** - Revealer of truth, reflecting what others are - or are not ready to see.
- **Anchor** - Stabilizer, offering peace and moral clarity in turbulent times.
- **Weaver** - Storyteller who connects patterns and reveals meaning.
- **Guide** - Mentor or elder, a catalyst for growth, grounded in spirit.
- **Seeker** - The student, traveller, adventurer, restless to uncover knowledge and deeper meaning.

Looking back, my life has danced between Protector and Vessel. As a police officer, father, husband, and leader, I was called to shield others - sometimes with force, sometimes with compassion. Later, I became a Vessel too, carrying lessons drawn from scars and experience, pointing others back to themselves.

Here's the revelation: purpose is not fixed. It isn't a job title or a single destiny - it's how we embody our soul role through free will. My purpose wasn't "police officer." It was Protector. And my choices determined whether I protected through fear and control, or through love, courage, and service.

When I finally saw this, I realized something liberating: every failure and triumph was not a detour - *it was the curriculum.*

Life may feel chaotic, stitched together by coincidence, but when we step back, we can see the threads forming a tapestry. Our lives are not accidents; they are cycles designed to remind us of who we are becoming.

Life in Cycles: Patterns of the Soul

According to numerology, life unfolds in cycles -predictable rhythms of growth and renewal. Out of curiosity, I mapped mine in sevens, and the pattern was undeniable:

- 7: Learned to read and write.
- 14: Chose subjects that shaped my path.
- 21: Took my first leadership role as a shift sergeant.
- 28: Promoted; began community outreach.
- 35: Emigrated to Canada; started anew.
- 42: Became Director.
- 56: Role expanded; lost sight in one eye.

These milestones weren't about possessions or milestones of status - they were about responsibility and transformation. Each cycle brought more opportunity to protect, serve, and grow. My soul role was written across decades like chapters in a novel. Each cycle wasn't a test to pass, but an invitation to rise.

This awareness brought peace. Now, I can look ahead and anticipate the next turning point, knowing another layer of growth waits beyond it.

If you're curious about your own cycles:

1. Calculate your cycle rhythm number.
2. Map your major life events against it.
3. Look for the patterns.

Example:
Birth date: 12 May 1971
(1 + 2) + (5) + (1 + 9 + 7 + 1) = 3 + 5 + 18

(3) + (5) + (1+8) = 17

Reduce 17 to single digits and add them together : 1 + 7 = 8
Your life cycle number would follow patterns of 8 years.

Here's the truth: when you recognize your cycles, you stop fearing change. You see it as part of a larger design - not punishment, but a rhythm calling you into alignment with who you already are.

The Fire, the Ashes, and the Light

If you've come this far, thank you.

You've walked through my fire - some blistering, some illuminating - and seen what was left in the ashes.

But this chapter isn't about my story anymore. It's about yours.

Picture us sitting across from each other, coffee between us - no rank, no titles. Just two souls comparing notes on what it means to live, stumble, protect, and rise again.

I don't claim to have all the answers; I've been more investigator than preacher. But I know this: life constantly drops clues. If we don't stop noticing them, the lessons pass us by like unmarked evidence left at a crime scene.

So, let's hold up the mirror together.

The Soul Roles We Carry

Looking back, one theme screamed through my life: Protector - of community, coworkers, family, even strangers. Sometimes I succeeded, sometimes I failed, but the role never left me. It was written in my soul.

Not every soul is called to protect. Maybe yours is different:

- **Anchor**: Steadying the storm, giving others a sense of home.
- **Mirror:** Showing people their truth - sometimes the wake-up call, sometimes the gentle reminder.

- **Vessel:** Channeling wisdom, faith, or creativity that flows through you.
- **Weaver:** Connecting stories or patterns others miss.
- **Guide:** Mentoring or radiating a presence that sparks transformation.
- **Seeker:** A restless soul, searching for meaning and wisdom.

Reflection – Through The Looking Glass

Some live their entire lives in one role; others shift with the season or lesson.
So ask yourself: What has life been calling you to become?
Look at the turning points - the extremes - they leave clues.

The Pillars of Our Lives

Certain themes returned so often they felt like pillars holding up my life. See which echo in yours:

- **The Guardian:** How have you safeguarded others - or your own soul?
- **The Sanctuary:** Where do you feel safe? Which sanctuaries have you built or lost?
- **The Fire of Extremes:** What crossroads forced your greatest choices?
- **The Mirror**: Who has reflected your truth back to you, and did you face it?
- **Legacy:** What echo will your life leave when you're gone?

Perspective shapes everything. As a balding man once joked, "I don't have much hair, yet if a few strands land in your soup, you'll shout, Waiter, there's a lot of hair in my soup!" Life is like that - the frame matters more than the facts.

Exercises for the Journey Ahead

If you're willing, let's turn reflection into clarity together. Don't rush - take one at a time and let them unfold.

1. **Your Life in Cycles** - Use your birth date to find your rhythm. Mark the milestones and look for recurring lessons.
2. **The Soul Role Map** - Identify the roles that describe your journey. Are you living true to them today?
3. **Sanctuary Inventory** - Where do you feel most safe? What threatens that safety now?
4. **The Fire Test** - Recall one defining moment. What truth did it force you to face? How did it shape your choices?
5. **Dialogue with Your Future Self** - Ask your wiser self: What are you proud of? What do you regret? What do you want me to do differently today?

Gentle Prompts Along the Way

- *When was the last time you felt truly safe?*
- *Which soul role has life been shaping in me?*
- *What lesson keeps repeating itself?*
- *If my story ended tomorrow, what story would others tell about me?*
- *What "truths" about myself have I outgrown?*

Reflection can be heavy, but it isn't about fixing everything - it's about noticing. About daring to hold the mirror steady long enough to see the truth.

I've lived my life as a Soul Protector and Guardian. Yours might be different, but every role carries wisdom and purpose. No matter how many sanctuaries we lose or rebuild, every soul has the chance to grow.

Your life is not a verdict - it's a canvas. The brush is still in your hand.

If this feels foreign, start small: sit quietly, breathe, and listen to the inner voice. If you want structure, I've written guided practices and meditations in the Appendix to help you begin.

The Many Faces of a Soul

For most of my life, I believed I was one thing: a Protector. That role fit so tightly it felt like my only skin. But writing this book became its own mirror, forcing me to sit still and see differently. Unknowingly, I have spent my entire life as a Seeker, searching for wisdom and meaning ever since I was a young child.

Our souls don't come here to be only one thing. Sometimes they choose many roles, stitching them together within one magical lifetime. Protector was my loudest role - forged in danger, where hesitation could mean death. But I was also a Vessel, carrying intuition I didn't understand until later; a Mirror, showing others their choices by the way I lived mine; an Anchor, grounding loved ones in storms; and now, a Weaver of stories using the fabric of my life's experiences.

Some souls may focus on one lesson. Others, like mine, taste many, carrying their contradictions until the pattern reveals itself in hindsight. For years I thought I was just surviving the extremes, but now I see the exquisite design. Each role mattered. Each served the whole.

If you're wondering about your own role, don't rush to name it. Maybe you're a Protector in your family, a Mirror to your friends, an Anchor at work, and a Vessel in quiet prayer. Your soul may have chosen them all - to experience the fullness of life.

You don't have to decide who you are once and for all. Your soul isn't finished yet. It's still weaving, still reflecting, still protecting, still carrying.

One day, when you look back, the roles you thought were separate will reveal themselves as threads of the same design.

And with that understanding, I close this story not just as a Protector, but as all the roles my soul has lived - grateful for every lesson, every scar, every moment that brought me here. If I've learned one truth, it's that strength is never one-dimensional. We are far more complex - and maybe that's the point: that in living, choosing, stumbling, and rising, we discover how many ways a soul can express itself.

Mine was forged in fire, but yours will be no less sacred.

May you find your reflection in these roles, and see your scars not as failures but as proof of a life deeply lived.

Don't Sweat the Small Stuff

I once knew an old man who grew increasingly afraid as the years caught up with him. He carried the weight of his past like a stone around his neck, haunted by a lifetime of infidelity. Convinced that God would punish him, he sought redemption by burying himself in church ritual to outrun his guilt. He performed piety as penance. He volunteered, he prayed loudly, he presented himself as devout. Yet beneath that performance was a man still bound by dishonesty, resentment, and judgment.

When he finally died, the priest spoke the expected words of comfort from the pulpit, but the people in the pews knew a different story. They knew the other side of him - the one he never truly surrendered.

We all stumble. We all make mistakes. We all carry regrets. But if we cling to them, they become prisons that keep us from living fully. We are not defined by our faults. We are the sum of our choices, and every choice has led us to this eternal moment of Now. This is the vibration we emit, the energy we radiate into the world.

Regret only dulls that energy, casting shadows where light is meant to shine. Energy cannot be destroyed; it can only be transformed. The real question is not whether you have failed in the past - it is: What will you transform your energy into today? And what story, what fear, what excuse is still stopping you?

I know some will see my vulnerability as weakness. It is easier to listen to the polished voices - the men with sculpted physiques, veneered smiles, and seven-figure salaries. But that is not me. And I believe that is not what the world truly needs. The world is full of imperfect, ordinary people - people like you and me - stumbling forward, trying to make sense of life, trying to keep walking even when the road is scorched and uneven. Wisdom does not only come from perfection. More often, it comes from the broken places, from the people who have known both despair and resilience.

The fire of my life has left deep scars. And yet, when I look back, I see not only wounds but blessings - moments of love, achievement, and grace that would never have unfolded if I had surrendered to despair twenty-two years ago. Hold that: If I had ended my life, I would have missed out on discovering these soul identities and all the wisdom I now carry from experiences that arrived as doorways cloaked as storms – and you would not be reading this book.

We are all damaged goods in the embers of life's inferno. Some cups bear only scratches. Some carry cracks, visible and deep. And some have been shattered completely, pieced back together with resilience, still capable of holding water, still capable of serving their purpose. The beauty is not in their perfection but in their survival.

In recent years, I have seen how COVID carved its mark on so many lives. I am independent by nature, but I know others who depend deeply on human contact, and when that was taken from them, their mental health suffered greatly. One of them reached out to me not long ago. He just wanted to talk. So I gave him my time, and I listened. Slowly he confessed how isolation had broken him, how he needed connection to feel alive again. His words reminded me of a truth we often forget: none of us is meant to carry the weight of life alone.

If you ever find yourself isolated, hopeless, or drowning in silence, reach out. Call a friend. Speak to family. Seek professional help if you need it. Ask for connection. There is no shame in saying, "*I cannot do this by myself.*" Perspective can be borrowed. Strength can be shared. And once you find it, you can lift yourself again and keep marching forward, because life still has lessons waiting for you - and they are worth living for.

Closing Reflection - What the Darkness Taught the Light

When I look back over the landscape of my life, I see now that nothing was wasted. Not the wounds, not the danger, not the nights that felt too heavy to carry. Every chapter that once seemed disconnected was quietly preparing the next. The child who felt misplaced was learning to listen. The young man walking into violence was learning to see. The protector I became was simply the boy I once was, grown into his purpose.

It took me years to understand that life was never testing my strength. It was refining my awareness - polishing the parts of me I didn't yet know were mine.

Trauma showed me how fragile a human being can be.

Presence showed me how resilient a soul can be.

And in the stillness between those truths, I began to recognise the person beneath the armour.

The work I did - the darkness I walked through - was not a measure of toughness. It was a curriculum in compassion. It taught me that courage is not loud, and wisdom is not always gentle. It taught me that a person can break open and still remain whole in ways the world does not recognise.

Policing did not create the protector in me. It revealed him. I once believed my job was to stand between danger and the innocent. Now I know the deeper task: to stand between fear and possibility, between despair and meaning, between the life we inherit and the life we choose.

There is a point in every journey where survival is no longer the goal - Awakening is. What I once tried to forget has become the very thing I understand best.

Trauma alone does not make wisdom. Pain only becomes meaning when the heart learns how to translate it.

Pain does not arrive to harden us. It arrives to reveal us. It clears what was false, sharpens what was true, and leaves us with a quieter, steadier strength - the kind that does not need to announce itself.

If I could offer only one thread from everything I've lived, it would be this:

Your past is not a prison. It is a place of initiation.

And every step you thought would break you was teaching you how to walk in a new way.

In the end, nothing I survived defines me.

What defines me is the person I became while learning how to hold darkness without letting it dim my light.

That is what the journey has shown me.

Not what the fire took - but what it revealed.

Acknowledgment

Life rarely explains itself in a single moment. Understanding arrives later, disguised as hindsight. Writing this has been more than crafting a book; it has been walking barefoot across the coals of memory, each step burning, yet each step carrying me closer to healing. These pages are not just a record of survival - they are a testament to the lessons hidden inside pain, to the strength forged in fire, and to the grace that carried me when I could not carry myself.

For every shadow I faced, there was a spark of light waiting to be revealed. For every wound I revisited, there was a deeper understanding that stitched it closed. The act of writing has been both a reckoning and a release - a sacred conversation with the past, and a quiet pact with the future.

I give thanks for the *unseen hands* that guided me in this telling - for memory that refused to be silenced, for the courage that returned each time I doubted, and for the mysterious way clarity arrives when one dares to speak their truth.

Above all, I am grateful for presence - divine, human, and ancestral. For those who walked with me in spirit. For those who challenged me in flesh. For those whose lives brushed against mine long enough to leave a lesson behind.

I often think of Mrs. J's cruel little poem - the one that made me walk a "*path of driven snow*" - and of my mother's rueful jokes about my looks and brains. Those two small, strange teachers taught me the same thing: perspective can be a cutting tool and a balm at once. They kept me honest, taught me to laugh at my own vanity, and reminded me that humility and humour are as essential to survival as courage.

If this work carries any weight, let it be this: that even in the darkest chapters, no soul is truly alone. That gratitude itself can be a form of survival. And that the act of remembering is not just about the past - it is a compass pointing us back to who we were always meant to be.

In the quiet after crisis, I learned that survival isn't triumph - it's responsibility.

You emerge from the flames carrying not just your own life, but the weight of every life you touched along the way.

At first, I mistook survival for strength. Now I see it for what it is - a second chance to live more honestly. To admit fear when it shows up. To love harder whenever I can. To stop being my worst critic, and to be grateful for the lessons that have shaped my humanity.

Meaning isn't found at the end of the fire - it's found in who you become walking through it. The fire stripped me down to what was real. It took away the noise, the performance, the false ideas of control. And what it left was humility, grace, unapologetic truth, and heart that still believes in goodness.

Maybe that's what the fire teaches in the end:

That being alive is not about being unburned.

It's about walking forward, scarred and awake, and still choosing to build something beautiful on the ground that was once ash.

What the fire takes, the soul remembers - and what the soul remembers becomes your light.

And to you, the reader - thank you for walking this road with me. By turning these pages, you've not only witnessed my journey, but you've allowed my story to touch yours. If even one reflection has sparked healing, courage, or clarity in your own path, then this book has served its purpose. We are connected now - not by chance, but by the quiet design of something greater.

If you've walked with me this far, know that the journey isn't finished. The meditations I've included at the back of this book are invitations - not instructions. They are doors. I hope you'll step through them.

The Appendix

Part I

Messages from the Other Side

Preface

This appendix contains details that are sacred to me. When I first began assembling related material, I experienced a physical and emotional response that felt like a request - an insistence - that Greg's story be kept apart from JC. Out of respect for that feeling and the memory of those involved, I have kept these memories separate in appendix. Their energies are incompatible. If you read both, know this was done deliberately: to honour what is private, to protect what is tender, and to preserve the integrity of a life that touched mine deeply.

The Full Story

In 2002, the most unusual and meaningful case of my policing career unfolded - a case that forced me to confront not only the darkest corners of human violence but also the possibility of guidance from beyond this world.

To fully understand, we must rewind seven years. Back then, I was SWAT trained and working in an elite crime prevention unit. Acting on intelligence about a hijacking suspect hiding in a rural area, we rolled in and immediately took fire from inside the house. I was part of a three-person team that breached. Inside, we found Sibongiseni, hands raised in surrender. Later, searching the room, we discovered the revolver he'd emptied at us and shoved under the bed. Alongside it: a hijacked vehicle and ammunition.

Months later, after he had skipped bail, we raided the same house at 2 a.m. He escaped through a window as his brother lied to us about his whereabouts. From the dark hills above, boulders rained down on us - our vehicle windshield smashed, forcing us to retreat. He was eventually arrested and served seven years before parole.

The Call Out

Fast forward to a Saturday morning in 2002. My day off was interrupted: *" Inspector! – You need to come to the station, Greg B has been killed."* Greg, a respected town planner and community watch leader, was known to me. His home had been burgled. Instead of calling police, he and a neighbor followed the trail into the nearby nature reserve, locating stolen goods. The neighbor left after hours; Greg stayed remained behind – intent on catching them himself. Alone, determined and with no support. By dawn, he was dead - shot multiple times by unknown assailants.

At the scene, there were hints of multiple shooters, maybe two weapons. Limited clues: a TV with possible fingerprints, some scattered property. Forensic analysis usually took weeks to determine, which gave us no certainty at that point in time. With no national ballistics database, at best a weapon might tie to another crime. Greg's widow, Jenny B, was distraught. Against every bit of training, I promised her I'd catch his killers.

The Investigation Begins

We worked nonstop, canvassing informers, posting rewards. Within 24 hours two names surfaced. One was Dlamini, a notorious hitman I'd arrested years before, wanted for the assassination of a high profile and controversial political figure Sifiso Nkabinde, and attempted murders of Metro K9 officers. Dangerous, but unlikely tied to Greg's murder. The other: Sibongiseni Mchunu. His name tugged at my memory. Reports said he'd been drunk, bragging about shooting a white man. Nothing concrete, but it was all we had. We planted an informer near his home and provided him with a cell phone to hold observation.

By Monday, word came: Sibongiseni was there, with groceries, flush with cash. We pulled together a six-man team, Metro K9 included. That evening, my wife - who rarely commented on my work - urged me to call Verna, a psychic I'd once known through hypnotherapy training. Skeptical, I resisted. But her insistence was unusual, so I relented.

A Divine Conversation

At 9:30 p.m., I dialed Verna. She lived 100km away. No details of the case had been made public. The conversation still echoes in me:

Malcolm: *"Hi Verna, it's Malcolm. Do you remember me?"*

Verna: *"Yes, of course."*

Malcolm: *"Sorry to call so late, but I'm on a murder case. Two possible suspects. I need to know if you sense danger for me tonight - and if you have any intuition about them."*

Verna: *"What's the victim's name?"*

Malcolm: *"Greg B."*

Verna: (pauses) *"Okay... Greg is almost embarrassed. He's saying, 'How did untrained people overpower me like that?' There were three suspects. One is only fourteen years old. Do you know that?"*

Malcolm: *"No. I suspected maybe two, but we have no details."*

Verna: *"Yes. Fourteen. A lookout. Not part of the actual killing, but he was brought along."*

Malcolm: *"What else?"*

Verna: *"Greg says he hit the shooter in the left eye fighting for his life and the cut has become infected. He won't go to a hospital out of fear. This is the worst crime he's ever committed - he hasn't killed before. And... there's a white van. Important, though not part of the crime. Are you writing this down?" "He has an unkempt scraggly beard and he is thin"*

Malcolm: *"What about the other suspects".*

Verna: *"The other suspect is older and stocky carrying a bit of weight. I see him with gun and he is grinding it with a stone or some kind of grinder"*

Malcolm: *" Can you describe that gun?"*

Verna: *"Yes it is a short small gun, with a round piece"*

Malcolm: "*Like a revolver?"*

Verna: *"Yes it has a cylinder"*

Malcolm: *"Yes. What about the names? Dlamini?"*

Verna: (sharp intake of breath) *"Terrible energy. Very dangerous. But not your guy for this case."*

Malcolm: *"Sibongiseni M.?"*

Verna: (immediately) *"Yes. That's him. His brother knows. But he's afraid of him."*

Malcolm: *"Where is this coming from?"*

Verna: *"From Greg! And one more thing, you won't find him at the first place you look. But you must persevere, because you will get him. And even if you don't get him tonight, it is his destiny that he will be caught. His mouth will give himself away".*

I hung up unsettled. She hadn't told me whether I would die that night. I decided not to ask. I was so focused on capturing everything she had said accurately. I didn't have time to ponder how this was even possible, or whether any of it was accurate. I was haunted by what was possibly true. Greg had been in the army reserve as a Major and would have been embarrassed if some low life criminal bested him. Her other comment of his mouth giving him away was consistent with why we had identified him as a possible suspect, he had boasted about killing someone. There were so many details that would have to be proved, and I grew skeptical because one thing was certain. We had him under observation, so how could Verna say he would not be at the first place we checked? Should I mention this to anyone or keep it to myself?

The Hunt

I shared every detail I had scribbled down with my team during the midnight briefing before the raid – our calm before the storm. Some laughed, others frowned, but when the night unfolded, every detail began to fall into place.

At the first raid, Sibongiseni was missing. His girlfriend pointed us to his brother's house - Phumlani's. My blood chilled: I'd been ambushed here years before. Outside sat a white van. Coincidence? My partner grinned: "*Means nothing.*" But inside, Phumlani trembled when he saw me – we had history. He admitted his brother had become dangerous. We pressed him into helping. Hours passed, several false raids. Finally, in a small house, we found a man sleeping under a blanket. I ripped it away -Sibongiseni. Next to him, a bag with a CZ 75 pistol. I took him outside under a street light and noticed a large gash on his left eye. It was clearly infected and required stitches.

"*Do you remember me, Sibongiseni*?" "*Yebo*" (Zulu for yes) was the answer. *"I'm going to ask you just once - How did you get that?"* I asked.

"*Fighting with the boss when I killed him,*" he replied, cold and casual. He admitted there were three involved, one only fourteen. With that, every detail Verna had shared was validated.

I was so focused on his admission that I almost missed it: he was thin, with a wispy, unkempt beard - exactly as Verna had described – A fact I pointed out to my partners who were stunned. How did anyone know details of a case that the investigators didn't even know, and could this communication be coming from the afterlife? Was this Greg's gift to us? Proof of life after death in return for catching his killer? This is something movies are made of.

I asked the suspect to describe the others. He claimed that one was indeed 14, brought along to carry stolen goods and was not involved. The other, a stout man lived nearby and he promised to take us to him. Sibongiseni also mentioned that he had a gun. It was a revolver, Taurus 38 special and it had the serial number scratched off – an event that Verna had witnessed in her spirit communication.

One final detail – a shotgun in Greg's possession was missing. This would be another piece of evidence we needed. When the suspect was pressed – he pointed to a location where he had buried it – under the white van! When a search revealed it was no longer there, his brother Phumlani admitted to digging it up and burying it in a dry riverbank. We recovered the shotgun and entered it into evidence. It appeared that white van was indeed pertinent to this investigation after all. I looked at my partner who had scoffed at the white van earlier in the evening. His expression said it all.

We did not manage to find either of the other suspects and they subsequently fled to another part of the country and disappeared.

The next morning, I told Jenny B: we had her husband's killer. I'd kept my promise. Forensics confirmed the pistol we found was the murder weapon. Sibongiseni confessed, though later in court he recanted, claiming self-defense. The judge acquitted him of murder, convicting him only on firearms charges. He served eleven years of a fifteen-year sentence.

Blast From the Past

Years later, after I'd emigrated to Canada, a cop friend Michael, (the same one who rescued me from being locked in that police van fighting for my life) visited and told me of a local home invasion that had happened only a few houses from my old home: a husband shot in bed, his wife forced to help the criminals load stolen goods into their car.

He also told me about an unfortunate tragedy when innocent patrons were shot in a restaurant by armed robbers in another part of town. This story gave me an uneasy feeling, as if my soul were being prodded – take notice. When he went home, I was compelled to look up that home invasion because it had happened so close to my old home and I was stunned to see the shooter was arrested – his name – Sibongiseni. He had been released early from his 15-year sentence and immediately committed a home invasion and shot a husband as he lay in bed with his wife. The victim later died in hospital. Another senseless murder — and another echo of Greg's unfinished story.

Gratitude From The Other Side

The story wasn't done. A year later (11 years after the Greg's case), Verna emailed me out of the blue. During a reading for a stranger, she connected with the spirit of a young man killed in a restaurant robbery. That man was Greg's nephew who provided details of his unfortunate end. He said that he was with his uncle who was also murdered, and his name was Greg who wanted to give his own message: "*Please thank Inspector Malcolm Rowe for catching my killer.*" Verna immediately put it together and asked the full name of her client. Rod B, Greg's brother. She was once again reunited with Greg in a spirit communication and was compelled to email me and close this cosmic loop.

I wept. For Greg. For Jenny B. For the truth that the world is larger and stranger than evidence alone can capture. I believe Greg nudged the pieces into place - informers, details, even my friend's visit years later - to remind me.

One day, I'll share that cold beer with Greg - and I'll raise a toast to the strange, sacred ways our lives remain connected, even beyond this world.

Part II

JC & HV: The Devil's Couple

Background

JC came into my life as a larger-than-life figure. He carried himself with the confidence of wealth and the air of mystery that drew people in. Fluent in French, fond of the extravagant, he claimed to be a television producer, even suggesting he had co-created an international police reality show. He spoke often of inherited fortunes tied to weapons and diamond interests in Europe and Africa. Whether fact or fiction, he had money, and he flaunted it.

Alongside him was HV, his quiet, pale partner. Introduced to me as his wife, she appeared unassuming, almost shy, but her silence seemed calculated - the perfect foil to his bravado. Where he demanded attention, she absorbed it passively.

Lifestyle of excess

JC cultivated an image of opulence. Private jets, Ferraris, expensive hotels, and wild outings were part of his toolkit. He thrived on surrounding himself with people who admired what he projected. I was not impressed by his wealth, but I did observe his pattern: generosity wasn't kindness, it was leverage.

He offered me opportunities - to drive his Ferrari, to take out a loan with promises of impossible returns, to secure him a firearm for him under South African law's temporary lending allowance. Each time I declined, politely but firmly. At the time, I could not fully articulate why. In hindsight, I know it was intuition - the same voice that kept me grounded when his stories tempted disbelief.

The darker truth emerges

It didn't take long for cracks to appear. JC hinted at adventures that blurred the line between truth and invention: military service, prison escapes, shadowy deals with politicians. Some were obvious exaggerations, others felt like boasts disguised as hypotheticals.

The reality was far darker. Rumors surfaced that JC had conned wealthy businessmen. One in particular was defrauded of millions, later lured to a hotel in Brussels, and murdered. JC and HV became fugitives, living in South Africa in plain sight, rubbing shoulders with senior police and political figures. Stories of corruption and protection at the highest levels swirled, making his freedom feel almost untouchable.

A later search of his residence revealed chilling evidence: detailed notes, including what was described as a "*hit list*." The man who had once waxed philosophical on my porch about the thin line between cop and killer had, it seemed, long since crossed it.

The mask slips

JC liked to toy with people. He once told me he wanted to make a film about a man who had been shot and disposed of, smiling as if it were just an idea. He named his favorite band as "*The Artful Dodger*," a wink to his own life of deceit. Looking back, these weren't casual comments. They were boasts dressed as jokes, small windows into the truth he otherwise hid.

He also confessed that he had no true friends. Money, he said, made people betray him. That confession, I believe, was genuine. He was a man who could not allow anyone to see his real self - and so he was condemned to isolation, even in company.

JC was arrested in Johannesburg – but his incarceration would be short lived. An unidentified woman who I believe was his wife – walked into the jail, disguised as a superintendent. She presented false transfer papers, and they walked out of the prison and onto his private jet – making their escape exactly as he has fantasized on the porch. The couple were free and back on the run.

The fall

Eventually, JC and HV's freedom ended after 23 years at large. Their names surfaced internationally when they were arrested in West Africa, decades after their crimes. By then, media outlets had branded them the "*Devil's Couple*." HV became the first woman ever placed on Interpol's 10 Most Wanted list. JC, once lean and flamboyant, appeared in photographs older, hunched, his expression blank. HV, once the delicate woman I'd met in hotels, looked gaunt and sickly. The years had stripped them of glamour, leaving only the residue of their choices.

HV reportedly struck a deal during extradition proceedings, claiming manipulation by JC and citing illness. JC was convicted of murder and fraud; finally held accountable for the trail of destruction he left behind.

A Cautionary Reflection

I often think about what might have happened had I taken that loan, or lent him a firearm, or accepted his invitations to cross a line. My life could have taken a disastrous turn. Instead, I trusted my instincts, resisted the lure of wealth, and maintained a boundary he couldn't manipulate.

JC was, in many ways, a mirror held up to me. He represented the extreme edge of the path I could have chosen had I ever let my darker impulses rule. I saw in him the embodiment of wasted intelligence and squandered charisma - proof that living as a lie corrodes the soul.

He once saw me as a kindred spirit, perhaps because he glimpsed in me the protector's darkness I carried into battle as a cop. But where mine was harnessed to shield others, his was unleashed to exploit them. That difference - intent - is what defines us.

The lesson he leaves me with is simple: wealth without honesty is rot, charisma without truth is poison, and no amount of mystery can protect a man from the judgment of time.

Part III

Self-Reflection Roadmap

This appendix is designed as a toolkit. Use it whenever you feel the need to pause, realign, or rediscover your soul's purpose.

1. Soul Roles at a Glance

Consider which of these resonates most with your life experiences:

⇨ Protector: Guardian of people, energy, or truth. Defender of the vulnerable.
⇨ Anchor: Brings grounding, peace, and stability when others are lost in chaos.
⇨ Mirror: Reflects truth back to others - sometimes as a wake-up call, sometimes as affirmation.
⇨ Vessel: Channel for wisdom, creativity, or spirit that flows through more than from you.
⇨ Weaver: Sees patterns and connections others miss; tells stories that reveal hidden truths.
⇨ Guide: Mentor, elder, or presence that pulls others forward with wisdom and humility.

Ask yourself: Which role (or roles) feel most like me? Which show up again and again in my story?

2. Life Cycle Mapping

Your life often moves in repeating cycles (7, 8, or another number depending on your date of birth).

- Write down your age in increments (e.g., 7, 14, 21, etc.).
- Note the major events, challenges, or transitions at each point.
- Look for recurring themes - do they line up with your soul role?

3. Sanctuary Inventory

- Where have I felt most safe, supported, or whole? (people, places, routines)
- What threatens my sanctuary now?
- What small step could I take today to rebuild or strengthen it?

4. The Fire Test

Think of one extreme or defining moment in your life. Ask:

- What truth did this moment force me to face?
- How did it shape my choices afterward?
- What would I tell my younger self standing in that fire?

5. Dialogue with Your Future Self

- Imagine yourself 20 years older, calm and wise.
- Ask them three questions:
    - What are you most proud of me for?

    - ⌘ What do you regret?
    - ⌘ What do you want me to do differently today?
- Write their answers as if they're speaking directly to you.

6. Gentle Prompts to Carry

Keep these questions close. Reflect on them during quiet moments:

- ⌘ When was the last time I felt truly safe?
- ⌘ What lesson keeps repeating in my life?
- ⌘ Am I resisting or embracing my soul's role?
- ⌘ If my story ended tomorrow, what story would others tell about me?

Closing Thought

This roadmap is not a one-time exercise. It's a compass you can return to again and again. As your story unfolds, your answers will change - and that's the point. Growth is proof that the soul is alive and learning.

Part IV

Meditations

Short Grounding Meditations

I've created these short, grounding guided meditations with you in mind - for those times when life feels busy, and all you need is a pause to feel fully present. Let them be gentle companions whenever you wish. You can read them, visualize them, or record them to experience with your eyes closed - whatever feels right for you. These quiet, tender moments are my little gift from my heart to yours.

1. **The Sanctuary Within** – finding your soul's safe place
2. **The Flame of Resilience** – strengthening your inner fire
3. **The River of Release** – letting go of burdens
4. **The Mirror of Truth** – seeing yourself honestly and with compassion
5. **The Legacy Path** – walking with intention and purpose
6. **The Circle of Gratitude** – widening the heart through thankfulness

1. Guided Meditation - The Sanctuary Within

Take a moment now to sit comfortably. Rest your hands gently on your lap. Close your eyes if that feels safe, or simply soften your gaze.

Breathe in… slowly, deeply.

Breathe out… let your shoulders drop.

Again - inhale… filling your lungs with calm.

Exhale… letting tension melt away.

One more time - breathe in peace…

Breathe out release.

Now imagine yourself standing in front of a gate. It may be wooden, or iron, or perhaps just an arch of trees. This is no ordinary gate - it is the entrance to your inner sanctuary, a place of deep rest that belongs only to you. No one else can enter without your invitation. This is your soul's safe place.

When you are ready, **breathe in… step forward…** and as you **breathe out,** walk through the gate.

Notice what you see around you. Are there tall trees swaying gently? Do you hear water flowing nearby, or birds singing overhead? Perhaps you smell fresh grass, flowers, or the clean air after rain. Take a moment to let the scene form around you, exactly as it needs to be.

Breathe in… take in the colours and shapes.

Breathe out… let the world outside fall away.

Look for a resting place here. Maybe it's a bench, a smooth rock, or a soft patch of grass. Go to it, and sit down in your mind's eye. Feel the solid ground beneath you. Know that here, you are safe.

At the edges of your sanctuary, place symbols of protection. You might see a stone glowing with quiet strength. A small eternal flame burning with courage. A guardian animal - a wolf, a bird, perhaps even a beloved dog.

Whatever comes to you is right. These protectors stand watch, ensuring your peace remains unbroken.

Breathe in… feel their presence.

Breathe out… release any fear.

If your thoughts wander, gently bring them back to this place. Notice the way the light filters through the trees, or the way the air feels against your skin.

This is your sanctuary. It does not depend on the weather, the news, or anyone else's approval. It exists within you, always waiting.

Breathe in… gratitude.

Breathe out… peace.

When you are ready to leave, return to the gate. Take one last look around. Let yourself feel thankful for this space your soul has created. Know that you can return at any time — in stress, in sadness, or simply when you need to rest. The gate will always open for you.

Breathe in… carry the stillness with you.

Breathe out… step back into the world renewed.

And when you're ready, gently wiggle your fingers, open your eyes, and return - carrying the sanctuary within you.

2. Guided Meditation - The Flame of Resilience

Close your eyes.

Take a deep breath in through your nose… and out through your mouth.

Again, slowly - in… and out. Let your shoulders drop as if a weight has been set down.

Now, imagine yourself standing in a quiet, darkened space. In front of you is a single candle, its flame steady, unwavering. You step closer and notice that the flame is small, yet fierce. It does not flicker even when the air stirs.

This flame is your resilience. It has burned through every storm you've faced. It burned the day you thought you couldn't go on, and yet you did. It burned when pain tried to hollow you out, and still it lit your way forward.

Breathe in, watching the flame glow brighter.

Breathe out, feeling its warmth spread through your chest.

Now, bring to mind one moment in your life when you felt close to giving up - yet you rose. See that memory clearly. Offer it to the flame. Watch as the fire absorbs it, transforming struggle into strength, weakness into wisdom.

Whisper silently to yourself: I am stronger than what tried to break me.

Stay here a few breaths longer, basking in the warmth of your own endurance. When you are ready, carry this flame inside you, knowing it will never extinguish.

3. Guided Meditation - The River of Release

Close your eyes.

Breathe in deeply… and let it out slowly.

Imagine standing on the bank of a wide, gentle river. The water is clear, reflecting the sky. The current is steady, neither rushed nor stagnant.

In your hands, you hold a small bundle. Inside it are the burdens you carry - grief, guilt, anger, fear, regret. They are heavy, and they tire your soul.

Kneel by the water. One by one, untie the bundle. Take each burden in your hand. Name it softly: *"fear," "loss," "shame," "resentment."* No need to judge it - only to recognize it.

Now, place each one into the river. Watch as the current takes it from you. Notice how the water does not resist - it accepts everything without complaint, carrying it downstream, away from your heart.

Breathe in - feeling lighter.

Breathe out - letting go.

Stay here until your bundle is empty. When you rise, your hands are free. The river still flows, carrying what you no longer need to hold. Whisper to yourself: I release what does not serve me. I walk forward unburdened.

4. Guided Meditation - The Mirror of Truth

Close your eyes.

Breathe in slowly, filling your chest. Breathe out, emptying it fully.

Now picture yourself walking into a quiet room. In the center stands a tall, polished mirror. It glows softly, as if lit from within. You approach, hesitant at first, but with each step, you feel calmer.

When you stand before the mirror, you see not just your face, but your essence - your soul looking back at you. There is no hiding here. No mask, no pretense. Only truth.

Take a breath in. Let your reflection speak.

What does it want you to know? What part of yourself have you been avoiding? What gift in you have you neglected?

Stay with whatever arises - whether comfort or discomfort. Let the truth be heard.

Now, whisper back to your reflection: I see you. I accept you. I will honor you.

Watch as the mirror softens and glows brighter. You are not judged - only witnessed, fully and without condition. Carry this clarity with you as you leave the room.

5. Guided Meditation - The Legacy Path

Close your eyes.

Take a deep breath in… and let it out. Feel your feet planted firmly on the ground.

Now imagine yourself standing on a path stretching forward into the horizon. On either side are tall trees, their branches woven together like guardians. Each step you take, the earth remembers.

Look down. You see your footprints forming behind you - each one representing a choice, a moment, a story you have lived. Some prints are deep, carved by struggle. Others are light, marked by joy.

As you walk forward, imagine a loved one - perhaps a child, a friend, or even someone you have yet to meet - following this same path. They walk where you have walked. They learn from the steps you've taken.

Now ask yourself: What footprints do I want to leave behind? What echoes of my life will guide those who follow?

Breathe in - filling with purpose.

Breathe out - releasing doubt.

Whisper to yourself: My life matters. My choices ripple beyond me. I walk with intention.

As the trees bow overhead, know that your path is still being written, one deliberate step at a time.

6. Guided Meditation - The Circle of Gratitude

Close your eyes.

Take a slow breath in… and release it.

Now imagine yourself sitting in the center of a circle. Around you are the faces of those who have shaped your life. Some brought joy, others brought pain - yet all left you with lessons. See them clearly: family, friends, mentors, strangers, even those who tested you.

One by one, look at each face. Whisper softly: "*Thank you.*" Not because everything they gave was easy, but because everything they gave was part of your becoming.

Now let the circle widen. Beyond people, see the places that held you: a childhood home, a quiet corner of nature, a sanctuary where you healed. Whisper again: "*Thank you.*"

Let the circle widen still. Feel gratitude for your body - imperfect, scarred, but carrying you each day. For your breath. For the simple fact that you are here, in this moment, alive.

Breathe in gratitude, filling your chest.

Breathe out gratitude, sending it into the world.

Sit here a little longer, surrounded by this circle. Let it remind you: no matter how dark the journey, gratitude can light the way home.

Part V

Deep Immersive Meditations

Journeys Through Fire and Water are longer, immersive meditations crafted for those moments when you can truly gift yourself some time and space. Designed with a gentle self-hypnosis touch, they are best experienced when read aloud to a small group, or recorded so you can lie back, relax, and let the words guide you.

CAUTION: Make sure you are cozy and at ease - these meditations are for quiet, safe moments, **not while driving, using machinery or any other task that requires your undivided attention**.

Let yourself sink into the experience and simply be.

1. **The Garden Beyond the Fire** – a deep journey of self-esteem, resilience, forgiveness, and rebirth.
2. **The Water's Edge** – letting go of regret, integrating life's extremes, and rediscovering strength.

1. Full Meditation – The Garden of Renewal

Take a moment to find a quiet, comfortable place.
Somewhere you can sit or lie down without interruption.
Allow your body to rest, and your eyes to gently close.

Take a slow, deep breath in…
and let it go.
Again - inhale deeply, filling your lungs…
and exhale, allowing your shoulders to drop,
your muscles to soften.

With every breath, notice how your body begins to release
any tension it has been carrying.
Your chest opens.
Your jaw loosens.
Your hands grow warm and still.

And now, with each breath,
allow your mind to follow -
quieting, softening, letting go.

Imagine that with every exhale,
you are releasing something you no longer need.
And with every inhale,
you are drawing in calm, strength, and peace.

This is your time.
This is your sanctuary.

In your mind's eye, see yourself standing in a wide, sunlit meadow.
The grass sways gently in the breeze,
each blade catching the golden light.
Wildflowers scatter color across the field -

yellow, violet, white, red -
their petals trembling as butterflies drift between them.

Above you, the sky is vast and clear,
a perfect blue dome stretching endlessly.
The warmth of the sun touches your skin,
gentle, comforting, reassuring.

You notice how safe it feels here.
The air is fresh, scented with earth and flowers.
You take a deep breath in,
filling your chest with the scent of freedom.
And as you exhale,
you feel lighter, more at ease.

In the distance, you notice a small farmhouse.
Its walls are warm stone,
its windows glowing with soft light.
A narrow path winds from where you stand to its door,
inviting you forward.

You begin to walk slowly,
each step grounding you more deeply in calm.
As you approach, you notice the details:
the wooden door,
a pot of flowers on the step,
the gentle creak of the old hinges as you open it.

You step inside.

The air is cool and welcoming.
Inside, the farmhouse feels timeless,
filled with objects that speak of care and comfort.

A fire crackles gently in the hearth.
On a wooden table rests a bowl of fruit,
bright and fresh.
A woven rug softens the floor beneath your feet.

The space feels familiar,
as if you have always belonged here.
This is a place of safety,
a place where you can be completely yourself.

You wander slowly through the rooms,
each one carrying its own gentle presence.
And then you notice a staircase leading down.
The steps invite you deeper,
into a quieter part of yourself.

You place your hand on the wooden rail,
and begin to descend – feeling safe and secure.

With each step downward,
your mind grows quieter,
your body more relaxed,
your heart more open.

I will count for you now.
With every number,
imagine yourself drifting deeper inward,
toward the place where wisdom and strength reside.

Ten…
your shoulders soften.

Nine…

your breath is slow, steady, calm.

Eight…

your mind releases old noise.

Seven…

a deep sense of peace surrounds you.

Six…

each step carries you further into yourself.

Five…

halfway down, deeper still, safe and calm.

Four…

your body is light, your heart open.

Three…

your inner world expands before you.

Two…

you are nearly there.

One…

you step onto the final landing.

Ahead of you is a door.
Strong, wooden, waiting.
You reach for the handle.
It turns easily in your hand.

You open the door,
and step into another world.

You are standing in a secret garden.
It is unlike any place you have seen before.
The air is fragrant with blossoms -
jasmine, roses, lavender.
The sound of birdsong floats above you,
clear and pure.
Somewhere, a stream trickles softly,
its waters glinting in the light.

Trees arch gracefully overhead,
their leaves whispering with the wind.
The sunlight filters through the branches,
scattering golden patterns onto the path.

You walk slowly forward,
taking in the beauty of this hidden sanctuary.
Each step deepens your sense of calm,
your sense of belonging.

And then you see it:
a simple wooden bench beneath a great tree,
its branches stretching like open arms.
The bench waits for you,
welcoming you to rest.

You sit down,
feeling the strength of the tree at your back,
the earth steady beneath your feet.
This is your place.
Your place of healing,
of renewal,
of remembering who you truly are.

You take a deep breath.
And another.
Letting the peace of this garden
fill your entire being.

Now, as you rest on this bench,
listen.

Within you is a voice.
A true voice.
It is quieter than the noise of the world,
but stronger than all of it combined.
It is the voice that remembers your worth.

It says to you:
You are more than your mistakes.
You are more than your scars.
You are the sum of your resilience,
your compassion,
your courage to rise again and again.

Self-esteem is not about perfection.
It is not about the masks we wear,
the roles we play,
the approval of strangers.
It is about seeing yourself clearly -
all of your cracks,
all of your triumphs -
and knowing you are enough.

Like the cups repaired with gold,
your broken places shine with resilience.

Your scars are proof of survival.
Your wounds are proof of your willingness to live,
to risk,
to keep loving despite it all.

Forgive yourself for the times you faltered.
Forgive yourself for not knowing better
until you did.
Forgive yourself for carrying burdens
that were never truly yours.

You are not here to be flawless.
You are here to be whole.
And wholeness includes the shadows,
as well as the light.

As you sit in this garden,
imagine your self-esteem
growing like the tree above you.
Its roots sink deep into the earth -
unshakable.
Its trunk is steady,
its branches expansive.
And its leaves reach for the sky,
dancing in the wind,
so alive.

This is you.
Rooted.
Steady.
Expansive.
Alive.

Take a slow, deep breath.
And feel that truth settle into you.

Sit here a moment longer.
Feel the bench beneath you,
the earth holding you,
the tree protecting you.

Notice the birds still singing,
their voices weaving a hymn of resilience.
Notice the flowers around you,
opening freely without apology.
Notice how every part of this garden belongs.
And so do you.

When you are ready,
stand and walk slowly back toward the door.
Place your hand on the handle,
and step through.
Behind you, the garden remains,
always waiting,
always yours to return to.

You find yourself once again at the staircase.
And now, with each step upward,
you bring with you the strength,
the self-esteem,
the compassion you discovered.

I will count for you.
With each number,
you rise closer to the waking world,
carrying your new truth with you.

One…

energy begins to return to your body.

Two…

your breath deepens, steady and calm.

Three…

you feel lighter, stronger.

Four…

self-esteem rooted deeply within you.

Five…

halfway back,

clearer, brighter.

Six…

awareness expanding,

like the sky above the meadow.

Seven…

your body awakening,

your spirit steady.

Eight…

your eyes flutter gently,

but remain closed for now.

Nine…

nearly there,

peace and strength flowing through you.

Ten…

you step into the meadow once more.

The sunlight warms your face.
The flowers sway gently.
The sky stretches wide above you.
And you know, in every part of your being,
that you are enough.

Now, take a deep breath.
And as I count backward from ten,
you will return fully awake,
refreshed, calm,
and grounded in self-esteem.

Ten…
slowly awakening.

Nine…
energy returning to your limbs.

Eight…
breath deep and strong.

Seven…
awareness widening.

Six…
peace still within you.

Five…
body stretching gently.

Four…
eyes beginning to flicker.

Three…
mind clear and steady.

Two…
completely present.

One…
fully awake.

Open your eyes.
You are here.
You are whole.
You are enough.

2. Full Meditation – The Water's Edge

Close your eyes, and allow your breath to steady itself.
Let the rhythm of the inhale and exhale
become like waves - rising, falling, rising, falling.
You are safe here. You are at rest.

See yourself standing in a clearing,
surrounded by tall trees,
their branches reaching high into the sky.

Before you, a waterfall cascades down smooth rock,
its waters clear and bright.
The sound is constant, steady -
a song of release, of surrender.

You step closer.
Mist from the falling water cools your face,
settling gently on your skin.
The air smells fresh, alive,
like renewal itself.

The water has been flowing here for centuries,
always letting go,
always moving forward,
never holding onto what has already passed.

Stand for a moment,
watching the water fall.
Notice how easily it releases.
Notice how naturally it moves on.

And ask yourself quietly:
What is it that I still hold?
What regrets cling to me like heavy stones?
Am I ready to lay them down?

Take a slow breath in…
and as you exhale, imagine those regrets
falling into the water below,
carried away, dissolved, gone.

Now see yourself walking from the forest
to a wide, open ocean.
The horizon stretches endlessly before you.
The waves roll in and out,
each one erasing what was written on the shore.

Find a place to sit in the sand.
The earth beneath you is solid, grounding.
The ocean before you is vast, limitless.
Above, the sky opens into a canvas of light.

Here, at the meeting place of land and sea,
ask yourself:

Which extremes have shaped me?
Where have I known fire, and where have I known calm?
When did I stand at the edge of despair, and what pulled me back?

Breathe with the waves.
Let them remind you that everything rises,
and everything falls.
Pain rises. And it falls.
Joy rises. And it falls.
But the ocean itself remains -
unchanging, eternal, whole.
Just like you.

As you sit here,
the water stretching before you,
bring to mind the Soul Roles we carry -
those different callings of the spirit.

Are you the Protector,
standing between danger and the ones you love?

Are you the Mirror,
showing others the truth of themselves,
whether they are ready to see it or not?

Are you the Weaver,
tying together the threads of people and purpose,
creating patterns no one else can see?

Are you the Channel,
receiving wisdom from places beyond reason,
and bringing it into the world as guidance?

Or are you a shifting combination of them all -
Protector in one season,
Weaver in another,
always changing, always learning?

Sit with this question.
Allow the role, or the roles,
that are most alive in you now to rise gently.
And when they come,
acknowledge them,
honor them.
They are part of your essence.

As you sit by the water's edge,
consider these questions -
not to be answered quickly,
but to be carried with you,
like smooth stones in your pocket:

- *Where has absence shaped me as much as presence?*
- *When fear threatened to break me, did it cage me - or forge me?*
- *Which losses still whisper to me in the quiet hours, and what did they leave behind?*
- *Who do I stand before when danger circles? And who stands before me when I cannot?*
- *When anger rises like fire, do I let it consume me - or do I learn to light the dark with it?*
- *What embers still glow in the ashes of my past, asking me to breathe life into them again?*

Let these questions echo with the waves,
their answers not forced,
but unfolding gently in their own time.

Now, breathe deeply.
Let your hand rest gently on your heart.
Feel the steady rhythm within you.
That beat is proof of resilience -
a song that has carried you through every extreme.

Say silently to yourself, or whisper aloud:

I forgive myself for what I did not know.
I forgive myself for faltering, for stumbling.
I release regret. It has no claim on me now.

I honor the choices that shaped me.
I honor the strength that carried me.
I honor the compassion that grows in me still.

Your self-esteem does not come from being untouched.
It comes from being touched deeply,
by both fire and water,
by both loss and love -
and still choosing to rise.

The sound of the ocean grows softer now,
fading into the rhythm of your own breath.
The waterfall becomes an echo,
reminding you of the ease of letting go.

Slowly, bring yourself back to the room around you.
Feel the surface beneath you.

Notice your breath.
Notice your body.

Take one last deep inhale,
drawing in resilience, compassion, strength.
And as you exhale,
release anything that no longer serves you.

When you are ready,
open your eyes.
The water remains within you -
always flowing,
always renewing,
always reminding you:

You are resilient.
You are forgiven.
You are strong.
You are everything you choose to be.

Part VI

Soul Role Reflections

Have you taken a moment to reflect on the section "*Exercises for the Journey Ahead?*" Have you noticed the presence of one - or perhaps several - soul roles in your life journey? Now is your gentle invitation to choose one of these short meditations to explore it with curiosity and care. Which one calls to you most? Or experience them all one by one in your own time.

1. **The Protector** - courage as presence, standing for others and receiving protection in return.
2. **The Mirror** - reflecting truth with compassion, inward and outward.
3. **The Weaver** - creating meaning by bringing together the threads of people and purpose.
4. **The Vessel** - listening, receiving, and carrying wisdom from your inner self.
5. **The Anchor** - bringing peace, stability, clarity and dependability.
6. **The Guide** - providing direction, grounding, sparking spiritual growth.
7. **The Whole Self** - exploring all your potential soul roles.

1. The Protector Meditation

Close your eyes.
Take a slow breath in - and let it out.

Imagine yourself standing at the edge of a forest.
The air is crisp, alive with birdsong.
Ahead of you, a small fire flickers in the distance.
It is not a fire of destruction,
but a fire that signals others may need warmth,
may need protection.

You step forward.
With each step, your spine grows taller,
your chest broader,
your presence stronger.

The Protector in you awakens.
Not with aggression,
but with clarity.
You are the one who stands between chaos and the vulnerable.
You are the shield when others cannot defend themselves.

Take a moment to remember:
Who have you stood for?
Who have you protected in moments of danger,
seen or unseen?

And just as important:
Who has stood for you?
Can you allow yourself to feel their presence now,
standing behind you,
a circle of protection that includes even you?

Breathe into this truth:
Strength is not in domination.
It is in protection.
It is in service.
It is in love made visible through courage.

Rest here a little longer,
feeling both the strength you give
and the strength you receive.

When you are ready, open your eyes.
Carry this quiet power with you.

2. The Mirror Meditation

Close your eyes and breathe deeply.

Picture yourself beside a still lake at dawn.
The water is calm,
a perfect mirror of the sky.

As you gaze into the water,
you see not only your reflection,
but the truth of who you are beneath the surface.
No masks.
No pretense.
Only what is real.

The Mirror in you does not deceive.
It reflects.
It shows others - and yourself - what is.

Think for a moment:
Whose truth have you reflected in your life?

Whose hidden strength, whose hidden wounds,
have you revealed simply by standing before them?

Now, let the mirror turn inward.
What do you see in yourself
that you have been avoiding?
What truth needs acknowledgment,
not judgment,
but honest seeing?

Breathe.
Know that to mirror truth is not cruelty -
it is compassion.
It is offering clarity where confusion reigned.

Sit with this gentle knowing:
You are both the one who reflects
and the one reflected.
Both matter.
Both are sacred.

When you are ready, open your eyes.
Carry truth with kindness.

3. The Weaver Meditation

Close your eyes.
Take a slow, grounding breath.

See yourself in a quiet room.
Before you is a loom,
its frame holding many threads -
threads of different colors, textures, strengths.

Some threads represent people in your life.
Some represent moments, lessons, memories.
Some are bright with joy.
Some are dark with sorrow.
All are part of the tapestry.

The Weaver in you lifts a thread,
ties it gently to another,
and begins to weave.
With patience, with care,
a pattern begins to emerge.
It may not be obvious yet,
but it is beautiful in its wholeness.

Ask yourself:
Which threads am I weaving now?
Am I bringing together people, ideas, moments,
that once seemed separate?
What pattern is slowly forming in my life?

Breathe deeply.
Know that your weaving has purpose,
even when you cannot yet see the full design.

Rest in the quiet truth:
You are a Weaver.
You create meaning, connection,
and beauty that outlasts you.

When you are ready, open your eyes.
Step back into life with patience for the pattern.

4. The Vessel Meditation

Close your eyes.
Breathe slowly, deeply.

Picture yourself on a hilltop at night.
Above you, the sky is vast and alive with stars.
Each one a point of light,
each one a message waiting to be heard.

The Channel in you is open,
listening, receiving, translating.
You are a vessel for wisdom
that does not begin or end with you.

Take a moment to notice:
What do you feel drawn to receive now?
What quiet whisper moves through you,
wanting to take form as words,
as action,
as compassion?

Do not force it.
Simply allow it to arrive.
Perhaps it is a memory.
Perhaps it is an image.
Perhaps it is only a feeling.

Whatever comes, trust it.
This is your channel speaking.
This is your gift.

Rest in the knowing that you do not need to own wisdom
to share it.

You need only to be open,
humble,
willing.

When you are ready, open your eyes.
Step forward as both receiver and messenger.

5. The Anchor Meditation

Close your eyes.
Take a slow, grounding breath.
Feel the earth beneath you - steady, unshaken.
Picture yourself as a great tree,
roots stretching deep into the soil.
No matter the storm,
you remain upright, strong, at peace.

This is the Anchor in you -
a stabilizer, bringing clarity when waters are muddy,
peace when the world feels chaotic.
Your presence is a home,
a place of safety for others to return to.

Ask yourself:
When have I offered steadiness to someone lost in the storm?
Where in my own life do I need to anchor more deeply?

Breathe again.
Feel the calm of belonging,
the peace of being rooted.
Know that the Anchor in you is not stillness without purpose,
but stillness that steadies the whole.

When you are ready, open your eyes.
Carry this grounding presence with you,
a quiet refuge for yourself and others.

6. The Guide Meditation

Close your eyes.
Breathe slowly, with intention.
See yourself at a crossroads,
where others have gathered, uncertain which way to go.
In your hand, you hold a flame -
not blazing, but steady, warm, sure.

This is the Guide in you.
The moral compass that points toward truth.
The elder voice that sparks awakening.
The mentor who walks beside others,
not ahead, not behind.

Ask yourself:
Where am I being called to kindle light for others?
Whose growth is waiting for my gentle guidance?
And where do I need to listen
to the wisdom rising from my own spirit?

Breathe deeply.
Feel the courage and the compassion of the Guide.
Together, they invite,
they illuminate,
they catalyze growth without force.

Rest for a moment in this knowing:

You are both flame and compass,
both mentor and fellow traveler.

When you are ready, open your eyes.
Step forward with humility and courage,
ready to guide by example,
ready to spark light where it is most needed.

7. The Whole Self Meditation

Close your eyes.
Take a long, slow breath in … and let it go.
Settle into stillness.
Allow your body to soften,
your heart to open,
your spirit to listen.

Now, invite the **Protector** within you.
Feel its presence rise -
the part of you that holds safe boundaries,
that shields with love, not fear.
Ask yourself:
Where have I protected myself or others with kindness?
How can I honor the strength of this guardian within me?
Rest for a moment in the reassurance of safety.

Next, meet the **Mirror**.
Imagine standing before it,
its surface clear and gentle.
It does not distort.
It reflects truth as it is,
softened with compassion.

Ask yourself:
What truths am I ready to see in myself?
What truths have I helped others to see?
Let clarity settle, free of judgment.

Now, let the **Weaver** appear.
See the threads of your life - joy, sorrow, lessons, love -
all being woven into a larger design.
Each strand matters.
Each has its place.
Ask yourself:
Which threads am I weaving now?
What greater meaning might they hold?
Trust the beauty of a tapestry not yet complete.

Welcome the **Vessel**.
Feel yourself as open, spacious, receptive.
You do not need to strive;
you simply need to allow.
The Vessel in you makes room
for wisdom, love, and spirit to flow through.
Ask yourself:
What am I being called to receive?
What can I hold without clinging,
so it may pass through me as blessing?

Now, sense the weight of the **Anchor**.
Rooted deep into the earth,
it steadies you through chaos,
offering clarity when all feels uncertain.
Breathe deeply and feel yourself sink into the earth,
Strong and dependable.

Ask yourself:
Where in my life do I need to root more deeply?
Where do I offer steadiness to others?
Feel the peace of being a place of belonging.

Finally, turn toward the **Guide**.
See its lantern-light ahead -
not blazing, but steady.
It is the compass of your soul,
an elder presence within you,
pointing toward growth and spirit.

Ask yourself:
Where am I being called to lead by example?
Who might be waiting for my gentle light?
Rest in the knowing that the Guide in you is never lost.

Take a deep breath now.
Protector, Mirror, Weaver, Vessel, Anchor, Guide -
all alive within you.
Each sacred.
Each necessary.

Each waiting to be discovered within you
Together they form your whole self.

Rest here in harmony for a moment,
feeling the strength of your completeness.

When you are ready,
open your eyes.
Step back into the world carrying this wholeness,
a living harmony of all your soul roles.